Travel Agency Law

Travel Agency Law

John Downes and Tricia Paton

 LONGMAN

Addison Wesley Longman Limited
Edinburgh Gate, Harlow
Essex CM20 2JE, England
and Associated Companies throughout the world

© Longman Group UK Limited 1993

First published in Great Britain 1993
Second impression 1995
Third impression Addison Wesley Longman Limited 1998

ISBN 0 582 36847 2

British Library Cataloguing-in-Publication Data
A catalogue record for this book is
available from the British Library.

Library of Congress Cataloging-in-Publication Data
A catalog entry for this title is
available from the Library of Congress.

Set by
Produced through Longman Malaysia, PA

Contents

In memory of our fathers,
James Martin Downes and John Martin Carroll.

Introduction

This book is aimed at students taking BTEC and SCOTVEC Travel and Tourism courses and is also suitable for those preparing for the Certificate of Travel Agency Management (COTAM). It deals with the general principles of law, focusing on the legal regulation of Tour Operators and Travel Agents.

In Chapter 1 we consider the meaning of 'Law', the distinction between civil and criminal law and the sources of law-making. There are three legal systems in the United Kingdom: the English Legal System (England and Wales); the Scottish Legal System; and the Northern Irish Legal System. The background to these separate legal systems, their court structure and legal professions is considered in Chapter 2. It must be pointed out that the law stated in the text is applicable throughout the United Kingdom except where specified otherwise. The Northern Irish Legal System is based upon English Law and the law and terminology of both systems are basically the same. The Scottish Legal System has been substantially influenced by Roman Law; however, in the area of law outlined in this text, the differences are few and these are indicated. The terminology of Scots Law is quite distinct from that of the other two systems.

The different types of business organisation are discussed in Chapter 3, with particular consideration given to the powers and duties of partners and directors. In Chapter 4 the legislation governing business premises is considered. In Chapter 5 the respective roles of the Tour Operator and Travel Agent are examined and principles of the Law of Agency applied to the relationship between them and their rights and duties vis-à-vis the consumer. Chapter 6 focuses on Fair Trading and Consumer Protection legislation, and also deals with the roles of the Office of Fair Trading, the Association of British Travel Agents (ABTA), and the Tour Operators' Study Group.

The Package Travel, Package Holidays and Package Tours Regulations 1992 came into force on 31 December 1992. These regulations do not replace the existing Common Law principles, except insofar as those principles are inconsistent with them. Furthermore, they only apply to those transactions defined in them and, thus, there are other transactions which Tour Operators and Travel Agents enter into which are not governed by the Regulations. The Regulations are discussed in Chapter 8. The general principles of the Law of Contract are outlined in Chapter 7. It is important to consider these two chapters together. In Chapter 9 the methods of Dispute Settlement are discussed and previous package holiday cases considered. Chapter 10 deals with contracts of carriage of passengers and their luggage and, in particular, the application of International Conventions. Insurance is dealt with in Chapter 11, and in

Chapter 12 we look at the application of Employment Law to the travel industry.

This book is intended as an introduction to Travel Law. A handbook for travel industry practitioners is currently being prepared by the authors, and will also be published by Pitman Publishing.

Whilst every effort has been made to ensure that the information contained in this book was correct as at 31 January 1993, no responsibility can be accepted by the authors, printers or publishers for any errors or omissions which may have occurred inadvertently.

The authors wish to thank Joyce Mathers and Lesley Burnett for their assistance in the preparation of the text.

John J Downes and Tricia A Paton
31 January 1993

1 Introduction to Law

GLOSSARY

by-laws Regulations made by local authorities and public corporations.

civil law The law which governs agreements and relationships such as contracts and marriage. It provides remedies for those who have suffered some loss as a result of another's failure to comply with his or her obligations.

common law Principles of law which the courts have evolved over the centuries.

criminal law That part of the law governing wrongdoings which the state prohibits and which provides punishments for those who commit crimes or offences.

defendant Person prosecuted in a criminal case. Also the person against whom a civil action is raised (England, Wales, Northern Ireland).

defender Person prosecuted in a criminal case in Scotland. Also the person against whom a civil action is raised.

delegated legislation Power given by Parliament to government ministers, local authorities and public corporations to make law.

law Rules made by Parliament, government ministers, the courts and local authorities which are binding on all of us.

plaintiff Person who raises a civil action (England, Wales, Northern Ireland).

prosecutor Official who raises a criminal prosecution.

pursuer Person who raises a civil action in Scotland.

sanction A penalty imposed for non-compliance with the law.

statutory instrument Regulation made by government minister.

AIMS

(a) To explain what 'law' is.
(b) To explain how the law works.
(c) To consider briefly how the law is made.

The legal background

There is an important legal maxim which lawyers use:

ignorantia juris neminem excusat.

What it means is 'ignorance of the law excuses no one'.

It is not sufficient for a travel agent to say to the judge that he or she did not know that what was done was against the law or that he or she is liable to compensate clients for mishandling a booking. It is presumed that everyone is aware of the whole of the law. This is known as a legal fiction.

Not even the most eminent judge could be fully familiar with the whole of the criminal and civil law; nevertheless, it is important for those wishing to pursue a career in the travel and tourism industries to understand the basic principles which govern the work that they do.

It is not our purpose to train readers to become lawyers but to inform them about the legal environment in which the travel industry operates and the application of Acts of Parliament and other regulations to the day-to-day business of a travel agent and tour operator.

The law

There are many rules which govern our lives but not all of them are *laws*. Students know that there are college rules, and at the start of their courses they probably have to sign an agreement to obey them. Trainees or those on day release will have an agreement with their employer by which he or she undertakes to ensure that training is properly supervised or agrees to allow trainees to attend college at specified times. There are examination regulations. There are rules on health and safety in the college and workplace. There are notices in the local park referring to by-laws, for example requiring that dogs be on a leash. Most people will now be aware that they have to pay the council tax. All of these are rules, but not all of them are *laws*. Let us consider which are which.

College rules

A college is entitled to make rules about the conduct and behaviour of staff and students on its premises. It can require people to agree to be bound by them. If they fail to do so they can be expelled from the college or dismissed from their employment. These are not laws, although the college can enforce them. However, if these rules are in conflict with a law (e.g. they discriminate on grounds of sex or race) they are invalid.

Traineeships and day release agreements

Those members who are on a training scheme will have an agreement with their employer whereby they have agreed to work under supervision and to do the tasks they are given. The employer has undertaken to ensure that trainees are properly supervised and trained. Those who are studying on a day release basis will have an agreement with their employer whereby he or she has undertaken to allow time off for study. The trainees have undertaken to attend the college and do the work required on the course. These are voluntary agreements. They are considered in law to be a *contract* and either party can enforce them. They are not law but there are legal remedies if either party breaks the agreement.

Examination regulations

In the same way that colleges can lay down rules, so too examination boards can make rules governing the conduct of examinations (e.g. students must not talk to one another during the exam). If one does not comply with these rules, one's examination may be invalid. Once again, these regulations are not laws – they are rules which students have voluntarily agreed to be bound by.

Health and safety regulations

There will probably be notices in college dealing with matters of health and safety. Fire notices will be prominently displayed. The Health and Safety at Work, etc. Act 1974 requires the college to ensure the health and safety of staff and students. It lays down standards that are to be achieved. It is for the college authorities to set out a policy as to how this will be achieved on their premises. The policy will contain rules which everyone entering the premises must comply with. The college is entitled to enforce this because the Act requires it to make reasonable rules on these matters.

By-laws

Local authorities are entitled to make rules governing parks and recreation facilities under their control. Although these specific rules were not made by Parliament they are laws and there will be penalties, such as a fine, for breaches of them. These penalties are imposed in the courts. This is because Parliament has given the local authority power to make rules, called *by-laws*, which have the full effect of law.

Council tax

We are required to pay the council tax unless specifically exempt. If we do not, ultimately we may be taken to court and our goods could be seized and sold to meet the tax. This is the law, laid down in an Act of Parliament.

In the examples which have just been given it is clear that there are some rules to which we voluntarily agree but there are others which are imposed on us whether we like it or not. A student voluntarily chooses to undertake a course, study or enrol in a traineeship – he or she voluntarily consents to the college rules, the examination regulations, the contract for employment or traineeship. The rules for health and safety, the by-laws and the council tax are imposed on us all, whether we are in favour of them or not. These are *laws*. It can be seen that laws are rules made by Parliament, the courts or local authorities which are imposed on us and there are sanctions if we do not comply with them.

Sanctions

We know from an early age that parents who want us to comply with their rules need to have some penalty if we fail to do so. We learned quickly from the 'no pocket money this weekend' situation that ultimately they can impose their authority. Perhaps we were good children who did what our parents wanted because it was correct. More probably we did what they wanted because we did not want to forfeit our pocket money. The lesson that we learnt was that there is no point in having rules unless there are measures to enforce them.

Employers or college authorities who do not comply with the Health and Safety at Work, etc. Act 1974 may be subject to a fine or, ultimately, a term of imprisonment. These are penalties for non-compliance. Employers who do not comply with the terms of the contract of employment may be required by an industrial tribunal or court to compensate employees. Employers in turn are legally entitled to dismiss employees who fail to do what they have undertaken.

These penalties are known as *sanctions*. In the one case they are criminal sanctions involving fines or imprisonment, in the other two cases they are civil sanctions involving compensation or dismissal.

SUMMARY Before we go on to consider this distinction between civil and criminal law, let us summarise what we have considered so far.

(a) It is no excuse to tell the judge 'I didn't know'.

(b) It is no excuse to be ignorant about one's legal obligations.

(c) There are many rules which govern our lives but not all of them are laws.

(d) Those rules to which we have agreed are not laws although they may be enforceable in the courts.

(e) Laws are made by Parliament, local authorities and the courts and are imposed on us whether we agree with them or not.

(f) If we do not comply with the law a sanction will be imposed.

(g) In the case of criminal laws, we may be required to pay a fine or might be imprisoned.

(h) In the case of civil laws, the sanctions will involve compensation, dismissal and other legal remedies which are discussed below.

Criminal law

We tend to think of the criminal law as being concerned with wrongdoing, and so it is. However, there are many wrongs which are not considered to be crimes. Most of us would agree that telling lies is wrong but not every lie amounts to a crime. It is only a crime in certain circumstances (e.g. telling lies in court is the crime of perjury). A view of what is right and what is wrong is a matter of personal belief, influenced by philosophy, religion, morality or ethics. The criminal law, however, is concerned with those wrongs which the state will not tolerate. These crimes have been defined by Parliament or identified by the courts. If we breach the criminal law we will incur a penalty such as a fine or a term of imprisonment.

The main aim of the criminal law is to punish the offender. It does not, as a general rule, provide compensation to the victim. There are criminal compensation schemes but these are rather limited. Victims can raise a civil action against those who caused them to suffer loss.

Generally, it is the Crown that prosecutes the offender in court. The victim can raise a private prosecution but these are very few in number (and virtually unknown in Scotland). The official bringing the prosecution on behalf of the Crown is known as the *prosecutor* and the person being prosecuted is the *defendant* (defender, in Scotland).

Example

Adam booked a 'weekend break' holiday for himself and his wife. The brochure indicated that they would be accommodated in a four-star hotel in central London. They would be provided with rooms with 'refreshment facilities, telephone and television'. In fact the hotel had only a two-star rating. It was ten miles from the centre of London and although the rooms did have a telephone they did not have a television or refreshment facilities.

It would appear that the tour operator has contravened the provisions of the Trade Descriptions Act 1968. This Act is part of the criminal law, providing penalties for those contravening its provisions. The tour operator will be prosecuted by the local trading standards department. If the prosecution is successful the tour operator will have to pay a fine.

Generally, the criminal law will not award Adam any compensation for his disappointing holiday. Adam can raise an action for damages in the civil courts.

Note: In Scotland, the prosecution will be conducted by the Procurator Fiscal.

Civil law

We have seen that voluntary agreements which we have entered into can be enforced in the courts. The purpose of civil law is to encourage people to comply with voluntary arrangements and to provide remedies when one party fails to do what he or she has agreed to do. Civil law governs such matters as contracts, partnership agreements, company law, commercial transactions, marriage, bills, sales of property, etc. It provides rules about how such agreements are to be made, how they are to be enforced and the remedies available to the parties involved.

The main remedies of the civil law are to require parties to comply with their obligations (e.g. to hand over a car which has been repaired), to provide compensation in the form of damages, to enforce payment of debts. It is not the purpose of civil law to punish the party who has broken an agreement.

The person who raises a civil action is called the *plaintiff*. The person against whom the action is raised is called the *defendant*. The Crown, the police or the trading standards department have no role to play in a civil action. Civil actions are known as *litigation*. In Scotland the person who raises the civil action is known as the *pursuer*, the person against whom it is raised is called the *defender*.

Example

In the case mentioned above Adam could raise a civil action against the tour operator to obtain damages for misrepresentation and breach of contract.

So, the civil law and the criminal law are entirely separate and the criminal courts are separate from civil courts.

The differences may be summarised as follows:

(*a*) *Criminal law*
    (i)   prohibits conduct which the state outlaws;
    (ii) provides penalties for those who commit crimes;
    (iii) does not generally compensate the victim.
The official who raises the prosecution is the *prosecutor*.
The person against whom the prosecution is raised is called the *defendant* (defender, in Scotland).

(*b*) *Civil law*
    (i)   regulates agreements, relationships and activities of individuals and groups;
    (ii) provides compensatory remedies such as damages for those who have suffered loss as a result of another's breach of obligations.
The person raising the civil action is called the *plaintiff* (pursuer, in Scotland).
The person defending the civil action is called the *defendant* (defender, in Scotland).

Many wrongdoings are referred to as 'offences' (e.g. offences under the Road

Traffic Acts and under the Trade Descriptions Act). These are part of the criminal law.

'Crimes' are wrongdoings which have been prohibited by law for a long period. They have always been recognised as inherently wrong (e.g. murder or rape).

'Offences' are wrongdoings which are not inherently bad but which Parliament has sought to prohibit in furtherance of a policy such as consumer protection, road traffic regulation or health and safety, etc.

The penalties for committing an offence are laid down in the Act of Parliament which created them. As with crimes, the penalties are fines and/or terms of imprisonment.

Sources of law

Most people think that law is made by Parliament and it is true that many Acts of Parliament are passed each year. However, there are many laws which govern our lives which were not made by Parliament but nevertheless must be complied with. Regulations made by government ministers, local authorities and by public corporations such as British Rail are included in this category.

In addition, courts interpret Acts of Parliament and also set legal precedents which are binding. The EC is increasingly important as a source of law.

Let us consider each of these sources of law.

Legislation

These are laws made by Parliament. Political parties put forward programmes for legislation in their manifestos. The party which wins an election becomes the government of the day and its programme for legislation is then put before Parliament. A proposed Act of Parliament is called a *bill* while it is being considered and debated. Once it has been passed by the House of Commons and the House of Lords and has received the Royal Assent (approval by the Queen – a formality) it becomes an Act of Parliament.

There are many Acts of Parliament regulating all forms of business and commercial activity (e.g. the Companies Act 1985) and these apply to the travel and tourism industry as they do to other industries. However, there are very few Acts of Parliament which apply only to the travel and tourism industry (e.g. Air Travel Reserve Fund Act 1975 or the Hotel Proprietors Act 1956).

Delegated legislation

In the last 100 years the state has increasingly taken on responsibility for the well-being of its citizens by increasing its activity in fields such as housing, education, employment, health, consumer protection, welfare, etc. The constant need for change and growth in these areas means that it is no longer possible for Parliament to enact all of the necessary laws and regulations itself.

Thus Parliament may delegate the powers to make laws to other bodies such as government ministers and local authorities.

An Act of Parliament may set out general rules and empower a government minister to provide more detailed regulations. The Development of Tourism Act 1969 provided that financial grants could be made available for certain types of tourism and hotel development. The Act empowered government ministers (Secretary of State for the Environment/Secretary of State for Scotland/Secretary of State for Wales) to make regulations with the full force of the law. This type of delegated legislation is known as a *statutory instrument*.

Local authorities such as county councils, borough councils and district councils (regional councils and district councils in Scotland) are empowered to make laws for their specific area. These laws are called by-laws and are enforced by the courts. Thus, for example, local authorities are empowered, by the Shops Act 1950, to make regulations concerning opening hours.

Judicial precedent or case law

In the past, legislation formed only a small part of United Kingdom law. Most of the law was common law (i.e. law made by the courts). Although the volume of legislation has increased considerably, the legal systems of the United Kingdom are still largely common law systems in that much of the law has evolved over the centuries.

When a judge makes a decision on a case he or she must give legal reasons for that decision. It is important that such decisions should be consistent. Once a case has been decided and a reason given for that decision then if another case comes before the courts involving the same basic points, similar reasoning should be applied. The decision in the first case sets a precedent which must be followed in subsequent cases involving the same basic circumstances.

It is important to note that a court is only bound to follow a decision laid down by a superior court. It is not bound by decisions of courts of equal or lower standing in the court hierarchy.

Example 1

A man purchases a package holiday involving a two-week stay at a hotel at Morlialp in Switzerland. The brochure contained several statements as to what was included in the package holiday. It indicated that the hotel had a warm friendly atmosphere, that the proprietor spoke English, that guests would be provided with 'afternoon tea' that skiing equipment could be hired and that there would be a yodelling evening.

On return from the holiday the holidaymaker raised an action for damages for not having been provided with what was indicated in the brochure. He included in his claim compensation for disappointment at not having been provided with the holiday which he had booked.

His claim was successful and the damages awarded included compensation for the loss of enjoyment which he suffered. This case, *Jarvis v Swan Tours Ltd* (1973), was most important because it created a precedent that holidaymakers who have an unsatisfactory holiday may claim not only for financial loss (e.g. the cost of the holiday) but also for disappointment and loss of enjoyment.

Example 2

Barbara purchases a holiday comprising a coach tour of Spain. The brochure indicated that the tour would include visits to Toledo to see El Greco's paintings, the Prado art gallery in Madrid and the Escorial Palace.

Whilst in Spain the passengers were informed that the itinerary had been changed. Instead of visiting Toledo they would visit a fish-canning factory in Tarragona; instead of visiting the Escorial they would have a half-day sight-seeing tour of Benidorm; and although they would be making a brief visit to Madrid, it would be to see the home ground of Real Madrid, not the Prado.

On her return, Barbara sued the tour operator. Her claim was not only for a refund of the price of her holiday but also for compensation for the frustration, disappointment and loss of enjoyment which she suffered. If she could prove the facts of her case she would be entitled to succeed, citing *Jarvis v Swan Tours* as a precedent. It does not matter that in that case the details were different (i.e. that Jarvis was a man not a woman, that his holiday was in Switzerland not in Spain, that his was a winter holiday whereas Barbara's was during the summer). It still involved the same basic legal principle.

European Community (EC) law

 The United Kingdom joined the EC in 1972. The European Communities Act 1972 provides that all rights and obligations created under the treaties of the EC form part of United Kingdom law. Thus, for example, article 119 of the Treaty of Rome provides that 'men and women shall receive equal pay for equal work'. In 1979 a woman raised an action against her United Kingdom employer to pay her the same wage as was paid to her male predecessor. She took her case to the European Court of Justice and was successful, notwithstanding the fact that the equal pay legislation in the United Kingdom did not entitle her to the same pay as her male predecessor. The court held that the relevant article of the Treaty was part of United Kingdom law.

It is not only the EC treaties which are binding in the United Kingdom but also regulations made by the Community. The EC may issue directives which require member states to achieve a particular result within a set time limit but leave the choice of method and detail to the individual states. Thus, the Directive on Package, Package Travel, Package Holidays and Package Tours did not automatically become part of its law but the United Kingdom has been given a certain period within which to introduce the proposals. The government implemented the provisions by way of regulations under section 2(2) of the European Communities Act 1972.

The European Court of Justice deals with disputes concerning EC law. Its decisions are binding on the parties to the action.

SUMMARY   We have covered a considerable amount of material in this section, so, before going on to the assessment questions, let us pause for reflection.

(a) Laws passed by Parliament are known as Acts of Parliament or legislation.

(b) Parliament may have empowered a government minister to make regulations on specific matters.

(c) Regulations made by government ministers are known as statutory instruments.

(d) By-laws are made by local authorities and public corporations.

(e) Judges are bound to follow rules of law that have been formulated by the courts.

(f) These 'precedents' or case law only have to be followed if the case before the court involves the same principle(s) as the previous case.

(g) The treaties and regulations of the EC are part of United Kingdom law.

(h) EC directives set out objectives to be achieved by member states.

Now test yourself with the assessment questions which follow.

SELF-ASSESSMENT QUESTIONS

State whether the following statements are correct or incorrect

1. A person cannot be held liable for failing to comply with a legal requirement of which he or she was unaware.

2. Sanctions act as a method of ensuring compliance with the law.

3. The sanctions imposed by the civil law include fines and sentences of imprisonment.

4. A person who is seeking damages must raise an action in a civil court.

5. Cases are raised in the civil court by the plaintiff (the pursuer, in Scotland).

6. A bill is a proposed Act of Parliament.

7. A statutory instrument is a regulation made by a government minister.

8. By-laws are merely local rules that are not enforceable in the courts.

9. If a point of law has been settled by a higher court, that decision must be applied by the lower courts to cases involving the same legal point.

10. EC regulations are part of United Kingdom law.

2 The Legal Systems of the United Kingdom

GLOSSARY   **jurisdiction** This is the authority of the court to deal with a particular case. It may be geographical (e.g. the authority of the court to hear cases arising within the locality) or it may be hierarchical (e.g. certain cases may involve matters which are reserved for the higher courts).

on indictment Such cases are heard before a judge and a jury and usually incur higher penalties than summary cases.

reparation When a party causes loss or injury to another he or she is required to make reparation to the victim (i.e. to pay a sum of money – 'damages'). This is dealt with under the law of tort; in Scotland it is part of the law of delict.

summary cases Cases heard without a jury. Usually these cases are less serious than those heard on indictment.

AIM   To describe the three legal systems of England and Wales, Scotland and Northern Ireland.

England and Wales

The English legal system

You will be aware by now that the English legal system has evolved over a long period of time. In fact, since AD 950 it has developed with no major break and no fundamental change.

English law is based mainly on 'precedent' or 'case law' (i.e. the rules of English law have been formulated by the courts over the centuries). This contrasts with other countries, such as France, which have a codified legal system (i.e. the law is set out in a code which has been enacted by the state).

Wales does not have a separate legal system because it was conquered by Edward I of England. The English legal and political system was, over the succeeding years, imposed on the Welsh people, culminating with the Laws in Wales Act 1530. When the judicial systems of England and Wales were amalgamated in 1830 the process was completed.

However, there is limited administrative devolution to Wales: the Secretary of State for Wales is a member of the Cabinet. The Welsh Grand Committee of MPs for Welsh constituencies scrutinises the activities of the Welsh Office.

The court system in England and Wales

The criminal courts

(a) *Magistrates' courts*. These courts deal with less serious matters such as breach of the peace, petty theft, disorderly conduct and minor offences. The majority of criminal prosecutions are brought in these courts. Justice is administered by *justices of the peace* or by *stipendiary magistrates*. If the case is heard by justices of the peace, there must be at least two, but not more than seven. Justices of the peace are not legally qualified and they are not paid but they do have a legally qualified clerk to advise them. Alternatively, the case may be heard by a stipendiary magistrate, who is legally qualified and paid. There are no juries in the magistrates' court.

The maximum penalties which may be imposed are a fine of up to £5,000 and/or six months' imprisonment. An appeal may be made to the Crown Court for a rehearing of the case, or to the Queen's Bench Divisional Court if the appeal is one on a point of law.

The magistrates' court has another important function. A person who is to be tried in the Crown Court *on indictment* (i.e. before a judge and jury) must first be brought before the magistrates' court for a 'preliminary hearing' to decide whether or not, on the face of it, there is a reasonable case made out against him or her.

(b) *Crown Court*. This court deals with all criminal cases above the level of those dealt with by the magistrates' courts. The most serious offences are heard by a High Court judge. Less serious offences are heard by a circuit judge. There is a jury of 12 persons and a majority verdict of 10–2 is sufficient to convict the accused. Appeals may be made to the Queen's Bench Division of the High Court.

(c) *High Court: Queen's Bench Division*. The court hears appeals from the magistrates' courts and from the Crown Courts. Further appeal lies from this court to the Court of Appeal.

(d) *Court of Appeal: Criminal Division*. This court hears appeals from the Crown Courts and the Queen's Bench Division of the High Court. The court comprises the Lord Chief Justice and Lords Justices of Appeal. Appeals from this court go to the House of Lords.

(e) *House of Lords*. This is the highest court of appeal. When acting as a judicial body the House of Lords comprises the Lord Chancellor and a maximum of 11 Lords of Appeal in Ordinary.

The civil courts

(a) *Magistrates' court*. The role of this court in civil law is very limited. It deals with the recovery of certain debts (e.g. income tax, gas and electricity bills, council tax), certain matrimonial disputes (e.g. separation orders and maintenance), and the granting of gaming and liquor licences. Appeal lies to the High Court.

(b) *County court.* Most civil actions are dealt with by this court. There are upper limits, however, on the size of the claims which may be made in this court (e.g. £50,000 maximum in a claim arising from a breach of contract). The court is usually presided over by a circuit court judge. Claims for less than £1,000 may be dealt with under the 'small claims procedure' in which event the case is heard by a recorder (part-time judge). It is not heard in open court and it takes the form of a simple arbitration. Neither party can claim legal expenses, however. Appeal from the county courts lies to the High Court.

(c) *High Court.* The jurisdiction of this court is unlimited (i.e. it can hear any kind of civil case). It is organised into three divisions.

The Queen's Bench Division deals with cases involving larger sums than can be heard in the county courts. The Commercial Court is a subdivision of the Queen's Bench which deals with commercial matters. There are approximately 45 judges in the Queen's Bench Division. The court may sit in any part of England and Wales that it wishes.

The Chancery Division deals primarily with cases involving land, company law and partnership. It is presided over by the Lord Chancellor, but in practice he usually sits only on appeals. Cases are usually heard without a jury and, as in the case of the Queen's Bench Division, the court may sit in any part of England and Wales.

As the name suggests, the Family Division of the High Court deals almost exclusively with family matters and, in particular, divorce.

Appeals from all three divisions of the High Court lie to the Court of Appeal (Civil Division), although in certain circumstances appeals may go direct to the House of Lords.

(d) *Court of Appeal: Civil Division.* The court hears appeals from the High Court. The court is presided over by the Master of the Rolls. Each appeal must be heard by at least three Lords Justices of Appeal. Decisions are by a majority. Appeals lie from this court to the House of Lords.

(e) *House of Lords.* This is the final court of appeal. Each appeal must be heard by a minimum of five Lords of Appeal in Ordinary. Decisions are by a majority.

The legal profession of England and Wales

The legal profession is divided into two branches: solicitors and barristers.

Solicitors are the more numerous branch of the profession. They deal with the day-to-day legal problems of their clients. The range of subjects with which a solicitor may be required to deal is very wide indeed. The solicitor may be engaged in court work, family law, conveyancing, company formation, tax, accounting, criminal law, etc. Increasingly, there is a trend towards specialisation. Solicitors may represent their clients in the lower courts. They must be members of the Law Society.

The main function of barristers is to represent clients in court. They have the right to be heard in any court including at 'the bar' of the House of Lords. Solicitors act as a filter for the legal problems of clients, most of which they can deal with themselves. Barristers can be instructed only by solicitors. Barristers may also provide solicitors with written legal opinions on their specialist areas. A barrister must be a member of the Bar Council, which is the governing body of that part of the legal profession. Barristers are also members of an Inn of Court (i.e. the Inner Temple, the Middle Temple, Lincoln's Inn or Gray's Inn).

SUMMARY

(a) The English legal system is based on rules which have been formulated by the courts.

(b) The English legal and political systems were imposed on Wales through conquest.

(c) The court system in England and Wales consists of two hierarchical sets of courts: the criminal courts and the civil courts.

(d) In the criminal court system the lowest court is the magistrates' court, which deals with minor offences like breach of the peace and petty theft.

   The next court 'up the ladder' is the Crown Court, which hears *all* those criminal offences above the ones heard in the magistrates' court.

   The next three courts – High Court (Queen's Bench Division), Court of Appeal (Criminal Division) and House of Lords – hear appeals.

(e) In the civil court system the lowest court is the magistrates' court, which deals with recovery of certain small debts.

   The next court 'up the ladder' is the county court, which hears the bulk of civil actions.

   Appeals from the High Court go to the civil division of the Court of Appeal and then to the House of Lords.

(f) The legal profession of England and Wales has two branches: solicitors and barristers.

Northern Ireland

 Following the partitioning of Ireland in 1920 the Government of Ireland Act 1920 established a Parliament of Northern Ireland (Stormont) for six of the nine Ulster counties in which there was a Unionist majority. The Parliament comprised the Queen, the Senate and the Commons. It had considerable devolved powers, including the power to make laws over a wide range of subjects.

Following massive civil unrest in Northern Ireland, Stormont was replaced by a 'power sharing' Northern Ireland Assembly. This in turn was dissolved following the general strike in the province in 1972. Northern Ireland is now governed by the Secretary of State for Northern Ireland and a devolved administration.

Although the legal system of Northern Ireland is separate from that of England and Wales, it is closely linked to it.

The law presented in the text applies to Northern Ireland unless specifically stated otherwise.

The court system in Northern Ireland

Criminal courts

(a) *Magistrates' courts.* The courts fulfil the same functions as the magistrates' courts in England and Wales. 'Preliminary hearings' are dealt with by resident magistrates. Appeal lies from these courts to the Crown Court.

(b) *Crown Courts.* These courts deal with the more serious criminal cases. They may also hear appeals from the resident magistrates. Cases are heard by a Crown Court judge or, in Belfast and Londonderry, by a resident magistrate. Appeal lies to the Court of Appeal.

(c) *Belfast City Commission or Belfast Recorders' Court.* This special court deals with criminal matters arising from acts of terrorism. Cases are heard without a jury.

(d) *Court of Criminal Appeal.* This court hears appeals from the lower criminal courts. It can order a retrial. The court comprises the judges of the Supreme Court. Appeal lies to the House of Lords.

Civil courts

(a) *Magistrates' courts.* These courts may also hear minor civil cases as they do in England and Wales. Appeal lies to the county court .

(b) *County courts.* Most civil matters are dealt with by these courts. The court sits without a jury. Appeal lies to the Court of Appeal.

(c) *Supreme Court of Adjudicature.* This court comprises the High Court, the Court of Appeal and the Crown Court. The High Court of Justice has similar functions to the High Court in England and Wales. It has the same subdivisions. The Court of Appeal hears appeals from the lower civil courts. Appeal from the Supreme Court lies to the House of Lords.

The legal profession of Northern Ireland

The legal profession is divided into solicitors and barristers, and these have the same functions as their counterparts in England and Wales. Solicitors must be members of the Law Society of Northern Ireland. There is a separate 'bar' from that of England and Wales. Barristers must be members of the Inn of Court of Northern Ireland.

SUMMARY

(a) Northern Ireland has a separate legal system from England and Wales.

(b) Although separate, Northern Irish law is closely linked to English law.

(c) The less serious criminal matters are dealt with by magistrates' courts.

(d) Crown Courts hear more serious criminal cases.

(e) Appeals from Crown Courts are heard in the Court of Criminal Appeal, with the possibility of further appeal to the House of Lords.

(f) Magistrates' courts hear minor civil cases.

(g) Most civil cases are heard in the county courts.

(h) Appeals from the lower civil courts are heard by the Court of Appeal with the right of further appeal to the House of Lords.

(i) The functions of the legal profession in Northern Ireland are divided in the same way as that of England and Wales.

Scotland

The Scottish legal system

The Kingdom of Scotland was entirely separate from that of England prior to 1707. For much of their history Scotland and England were enemies. Thus, the dominant influence on Scotland during the period in which the legal system evolved was France. There was an 'auld alliance' between the two countries. The French legal system, and indeed the legal systems of most of Europe, were based on Roman law and thus many of the principles of Scots law have a Roman origin.

In 1603 the Scots King James VI became James I of England and thus united the two kingdoms. The two countries remained independent although they shared the same monarch. By the Treaty of Union 1706 and the respective Acts of Union, Scotland and England were superseded by the new state, the United Kingdom of Great Britain. The two countries thereafter were represented by one Parliament. The treaty preserved the separate legal systems of the two countries 'for all time coming'.

Although the two legal systems have become closer since the Union of 1707 and Scots law has been considerably influenced by English law, there are still substantial differences between the two systems. These differences are highlighted throughout the text but now we will go on to point out some of the general differences.

Jurisdiction

The authority of the courts of England and Wales stops at the Scottish border. A tour operator based in England who wishes to sue a travel agent based in Scotland would have to raise the action in a Scottish court. Likewise a travel agent based in Scotland who wishes to sue a tour operator based in England will have to raise the action in an English court.

Case law

Precedents from the English, Welsh or Northern Irish courts are not binding on Scottish courts. However, courts will pay regard to decisions from these other British jurisdictions if they are based on areas of law common to all three systems (e.g. tax law).

Legislation

Scotland has considerable administrative devolution. Many functions of government are dealt with by the Scottish Office. The Secretary of State for Scotland has more wide-ranging powers than any other Cabinet minister, with the exception of the Prime Minister. There is a Scottish Grand Committee of Members of Parliament for Scottish constituencies who scrutinise the activities of the Scottish Office.

Thus, whilst most Acts of Parliament apply throughout the whole of the United Kingdom, some do not apply to Scotland. Even those which do apply throughout the whole of the United Kingdom may have separate provisions within them dealing with Scotland. Parliament also enacts legislation which applies only to Scotland (e.g. the Age of Legal Capacity (Scotland) Act 1991).

Criminal law

Scottish criminal law is entirely separate from that of England and Wales or Northern Ireland. Certain actions may constitute a crime in Scotland but not in England and Wales and vice versa. Private prosecutions are virtually unknown in Scotland. Prosecutions are conducted by the Lord Advocate or by the local Procurator-Fiscal. Scottish juries comprise 15 persons, not 12. In Scotland there are three possible verdicts – 'guilty', 'not guilty' and *'not proven'*. The latter verdict indicates that there is insufficient evidence to convict the accused, but the court wishes to indicate that it does not consider the accused 'not guilty'.

Civil law

Because of the needs of business and commerce between Scotland and other parts of the United Kingdom many aspects of civil law have become similar throughout the state. There are still many differences, however, between Scots and English civil law and these will be pointed out throughout the text.

Language

The Roman law influence on the Scottish legal system has left Scots law with much Latin terminology. In addition, many old Scots words are used as legal terms, e.g. caution – pronounced 'kayshun' and meaning a guarantee. Some Scottish terms are similar to those of England, Wales and Northern Ireland but they should not be confused. Thus, in Scots law it is 'pursuer' rather than 'plaintiff'; 'defender' not 'defendant'; 'aliment' not 'alimony'; 'arbiter' not 'arbitrator'; 'interdict' not 'injunction'.

SUMMARY   Points to remember about the Scottish legal system:

(a) The Scottish legal system has been considerably influenced by Roman law.

(b) The Treaty, and subsequent Acts, of Union preserved the separate Scottish legal system.

(c) The Scottish court system is separate from that of England and Wales.

(d) Most Acts of Parliament apply throughout the whole of the United Kingdom but they may contain special provisions for Scotland.

(e) Some Acts of Parliament do not apply to Scotland and others apply to Scotland only.

(f) Scottish criminal law is entirely separate from English criminal law.

(g) Scots law has its own legal terminology.

The court system in Scotland

Criminal courts

(a) *District courts*. These courts deal with less serious criminal offences such as breach of the peace, disorderly conduct and minor offences. The courts are presided over by justices of the peace, who are not legally qualified, or by a stipendiary magistrate, who is. There is a legally qualified clerk of the court to assist the justices. There are no juries in the district court.

   The maximum penalties are a fine of up to £2,500 and/or up to 60 days' imprisonment. If the case is heard by a stipendiary magistrate he or she

may impose a fine of up to £5,000 and/or three months' imprisonment.
Appeal lies to the High Court of Justiciary.

(b) *Sheriff court.* Most criminal cases are dealt with by the sheriff court. Less serious cases are heard on 'summary procedure' where the sheriff sits without a jury and can impose a fine of up to £5,000 and/or three months' imprisonment (six months for a second or subsequent offence or dishonesty). More serious cases are heard 'on indictment' under 'solemn procedure' where the sheriff sits with a jury of 15. The maximum penalty under solemn procedure is an unlimited fine and/or up to two years' imprisonment. The sheriff may remit the case to the High Court if he or she feels that a tougher sentence should be imposed.

Appeal lies to the High Court of Justiciary (Court of Criminal Appeal).

(c) *High Court of Justiciary.* This court can deal with any criminal offence committed in Scotland, including its territorial waters. Very serious crimes, including treason, murder and rape, can be dealt with only by the High Court of Justiciary.

The court comprises the Lord Justice-General, Lord Justice Clerk and Lords Commissioners of Justiciary. Sittings of the court take place in Edinburgh and on circuit. Scotland is divided into four circuits, centring on major cities and towns in the area.

There is no maximum penalty.

Appeal lies to the High Court of Justiciary as a Court of Criminal Appeal.

(d) *High Court of Justiciary; Court of Criminal Appeal.* This court hears appeals from the lower criminal courts. Cases are heard in Edinburgh by the Lord Justice-General or the Lord Justice Clerk and at least two Lords Commissioners of Justiciary.

There is no appeal from this court.

Civil courts

(a) *Sheriff courts.* Most civil cases are dealt with by the sheriff court as a civil court. Certain actions are excluded from this court, however, and these include actions for nullity of marriage, decrees of legitimacy and the winding up of companies with a paid-up share capital in excess of £120,000. There is no upper limit on the amount which may be claimed in the sheriff court but in practice claims for very large sums of money are usually raised in the Court of Session.

Scotland is divided into six sheriffdoms within which there are several sheriff courts. The Sheriff Principal has overall responsibility for the administration of justice within the sheriffdom. Cases are heard by sheriffs without a jury. Appeal lies to the Sheriff Principal or the Inner House of the Court of Session. Appellants may choose to make their appeal to the Sheriff Principal as the appeal will be heard locally.

Appeal lies from the Sheriff Principal to the Inner House of the Court of Session.

(b) *Court of Session*. This court sits in Edinburgh and comprises the same judges as the judges of the High Court of Justiciary. As judges of the Court of Session their titles are the Lord President, Lord Justice Clerk and Lords Ordinary. The court is divided into the Outer House and the Inner House.

The Outer House is a court of first instance (i.e. it hears cases which have not been brought before the lower courts). Cases are heard by a Lord Ordinary. In certain limited cases there may be a jury of 12 persons. The work of this court is dominated by actions for divorce, reparation and actions for damages.

Appeal lies to the Inner House.

The Inner House is subdivided into First Division and the Second Division. Both divisions have equal standing. The First Division comprises the Lord President and three Lords Ordinary. The Second Division comprises the Lord Justice Clerk and three Lords Ordinary. Each division hears appeals from the lower courts.

Appeal lies to the House of Lords.

(c) *House of Lords*. By convention, when hearing Scottish appeals two of the Law Lords hearing the case must be versed in Scots law.

The Scottish legal profession

The Scottish legal profession has two branches, solicitors and advocates. Solicitors have the same function as their counterparts in England, Wales and Northern Ireland. They must be members of the Law Society of Scotland. Advocates have the same functions as barristers. They must be members of the Faculty of Advocates.

SUMMARY   The key elements of the Scottish courts are:

(a) The less serious criminal matters are dealt with by the district courts.

(b) Most criminal cases are heard in the sheriff court.

(c) Cases in the sheriff court may be heard on 'summary procedure' (without a jury) or 'on indictment' under 'solemn procedure' (with a jury).

(d) The High Court of Justiciary deals with the most serious criminal cases.

(e) The High Court of Justiciary goes on circuit throughout Scotland.

(f) The High Court of Justiciary acting as a court of criminal appeal is the final court of appeal in Scottish criminal matters.

(g) Most civil actions are heard in the sheriff court.

(h) Appeals may be made to the Sheriff Principal and/or the Inner House of the Court of Session.

(i) The Outer House of the Court of Session is a court of first instance.

(j) The Inner House of the Court of Session hears appeals from the sheriff courts and the Outer House.

(k) The House of Lords is the final court of appeal in Scottish civil cases.

SELF-ASSESSMENT QUESTIONS

State whether the following statements are correct or incorrect.

England and Wales

1. English law is based on 'precedent' or 'case law'.

2. Wales has a separate legal system from that of England.

3. Cases which are to be heard 'on indictment' in the Crown Court receive a 'preliminary hearing' in the magistrates' court.

4. Most criminal cases are dealt with by the Crown Courts.

5. The verdict of the jury in the Crown Court must be unanimous.

6. Appeals from the magistrates' courts are heard by the Queen's Bench Division of the Court of Appeal.

7. The House of Lords is the highest court of criminal appeal.

8. The magistrates' courts have very limited civil law functions.

9. Most civil actions are dealt with in the county courts.

10. Claims for less than £1,000 may be dealt with under the small claims procedure in the county courts.

11. Cases involving large sums of money are heard in the Queen's Bench Division of the High Court.

12. The House of Lords is the highest court of appeal in civil cases.

Northern Ireland

1. Northern Irish law is closely linked to English law.

2. 'Preliminary hearings' in the magistrates' court are heard by resident magistrates.

3. Appeals from the Crown Court are heard by the Belfast City Commission.

4. The Court of Criminal Appeal can order a case to be retried.

5. The highest court of appeal in Northern Irish criminal cases is the House of Lords.

6. Magistrates' courts have no civil law functions.

7. Most civil matters are dealt with by the county courts.

8. The jury in the county courts comprises 12 persons.

9. The High Court of Justice has similar functions to the High Court in England and Wales.

10. The Supreme Court of Adjudicature is the highest court of appeal in Northern Irish civil cases.

11. The Northern Irish legal profession is divided into solicitors and barristers.

12. Barristers must be members of the Law Society of Northern Ireland.

Scotland

1. The Scottish legal system is based on that of England and Wales.

2. The Treaty of Union preserved the separate legal system.

3. Some Acts of Parliament do not apply to Scotland.

4. Minor criminal offences are dealt with by the magistrates' courts.

5. Cases dealt with under 'solemn procedure' in the sheriff court are heard by a sheriff with a jury of 15 persons.

6. Very serious criminal cases are heard by the High Court of Justiciary.

7. The House of Lords is the highest court of appeal in Scottish criminal cases.

8. Most civil cases are dealt with by the sheriff court.

9. The Sheriff Principal hears appeals from the sheriff court in civil cases.

10. The Outer House of the Court of Session is a court of appeal.

11. The Court of Session goes on circuit throughout Scotland.

3 Business Organisations

GLOSSARY

capital Money invested in a business.

creditor Person to whom one owes money.

debentures A loan given to a company by a person, the debenture holder, evidenced by a debenture certificate. The debenture holder is entitled to repayment in full of the sum loaned plus interest at the agreed rate. He or she is not entitled to a share of the profits but then the value of the certificate does not decrease when the company incurs losses.

injunction Court order preventing someone from doing something.

interdict Scottish equivalent of injunction.

legal capacity Certain individuals (e.g. young children and the insane) are considered to lack the understanding to enter into legal obligations (i.e. they lack legal capacity).

passing off To trade in such a way as to indicate a (false) connection with an existing business.

pro rata In proportion to each person's contribution.

secured creditor A person who has been given security for a loan. This security may be in the form of a mortgage over the debtor's property. If the debtor fails to pay the creditor will ultimately be able to sell off that property and meet the debt with the proceeds of the sale.

shares A right to a proportion of the profits based on one's capital investment in the company. It also represents one's degree of liability for the debts of the company.

title to property Power of control over property which is usually, but not always, held by the owner.

AIM We often refer to the 'travel agent' and 'tour operator' as if they were individuals. In fact, in the United Kingdom, most travel agents or tour operators are businesses where a number of people work. The travel agent may own his or her own business or be in partnership with others. The travel agency may be part of a 'multiple' (i.e. a large company with many retail travel agency branches throughout the country) or it may be a small private company. The purpose of this chapter is to consider these different types of business organisation and the legal rules which govern them.

The sole trader

A person may wish to set up in business on his or her own as a sole trader; for example, the corner shop or the local fish and chip shop. This is the 'one-man' business, which means that all the profits are the trader's and all the losses as well.

All a sole trader needs to do to set up in business is to find suitable premises from which to operate. Suitable, that is, for use as business premises under current planning legislation and regulations.

The sole trader, however, does have some legal regulations imposed on him or her with regard to the business name (the name he or she intends to trade under). If the trader does not intend to do business under his or her own name, but to use a business name, the Business Names Act 1985 must be complied with (e.g. where Con Tacts trades as 'Contacts').

The provisions of the Act which apply to sole traders are:

(a) Traders may not carry on business in Great Britain under a name which would be likely to give the impression that the business is connected with central or local government. The reason for this is to ensure that the public are not misled into believing that the business gets a grant of money such as that received by local authorities from central government.

(b) Traders may not use a business name which includes any word or expression which has been specified in the Company and Business Names Regulations 1981, for example: building society, insurance or royal.

(c) If a trader does wish to use a name specified in these regulations then it is necessary to write to the 'relevant body', if one is stated, for permission to include that word in the business name (relevant bodies include the Home Office and the Scottish Home and Health Department).

(d) A trader's name (e.g. Con Tacts) and address must be stated clearly on all business letters, written orders for goods or services, invoices and receipts and demands for payment, and he or she must display a prominent notice containing the name and address at any premises where the business is being carried on.

(e) When people ask for these details traders must be able to supply a business card stating their names and addresses.

(f) When traders choose a trading name this must not be like that of an existing business. The reason is that the public might confuse the two businesses.

Example

The sole trader decides to set up a travel business and trade under the name Contacts. However, another business called Computer Contacts Ltd is already established, specialising in computer dating. The sole trader may have a civil action brought against him or her for 'passing off'. This would entitle Computer Contacts Ltd to apply to the court for an injunction (interdict, in Scotland) to stop the sole trader using the name. It will then be necessary to choose another name; failure to do so would be contempt of court and make the trader liable to a fine or a term of imprisonment. Passing off does not apply if the sole trader trades under his or her own name (e.g. Con Tacts as opposed to Contacts).

Traders commit an offence if they contravene any of these provisions. Furthermore, if they do not display their true names in the ways described they may find it difficult to enforce their contracts.

Example

Contacts is owed £500 by Cheapo Tours Ltd. It raises an action against the latter for payment of the debt. Cheapo Tours Ltd may not have to pay the debt if it establishes that it could not find out the true name and address of Contacts.

SUMMARY

(a) The business name must not imply a connection with the government or a local authority.

(b) Certain words or expressions are prohibited (e.g. royal, insurance, building society) unless permission has been obtained from the relevant body.

(c) The sole trader's own name must be displayed on business documents, etc. and on a notice at the business premises.

(d) It is an offence to fail to comply with these regulations and it may also render contracts unenforceable.

(e) The business name must not be like that of an existing business.

Special characteristics of a sole trader's business

(a) Sole traders put their own money into their businesses and if more is needed they may be able to convince various financial institutions to lend them some. However, sole traders are under a disadvantage because they are very limited as to the ways of attracting capital: they cannot persuade people to invest in the business because they are not a company; nor can they bring in partners with capital.

(b) Sole traders' liability is unlimited, which means that they are personally liable for all the debts and obligations of their businesses, so that even their private property may be used to pay the debts of the business (e.g. if the business has £50,000 of debts to pay and the total value of the business is £20,000 the sole trader must make up the difference from his or her personal funds). Transferring private property to a spouse will not make it safe if it can be shown that this was done in order to defeat creditors.

(c) There is no requirement to hold an annual general meeting or to lodge an annual return and accounts. Sole traders may conduct their businesses with as little regulation as possible, though for tax purposes accounts should be checked by an accountant.

(d) Sole traders can cease to carry on their business whenever they like. They simply shut the door, sell up, pay their debts and liabilities and retire to the country with the remainder. If a trader dies, and his or her successor (spouse or child) does not wish to carry on trading, the business also ceases and the executors may either sell the business as a going concern or sell the assets to another business, first paying its debts and liabilities.

Insolvency

In the case of sole traders who cannot pay their debts, their businesses can be dissolved by the creditors, thus making them bankrupt. The procedure is contained in the Insolvency Act 1986 (or Bankruptcy (Scotland) Act 1985) and can be summarised as follows.

If a creditor is owed £750 or more by a sole trader the creditor will present a petition to the county court (sheriff court, in Scotland) to declare him or her bankrupt. The creditor has two choices:

(a) He or she may be able to propose a scheme of arrangement under which the trader pays the creditors so much in the £, e.g. there are debts amounting to £10,000 but the business is worth only £5,000, so he or she would propose to pay the creditors 50 pence for every pound owed. If the trader adopts this course he or she asks the court for an interim order, which, if granted, halts the bankruptcy proceedings. An accountant is appointed to run the business. If the creditors accept this appointment and the scheme of arrangement, the sole trader will not be declared bankrupt.

(b) If the trader cannot or does not propose a scheme of arrangement to the creditors or they do not accept it, the petition to the court goes ahead and he or she is declared bankrupt. The court appoints a trustee in bankruptcy who takes control of the sole trader's business. The creditors may appoint a committee from among themselves to work with the trustee. The trustee puts notices in local newspapers asking for the creditors to send in proof of their debts which the trustee will rank in order of priority as set out in the Acts. After the trustee's expenses and fees are paid there are certain preferential debts (i.e. income tax, PAYE deductions, VAT and car tax, wages, holiday pay and social security contributions of employees).

These debts are paid with the proceeds from the sale of the sole trader's assets and only when these and any secured creditors have been paid can the ordinary unsecured creditors receive any payment. The court discharges the sole trader three years after he or she has been declared bankrupt, though there will be no discharge if he or she has not been complying with the statutory provisions or not co-operating with the trustee.

Once the trader has been discharged, any debts not paid by the date of the discharge are no longer due, which means they are cancelled and he or she is free to set up in business again with a clean sheet.

SUMMARY The legal position of sole traders can be summarised as follows:

(a) Generally, there are no legal regulations to prevent people from setting up in business as sole traders.

(b) If they use trade names for their businesses, the Business Names Act 1985 applies, which means that the business name cannot be a prohibited one or one which the public might confuse with a government department or another organisation with a similar name.

(c) Traders must give written notice of their names and addresses to persons with whom they do business when requested to do so (e.g. by providing a business card). They must also display a notice with this information on their premises.

(d) Traders commit an offence if they contravene the Act.

(e) Attracting finance is a problem because they cannot ask the public to invest in their businesses or bring in partners.

(f) Sole traders have unlimited liability for the debts of the business.

(g) The business can be terminated whenever they wish.

(h) If sole traders cannot pay their debts they may be declared bankrupt unless they can propose a scheme of arrangement to the creditors. If they cannot do this the court declares them bankrupt and appoints a trustee who sells the business to pay the preferential debts and then the ordinary creditors. A discharge from bankruptcy is usually given three years after becoming bankrupt provided the regulations have been complied with.

Partnerships

Introduction

When someone wants to enter into business with another person, or several others, he or she could form a partnership to carry on the business. Con Tacts' travel business, for example, has been very successful; however, he needs more capital in order to expand. He cannot persuade any financial institution to advance him further loans so Con asks his friend, Sue, to be his business partner. Sue is to contribute an amount of capital and expertise in return for a share in the business. Sue and Con would then work together in the business, having drawn up a partnership agreement.

Nature of partnership

 Partnerships are subject to the provisions of the Partnership Act 1890. This Act defines a partnership as 'the relation which subsists between persons carrying on a business in common with a view of profit'.

What then are the general characteristics of partnerships?

(a) They come into existence when the parties agree the terms under which they will do business together. This agreement, which is a contract, may be oral or written or even inferred from the parties' acts. For Con's and Sue's agreement, common sense dictates that they should make a written partnership agreement. No particular form for this is laid down by law.

(b) The term 'business' implies that there is a course of business activity, even though this might be of a relatively short duration.

(c) The persons must have full legal capacity to enter into the partnership agreement.

(d) The business must be a commercial venture, trade or profession.

(e) The aim of this commercial venture must be a share in net profits, that is, profits less all the expenses and outgoings. Persons who get together in a society to prevent cruelty to pit ponies are not partners, nor are joint owners of property such as a husband and wife.

(f) A partnership, or firm, is the group of partners. Each partner is jointly liable with the other partners for all the firm's debts and obligations incurred while he or she is a partner.

Example

Jason, Kate and Sandra Moll are partners in the firm of Over Sea Travel. After initial success, sales steadily declined and the firm went bankrupt. The firm's debts amounted to £60,000 whilst the assets were valued at £30,000. Jason and Kate are also both personally bankrupt.

Mrs Moll has substantial private assets. The creditors can claim the £30,000 outstanding from her. Each partner is liable for the whole of the firm's debts.

Note: For the Scottish position re joint and several liability *see* p31.

Partnership property belongs to the partners, which means that when they die or retire there will be changes in the formal title to the firm's property.

The Rules of the Supreme Court allow firms to be sued in the firm name. This right already existed under Scottish common law.

(g) Section 4 of the Partnership Act 1890 provides that in Scotland 'a firm is a legal person distinct from the partners of whom it is composed'. This means that:

(i) the firm's debts are those of the firm; however, if it cannot pay, each partner is liable jointly and severally for those debts: jointly with the firm and the other partners, and personally (severally) – i.e. his or her own personal estate becomes liable to pay;

(ii) partnership property belongs to the firm; however, title to any heritable property (land, buildings) will be held by the partners in trust for the firm;

(iii) a partner can contract with the firm and the firm can sue and be sued on these contracts.

(h) If the partnership name does not contain the surnames of each partner it will be subject to the provisions of the Business Names Act 1985 and the same restrictions and disclosure requirements as is the sole trader. Thus, the names and addresses of all the partners must be prominently displayed in a notice and on all business letters and documents.

The firm may choose to carry on business in the name of the partners, even if this causes confusion with another business. If the name the firm chooses is the same as or similar to that of a competitor, then the firm may have an action brought against it seeking an injunction (interdict) to prevent it using that name.

(i) The firm is dissolved every time a partner dies or retires because he or she, or the estate, has to be repaid his or her capital and share of the profits. A new partnership agreement between the remaining partners is drawn up. Similarly, when a new partner comes into the firm a fresh partnership agreement between all the partners is entered into.

SUMMARY (a) Partnerships are subject to provisions contained in the Partnership Act 1890.

(b) Partnerships are created by an agreement between the parties, which may be oral, written or inferred from their actions.

(c) Partners must have legal capacity.

(d) The subject of the partnership must be a business and the partners must share net profits.

(e) Partners are liable jointly for the firm's debts and obligations, and partnership property belongs to them.

(f)   In Scotland a partnership has a separate legal personality; partners are jointly and severally liable; partnership property belongs to the firm.

(g)   The firm may be subject to provisions in the Business Names Act 1985.

(h)   The firm is dissolved when a partner dies or retires, or a new partner joins.

Powers of partners

In deciding when to become partners in a business one of the important things to discuss and agree upon is what areas of the business each partner will have special responsibility for and control (authority) over.

Example

One of the reasons Con asked Sue if she would consider going into partnership with him is because of Sue's skill and ability to negotiate good business contracts. Con's skill lies in managing the finances but he does not have Sue's flair for selling or negotiating. In their written partnership agreement they have expressly agreed that Sue will have control over the selling side of the business and Con will look after the finances.

However, besides these specific powers that individual partners may agree upon, the Partnership Act 1890 states that every partner has the power to make himself (herself) and the other partners liable for all the acts he or she does which are within the ordinary business of the firm.

In Con and Sue's case this means that if Con enters into a contract with a tour operator to sell holidays and the tour operator does not know that Sue and Con have agreed that Sue will control this side of the business, this contract will be binding on the firm. Sue and Con would not be able to get out of this contract (because Con did not negotiate as favourable terms as Sue would have done!) on the grounds that Con did not have the power to make that contract on behalf of the firm. The tour operator (third party) was not aware of any restriction on Con's powers and the contract is one which would be within the normal course of business of a travel agency.

If partners do agree any restrictions on their power, such restrictions have to be notified to all persons who deal with the firm, otherwise third parties may rely on the fact that the partner can bind the firm and the other partners for all acts which are within the normal course of the firm's business.

Any partner who contravenes such an agreement, where persons dealing with the firm were aware of the restrictions on his or her power, will be personally bound on that contract with the third party.

Thus:

(a) partners have to decide on the specific authority each will have;

(b) partners are liable with the other partners for all acts within the ordinary business of the firm;

(c) any restrictions on partners' authority should be notified to persons dealing with the firm.

Liability of partners

When Con was a sole trader he had the sole responsibility (liability) for paying the debts of the business and for carrying on the business. Now that he has a partner, Sue, they both share in the running of the business and the profits. Each is liable jointly with the other for all the debts and obligations of the firm incurred while a partner. If either dies, his or her estate will have to pay his or her share of the debts and obligations of the firm.

When a partner retires liability for transactions entered into while he or she was a partner persists, unless it is possible to show that he or she is no longer liable.

Retirement

Prior to retirement, a partner comes to an agreement with the other partners and clients to pay his or her share of the firm's debts and obligations. It is more common today, however, to have an indemnity clause in the partnership agreement which would state that in the event of retirement the remaining partners will take over the liabilities of the firm, thus doing away with the necessity of drawing up an agreement.

In Scotland the liability of the partners for the firm's debts and obligations is joint and several. This means that a creditor looks to the firm first for payment of the debt or obligation, so any action is first brought against the firm in its name (joint liability). Only if the firm cannot pay the debt or fulfil the obligation can an action be brought against a partner personally (several liability). That partner then has the right to relief *pro rata* from the other partners; that is, the other partners pay their share of the debt to the partner against whom the action for payment was brought.

Liability to third parties

If the partner, while engaged in the firm's business, harms another person or his or her property, the firm is liable in damages to that third party. The partner is also personally liable. The injured third party may thus bring an action for damages against the firm and/or the individual partner. The firm may then seek to reclaim the amount paid from the partner whose negligence caused harm to the third party.

The firm is liable not only when partners harm third parties or their property but also if a partner who received money or property belonging to a client then gambles that money away at the local casino or sells the property at the weekly auction sale. The firm has to make good the client's loss. However, for the firm to be liable for the client's loss the partner must have been acting within the scope of his or her authority. Thus, it would be within the scope of the authority for either Sue or Con to receive money from people coming in to book holidays. If either one uses that money for his or her own purposes (e.g. at the casino) the firm has to repay the money. The client may bring an action for repayment against the firm and separate and successive actions against the partners for compensation.

In Scotland victims first bring their claims against the firm and, if it cannot pay, they may then bring an action against an individual partner who is entitled to relief *pro rata* from the other partners.

SUMMARY

(a) When partners die their estate becomes liable for their share of the debts and obligations incurred while they were partners.

(b) Retiring partners are liable for their share of firm debts and obligations incurred while partners.

(c) In Scotland liability is joint and several.

(d) The firm is vicariously liable for harm caused to third parties.

(e) If money or property belonging to a third party is misapplied by a partner the firm is liable to make good the loss.

(f) The third party may bring an action against the firm and separate and successive actions against the partners for compensation.

(g) In Scotland victims first bring their claim against the firm and then against an individual.

Companies

The nature of companies

The law affords adult human beings the right to perform a number of legal functions such as entering into contracts and suing and being sued on those contracts. Companies, too, are viewed by the law as legal persons able to enter into contracts.

 The case which established the principle that companies have a legal personality is *Salomon v Salomon & Co. Ltd* (1897).

Salomon had a successful leather and boot business which he ran with his four sons. He then incorporated this business under the Companies Act 1862

and set it up as Aaron Salomon & Co. Ltd. The Act required at least seven shareholders as the minimum number of members of a company registered under the Act so he transferred six shares to his wife and family while he held the rest. Salomon entered into an agreement with the company for the sale of the business. A further £10,000 of the purchase price he loaned back to the company, which was to repay him later. The security for this loan was the assets of the company, which meant that if it defaulted on repayment of the instalments or went into liquidation the assets would be sold and the proceeds would be first used to repay Salomon his £10,000.

The new company did not prosper and had to go into liquidation. The debts of the trade (unsecured) creditors came to approximately £8,000 while the company's assets were approximately £6,000. These unsecured creditors then claimed that all the assets should be applied to repaying them what they were owed. Their grounds for claiming this were that Salomon and the company were in reality the same person and on this ground he could not lend money to himself or give himself a security over his own assets. The liquidator claimed rescission of the contract for the transfer of the business and disputed the issue of the secured loan. The House of Lords decided that the company was a separate legal person, thus the secured loan was a perfectly valid transaction. The company was separate from Salomon and so he could not be responsible for its debts. Therefore it was Salomon, as a secured creditor, who was entitled to the remaining assets in part payment of his £10,000 loan to the company.

Abuses

However, this principle of corporate personality has allowed abuses, with companies trying to avoid their legal obligations. This has led the courts to attribute acts or omissions to the shareholders and thus ignore the separate personality, as the case of *Gilford Motor Co. Ltd v Horne* (1933) illustrates.

Horne had been employed by the Gilford Motor Company and had agreed to the inclusion of a clause in his contract of employment which stated that he would not try to persuade the company's customers to transfer their custom to him should he set up in the same line of business himself.

Horne did leave this job and set up a similar business which he incorporated by registering it under the Companies Act. His next move was to send out letters from his company inviting his former employer's customers to do business with his organisation instead.

The Gilford Motor Company asked the court for an injunction to stop Horne, alleging he was in breach of his contractual obligations. Horne argued that it was not him but his company that was competing with Gilford and that his company was not a party to his employment contract with Gilford Motor Company.

The court granted the injunction against Horne and his company on the grounds that he could not use the company to evade his contractual liabilities.

Acts of Parliament, particularly the Companies Act 1985, the Insolvency Act

1986 and tax legislation, will also allow the courts to ignore the corporate personality.

Other characteristics of corporate personality

Besides this separate personality, companies also have the following characteristics:

(a) The company can be dissolved only by process of law; it is unaffected by the death of its shareholders.

(b) If the company is limited by shares or guarantee then a member's liability is limited either to the unpaid portion of his or her shareholding (if any) or to his or her guarantee.

(c) Shares in a company are generally freely transferable though there may be some restriction on transfer in the articles (i.e. they may have to be offered first to directors or other shareholders).

(d) A company may have as many members as it likes, though a registered company is subject to a minimum of one.

(e) A company must have a written constitution made up of a memorandum of association and articles of association.

(f) Companies can borrow for purposes which are within their objects clauses. They have additional methods of granting security for loans compared with patnerships and sole traders.

(g) Companies can generally be dissolved only by a formal liquidation.

(h) Companies have to pay corporation tax on profits and gains.

As the main form of business organisation in the United Kingdom today is the registered company, the law relating to registered companies being found principally in the Companies Act 1985 and case law, any further reference to 'companies' is to registered companies.

Types of registered company

Thus, there are various types of registered company.

Limited companies

Registered companies are most commonly limited by shares, which means that the liability of the members is limited because once they have paid the full nominal value of their shares, and any premiums that may be payable, they cannot be asked to pay any further sums in the event of the company being wound up on the grounds that it cannot pay its creditors.

Companies limited by guarantee

These companies are not usually commercial enterprises but, rather, clubs and societies. Their members are liable only to the amount stated in the company's memorandum, which will not exceed £100. This sum becomes payable only if the company is wound up while the person is a member, or within a year after he or she ceases to be a member, for payment of the company's debts and liabilities contracted before he or she ceased to be a member, and for the expenses of the winding up.

Unlimited companies

Members of these companies can be asked to pay sums to meet the liabilities of the company, but only if the company is wound up and has more liabilities than assets. This type of company is not very common because of this personal liability of the members.

Public companies

The Companies Act 1985 defines a public company as one having the liability of its members limited by shares or guarantee and having a share capital, with a clause in its memorandum which states that the company is a public one. The company name has to end with the words 'public limited company' or the initials 'plc' or the Welsh equivalent 'ccc'. The company must have an authorised share capital of at least £50,000, 25 per cent of which is to be fully paid up. This requirement has to be met before a public company can commence business. Public companies can offer their shares for sale to the public.

Private companies

These companies are not subject to the requirement as to a minimum amount of share capital and they can, therefore, commence business as soon as they obtain a certificate of incorporation from the Registrar of Companies. Their names have to end with the word 'Limited' or 'Ltd'. They are prohibited from offering their shares for sale to the public.

SUMMARY

(a) Companies have a legal personality separate from that of their members.

(b) The case of *Salomon v Salomon & Co. Ltd* (1897) established the principle of the separate legal personality of companies.

(c) Businessmen and women have abused this principle; therefore the courts will, on occasion, ignore the separate personality.

(d) Companies have other characteristics which make them different from sole traders and partnerships.

(e) Companies registered under the Companies Act 1985 are the most common type of company.

(f) There are various types of company registrable under the Act.

Constitution of a company

If Sue and Con have done really well in their partnership and expanded it by bringing in other partners (up to a maximum of 20) they may now find that they are having difficulty in attracting more capital. Therefore, if they wish to develop the business further they are going to have to consider incorporating it.

This means that they will form their business into a company.

A company, limited or unlimited, private or public, is formed by applying for registration to the Registrar of Companies (in Cardiff, for English and Welsh companies; in Edinburgh, for Scottish ones; in Belfast, for Northern Ireland).

Registration means having to send certain documents to the Registrar who checks them to see that the statutory (under the Companies Act 1985) requirements have been complied with. The Registrar then issues a certificate of incorporation, which means that from the date of issue the company is 'born'; it is a legal person able to do business and capable of exercising all the functions of an incorporated company.

The two main documents of a registered company are the memorandum of association and the articles of association.

Memorandum of association

The memorandum, which sets out the essential details of the company's relationship with the outside world, contains five main clauses:

(a) the name of the company;

(b) whether the registered office is situated in England, Wales, Scotland or Northern Ireland;

(c) the objects of the company – that is, what it is in business to do;

(d) a statement that the liability of the members is limited;

(e) a statement of how much authorised share capital the company has and its division into shares of a fixed amount.

If the business is a public company it will have an additional clause stating that it is a public company. If the company is one limited by guarantee there will be an additional clause stating the amount of the guarantee.

Example

Con and Sue decide that incorporating their business is the way forward for them. They could draw up a memorandum which might contain the following information:

(a) The name of the company shall be Contacts Limited.

(b) The registered office is to be situated in England (Wales/Scotland/Northern Ireland).

(c) The objects for which the company is established are: . . .(since the passing of the Companies Act 1989, the incorporators now have the choice – under section 110(1) – of having a traditional objects clause or a simple statement that the object of the company is to carry on business as a general commercial company).

(d) The liability of the members is limited.

(e) The share capital of the company is £30,000 divided into 30,000 shares of £1 each.

'We the persons whose names and addresses are subscribed are desirous of being formed into a company in pursuance of this Memorandum of Association, and we respectfully agree to take the number of shares in the capital of the company set opposite our respective names.'

Sue and Con then sign this form and opposite their signatures the number of shares each has agreed to take (usually one share). Then follows the date and the signatures of the witnesses to Sue's and Con's subscription.

Articles of association

The articles of association regulate the company's internal affairs and deal with such matters as the rights which attach to the various classes of shares the company might have; the powers of directors; the procedure at company meetings; winding up. Sue and Con do not have to write the articles. They may adopt those set out in Table A to the Companies (Tables A–F) Regulations 1985. Alternatively, they could adapt the articles in Table A to suit their company's needs. If they do this they must ensure that the articles are printed and numbered consecutively.

Both the memorandum and articles have to be signed by two persons in the presence of at least one witness.

These two documents may be altered by the company in general meeting, though there are statutory restrictions on this power to alter which safeguard the rights of shareholders and creditors. A company may alter its objects clause by special resolution, but this is subject to confirmation by the court (section 110(1) and (2) of the Companies Act 1989, replacing section 4 of the 1985 Act).

The articles may be altered by a special resolution passed by the members in general meeting. The statutory restrictions on this power safeguard the rights of the holders of various classes of shares in the company and can be found in sections 125–129 of the Companies Act 1985.

SUMMARY

(a) A business such as a sole trader's or a partnership may be incorporated.

(b) Incorporation is achieved through registration.

(c) The two main documents of a registered company are the memorandum of association and articles of association.

(d) Both the memorandum and articles may be altered, subject to statutory restrictions.

Liability of a company

Now that Sue and Con have incorporated their business, the company, Contacts Limited, has a separate legal personality and can enter into contracts in its own name and sue and be sued on these agreements. However, even though Contacts Limited has a legal persona it has no animate form so it has to act through agents. Sue and Con are the directors of the company and, as such, they are its controlling power; they are the agents through which the company works. Therefore, they have power to enter into contracts on behalf of the company.

Powers of directors

The directors of a company may decide that they will form a board of directors and elect one of their number as a managing director who will have power to make contracts on behalf of the company. Individual directors may have limits on their power to contract; for example, Con and Sue could decide that Con should have authority to enter into contracts in relation to the finances of the company, while Sue has the authority to negotiate contracts in relation to the selling of holidays.

If the director, or managing director, has power to enter into a particular contract, and it is within the objects stated in the objects clause of the memorandum, that contract will be binding on the company.

However, what would be the legal position if the director, or managing director, enters into a contract with a third party which is beyond his or her authority? The company would be bound by such a contract if it is one that a third party would expect to be within the ordinary ambit of authority of such a director (see *Freeman & Lockyer v Buckhurst Park Properties (Mangal) Ltd and Another* [1964] All ER 630).

 There is also the rule in *Turquand's Case* (1856). Here the articles of the company authorised the directors to borrow money on behalf of the company, first having obtained this authority by means of a resolution passed by the company in general meeting. The board of directors borrowed from the bank, but did not get the authority to do this by having the resolution passed.

The court held that the company was bound by this contract because the bank had no way of knowing whether or not a resolution had been passed. The bank was entitled to assume one had been passed.

Therefore, the rule is: when a person deals with a company in a transaction that is not outside powers laid down in the articles and memorandum, the company will be bound by that transaction even if there has been some irregularity in the internal management.

Finally, there is the situation of the company holding out (representing) to third parties that a director has more authority than that actually given him or her by the company – for example where a company allows a director to act with all the powers of a managing director when no managing director has in fact been appointed by the company. Third parties do not know of this internal irregularity. He or she has been held out (represented) by the company as being the managing director. Therefore, if a director does not in fact have the actual authority to enter into a particular transaction the company will be barred from withdrawing from that contract on the grounds that the director was acting outside his or her actual authority.

Besides having contractual liability, the company also has liability for the civil wrongs of the directors when they are acting on its behalf. If a director, in his or her capacity as director, causes harm to a third party or to his or her property, the company may be liable to compensate that third party.

A company can also incur criminal liability. Some legislation imposes criminal sanctions; for example, under the Trade Descriptions Act 1968 it is an offence to make false or misleading statements relating to the provision of services, facilities and accommodation in travel brochures. The company and every person responsible for that travel brochure is liable to a fine and/or a term of imprisonment. (This is discussed further in Chapter 6.)

SUMMARY   The liability of a company may thus be stated as follows:

(a) A company acts through agents – its directors.

(b) Directors have power to enter into contracts on behalf of the company.

(c) A company may have a board of directors with a managing director.

(d) Individual directors may have limits on their power to contract.

(e) A contract entered into by a director which is outside his or her authority binds the company.

(f) If a company seeks to withdraw from a contract, the third party may rely on the rule in *Turquand's Case*.

(g) If a company holds out a director as having more authority than he or she has in reality, then the company cannot put forward the plea that the director was acting outside his or her authority as grounds for withdrawing from the contract.

(h) A company may incur liability for the harm caused to a third party or his or her property.

(i) A company may incur criminal liability.

Directors' powers and liability

Directors have powers of management, which means that they should act with skill and care and in the best interests of the company as a whole. Some specific powers of management are:

(a) to appoint additional directors;

(b) to borrow;

(c) to convene meetings;

(d) to issue shares and debentures;

(e) to bring legal actions in the name of the company.

Directors also owe a fiduciary duty to the company because they are its agents. It means that they are liable to account to the company for any unauthorised profits that were made because of their position as directors. Directors are also liable for any loss suffered by the company as a result of their negligence. If they make an error of judgement, provided they were acting in good faith they will not be personally liable.

Therefore, if what directors do is within their powers and not fraudulent or dishonest, they will not be liable for loss. It has to be proved that the director failed to exercise discretion and judgement as a director.

Misapplication of company funds by directors makes them liable to make restitution or pay compensation to the company for the loss suffered.

When directors enter into contracts with third parties on behalf of the company they may be personally liable on those contracts. This situation would arise where a director enters into a contract for the company before that company has received its certificate of incorporation. For the director to avoid personal liability on such a pre-incorporation contract it must be clearly expressed in the contract that it was not intended that he or she should be liable.

The company can commit offences because the acts of those in control of the company become the company's acts, and may make it liable for criminal prosecution. It has been decided by case law that 'those in control' are the board of directors, the managing director and other officers who may have power delegated to them. Thus, directors and other company officers will be liable along with the company. For example, it is an offence for a director to authorise or permit contravention of the Companies Act 1985. The company is also liable.

SUMMARY

(a) Directors owe a duty of care to the company.

(b) Directors owe a fiduciary duty to the company.

(c) Misapplication of funds by directors makes them liable to pay compensation to the company.

(d) If directors enter into pre-incorporation contracts, they may be personally liable on them unless there is clear indication to the contrary.

(e) Directors and the company may be liable for criminal prosecution.

SELF-ASSESSMENT QUESTIONS

State whether the following statements are correct or incorrect.

1. The Business Names Act 1985 applies to sole traders if they trade under their own names.

2. Sole traders commit an offence if the business name gives the impression that it is connected with a government department.

3. Belinda Buckett wants to trade under the name 'The Buckett Shop'. This name would have to comply with the Business Names Act 1985.

4. Sole traders may avoid being declared bankrupt by proposing to pay their creditors so much in the £ under a scheme of arrangement.

5. By transferring ownership of family property to a spouse a sole trader removes it from the risk of being claimed by creditors in order to pay his or her debts.

6. In bankruptcy proceedings the preferential debts are paid in full before the ordinary creditors.

7. The law in relation to partnership is found in the Partnership Act 1890.

8. In England, Wales and Northern Ireland a partnership has a separate legal personality, whereas in Scotland it is merely the aggregate of the partners.

9. Betty and Alexandra are partners in an accounting firm. Alexandra, driving her car negligently on her way to work, knocks down a pedestrian. Betty is also liable for Alexandra's act.

10. The next day Alexandra is driving on firm's business and has another accident. A client, Milton Freeway, on whose behalf the journey is being undertaken, is a passenger in the car. He can sue the firm as well as Betty and Alexandra for injuries received in the accident.

11. When a partner retires from the partnership his or her liability as a partner also ceases from the date of retirement.

12. A firm may be liable in tort (delict) for the civil wrongs of partners.

13. In England, Wales and Northern Ireland the aggrieved parties may raise actions against individual partners for compensation. If their claims are not fully satisfied they may raise separate actions against the remaining partners.

14. In Scotland a third party raises an action for compensation against the firm.

15. A company can enter into contracts in its own name.

16. Promoters of a company act as its agents.

17. Directors who act beyond their actual authority but within the capacity of the company bind the company.

18. Directors acting within their powers and not fraudulently or dishonestly will not be liable for any loss suffered by the company.

19. A company can be liable for a civil wrong if it can be shown that the directors are acting as the company.

20. A company cannot commit an offence because it has no will of its own.

4 Business Premises

GLOSSARY

enforcement notice Notice served by the local planning authority when a building has undergone a change of use or has been materially altered without the necessary planning permission. It may also be served where permission has been obtained but the conditions laid down have not been complied with.

occupier The person who has the control of the building.

planning permission An express application made to the local planning authority for permission to alter certain aspects of a building.

trespasser Any person who is on premises without invitation of any kind and whose presence is not known to the proprietor, or someone who goes beyond the limits placed on visitors by the proprietor.

Introduction

Sometimes it may be necessary for a travel agent to convert the premises from which the business is to be run or to make some alterations to the structure. To do either of these things the travel agent must know the basic provisions of the planning legislation. We tell you what these are, and also about other legislation that affects business premises, so that you are aware of the duties the law imposes on the owner/occupier of business premises.

Planning legislation

 The law of planning is contained mainly in the Town and Country Planning Acts 1947 to 1977. In Scotland the main provisions are found in the Town and Country Planning (Scotland) Act 1972. There is also a large amount of subordinate legislation, made by both the Scottish and English legal systems. Generally, English and Scots planning law is similar, and for the most part the implications of the legislation for the travel agent are the same under both legal systems.

Change of use

One of the matters planning legislation covers is the use to which land and/or buildings are to be put.

Planning permission is required if a material change is to be made in the use of land or buildings. It is a matter of *fact* whether a change of use is 'material'. One of the criteria for judging this is the primary use to which a building is put, rather than any ancillary use.

Example

Oxbridge University Students' Association has a small travel office in the Students' Union building. The primary use of the building is for students' social recreation; the travel office is merely an ancillary use.

A modification to this requirement that planning permission is required for all material changes of use is that the Use Classes Order will generally permit changes of use within a particular class (defined in the Order) without planning permission. This is because changes within classes defined in the Order have little (if any) impact on the community.

The 'use class' to which a travel agency belongs is Class I (shops). This class includes shops, hairdressers, undertakers, post offices, repair and pet shops. It does not include garages, petrol stations, car showrooms, restaurants and cafés, betting shops, hotels or licensed premises. Organisations such as banks, estate agents and building societies are classified as 'financial, professional and other services'. Car hire and driving instructors' establishments are categorised as offices rather than shops.

If a change of use is trivial, planning consent will not be required.

When is planning permission required?

The travel agent will require planning permission:

(a) if it is intended to alter the structure of the premises;

(b) for external decoration for advertising purposes;

(c) for any alterations to a building that provide additional space below ground;

(d) to put up illuminated signs.

Internal alterations and maintenance do not require planning permission unless they affect the use to which the building is put, or its external appearance.

Certain specified types of development may be authorised by means of a Development Order made by the Secretary of State. Such 'developments' as greenhouses and garages, sewers, private roads and temporary buildings come into this category. They do not need a specific application for planning consent.

How do you get planning permission?

Planning permission is obtained by making an express application for it, to the local planning authority. An application form must be obtained from the authority, be completed by giving details of the proposed development and be lodged with copies of the plans. The planning authority notifies the applicant in writing of its decision. Conditions may be imposed on the applicant but these must be fair and reasonable.

Who may make an application?

Applications may be made only by the person who owns the premises, or has a tenancy of or other interest in them.

If a change of use is made, or alterations undertaken, without first obtaining permission, or in contravention of any conditions imposed, an enforcement notice may be served by the planning authority. Such notice may require the person to demolish the work or to comply with the conditions in question. Failure to comply with an enforcement notice may incur a fine.

Appeals

The applicant may be dissatisfied with the planning authority's decision, either because the application was refused or because conditions were imposed. In such a case notice of appeal may be given by the applicant within one month of the decision.

The appeal must be made to the appropriate Secretary of State: in England, the Secretary of State for the Environment; in Scotland or Wales, the Secretary of State for Scotland or Wales, as the case may be. The applicant/appellant will be sent a form in which to make a formal appeal. This must be completed and submitted together with the original planning application and plans. The Secretary of State will decide the appeal, though it is more usual for an inspector to be appointed to determine it. The planning authority will be represented in writing.

Once the appeal has been determined, a report is sent to the applicant. This decision is final unless a point of law is involved, in which event an appeal may then be made to the courts.

SUMMARY
(a) Planning law is contained mainly in the Town and Country Planning Acts 1947 to 1977 and the Town and Country Planning (Scotland) Act 1972.

(b) Planning permission is required if a material change of use of land or buildings is to be made.

(c) The Use Classes Order generally permits changes of use within a particular class without the need for planning consent.

(d) A travel agent belongs to Class I (shops).

(e) Planning permission is obtained by an express application to the local planning authority.

(f) Planning permission is also required for such matters as alterations to the structure, external decoration for advertising and illuminated signs.

(g) To obtain planning permission a form is completed and lodged with copies of plans with the local planning authority.

(h) Planning applications may be made by the owner of property or a tenant, or a person with an interest in it.

(i) An enforcement notice may be served if work is done without obtaining planning consent.

(j) The applicant may appeal against the decision of the planning authority.

Occupiers' liability

The law imposes duties on those who occupy, i.e. those who have possession and control of, land and buildings. These duties are described generally as 'a duty of care'. This duty is owed by the occupier to protect those who come on to property under his or her control. In England and Wales the duty of care is regulated by the Occupiers' Liability Acts 1957 and 1984.

To whom do the Acts apply?

An 'occupier' is not defined in the Acts. However, the commonsense criterion is applied: who was in control of the premises at the time the person was injured or suffered loss? The Acts are not confined to the occupier of land and buildings. Section 1(3)(a) of the 1957 Act states that it also regulates 'the obligations of a person occupying or having control over any fixed or movable structure, including any vessel, vehicle or aircraft'. Under this section therefore come things like cupboards, shelving, display cases, counters, chairs, stools, carpeting, flooring, doors, stairs, platforms and exhibits.

Section 2(2) defines the occupier's common duty of care:

> *a duty to take such care as in all the circumstances of the case is reasonable to see that the visitor will be reasonably safe in using the premises for the purposes for which he is invited or permitted by the occupier to be there.*

What is the duty?

The duty is to make the visitor, rather than the premises, safe. The Acts provide that the occupier must be prepared for children to be less careful than adults. The occupier would not, however, generally be liable to repairers, painters and decorators, electricians, plumbers and the like who, if they had exercised reasonable care and skill in carrying out their work, would not have been injured on the premises. It *is* the occupier's duty, though, to select competent contractors.

The Acts draw a distinction between a lawful visitor and a trespasser. A trespasser is a person who is on the premises without invitation of any kind and whose presence is either unknown to the occupier or, if known, is objected to. Into the category of lawful visitors come employees and customers, postmen and salesmen; statutory inspectors have tacit invitation on to premises and are therefore classed as visitors. It is quite lawful for an occupier to place limitations on where a person may go on the premises, and a visitor going beyond such limits is a trespasser. Thus, a customer who ignores a 'Staff only', 'Private' or 'No entry' sign may be considered a trespasser. These signs must, however, be clearly displayed.

These provisions apply only to lawful visitors. The common law rules in respect of trespass still apply, and the occupier may therefore take reasonable steps to exclude trespassers – including static deterrents such as spikes on the top of a high wall. Concealed deterrents such as mantraps are not permitted. Because the law of trespass has changed greatly over the past few years, it is accurate to state that the duty of care the occupier owes to the trespasser is very close to that owed to a lawful visitor.

 In Scotland the Occupiers' Liability (Scotland) Act 1960 applies. Scots law makes no distinction between visitors and trespassers. An occupier has a duty of care to take reasonable steps to ensure that any person (or his or her property) brought on to the premises will not suffer loss or injury due to any reasonably foreseeable danger. This duty, then, may also apply to trespassers.

SUMMARY

(a) In England and Wales the Occupiers' Liability Act 1957 imposes a duty of care on the occupier of premises.

(b) The occupier has the duty to protect the lawful visitor who comes on to the premises.

(c) The Act applies to the occupier of land and buildings, and also to those who have things like cupboards, shelves, display cases, carpeting and flooring under their control.

(d) In Scotland the Occupiers' Liability (Scotland) Act 1960 imposes a duty on the occupier to ensure that no harm or loss will be suffered by a person who comes on the premises.

(e) The harm or loss suffered must be as a result of any reasonably foreseeable danger.

Defective Premises Act 1972

The provisions of this Act apply to landlords. The Act places a duty on them to maintain and repair premises which they have let under a tenancy agreement.

What is the duty?

The landlord owes a duty of care to all persons who might reasonably be expected to be affected by defects in the state of the premises. This duty is to take such care as is reasonable in all the circumstances to see that these persons are reasonably safe from personal injury or from damage to their property which could be caused by non-compliance with the repairing obligation.

Who may sue the landlord?

Injured persons, whether visitors, trespassers or passers-by, as well as the tenant, may sue the landlord if their injury arose from the landlord's failure to repair the premises. The injured person must establish that the landlord knew, or ought to have known, of the defect. In an action brought by a visitor, trespasser or passer-by it would not be a defence to show that the tenant had not notified the landlord of the defect, although that could be used as a defence to any action brought by the tenant.

The Act does not apply to Scotland, but similar common law rules do.

Offices, Shops and Railway Premises Act 1963

In the 1950s and early 1960s there were several Acts of Parliament to regulate working conditions in factories and mines and other industrial premises. As the number of people working in the service industries steadily grew it was recognised that there was a need for improvement in their working conditions. The Offices, Shops and Railway Premises Act 1963 provides minimum standards in relation to safety, health and welfare. It does not deal with the safety, health and welfare of customers.

The Act defines an 'office' as 'being a building or part of a building, the sole or principal use of which is an office or for office purposes'.

'Office purposes' are defined as including 'administration, clerical work, handling money and telephone and telegraph operations'. It is clear from this that, unlike for planning purposes, a travel agent's premises are regarded by the Act as an office rather than a shop.

An exclusion was made for premises where only self-employed persons work or where only members of the family are employed. Also excluded are premises where the total number of hours worked in a week by the employees does not exceed 21. This latter exclusion may be relevant to the travel office in a student union or student association building.

What does the Act regulate?

The Act sets out minimum working conditions for those workers who come within the scope of its provisions. It also empowers the Secretary of State to make regulations in order to further its provisions. However, the Act will gradually be absorbed by new regulations made under the Health and Safety at Work etc. Act 1974.

What are the main provisions of the Act?

These are set out under a number of headings.

Cleanliness

The premises, furnishings, fixtures and fittings must be kept in a clean state. Dirt and refuse must not be allowed to accumulate. Floors and stairs must be cleaned not less than once a week by washing or, if it is effective, by sweeping or other method.

Overcrowding

No room in the premises should, while work is going on in it, be so overcrowded as to cause risk of injury to the health of persons working therein. There must be a minimum of 40 square feet of room space and 400 cubic feet of breathing space per member of staff. In making this measurement, ceiling heights above 10 feet and space occupied by permanent fixtures and fittings should be excluded. These space requirements do not apply to rooms frequented by members of the public, e.g. the public parts of the travel agency.

Temperature

Effective provision must be made for securing and maintaining a reasonable temperature in every room in which persons are employed to work, other than for short periods. The equipment used must not in itself cause discomfort or danger through fumes. In rooms to which the public does not generally have access, the temperature must be maintained at a minimum of 16° Centigrade. This temperature must be reached within one hour of the premises being opened for work that day. A thermometer, in proper working order, must be prominently displayed on each floor of the building in which work is being undertaken. Employees working in the part of the premises to which the public have access and where the temperature is lower than 16° Centigrade, are entitled to resort to an accessible place where they can find effective means to warm themselves.

Ventilation

A constant flow of clean fresh air, without draughts, should be provided. Alternatively, circulation of artificially purified air should be made.

Lighting

This should be of the right quality and quantity. The Department of Employment booklet *Lighting in Offices, Shops and Railway Premises* is useful in assessing the amount of light required. There should be an absence of glare and hard black shadows.

Sanitation and water

Toilets should be provided, should be accessible to persons employed there and should be sufficient and suitable for their use. They must be kept clean, properly maintained, effectively lit and ventilated. There should be separate toilets for both sexes.

A supply of clean running hot and cold water, soap and towels (or suitable alternatives) should be provided. These facilities should be kept clean, properly maintained, and effectively lit and ventilated.

A supply of wholesome drinking water should be available at suitable places, easily accessible to persons employed there. Where that water is not piped, it should be contained in suitable vessels and must be renewed at least daily. Steps should be taken to avoid contamination

Accommodation for clothing

There should be suitable accommodation for employees' outer clothing.

Seating facilities

Where employees, in the course of their work, have reasonable opportunities for sitting, without detriment to their work, suitable seating provision should be made for them. In the part of the travel agency premises to which the public has access the minimum seating places for staff working there is in a ratio of one seat to three members of staff. The seating must be of a safe and suitable design, construction and dimensions and should have a footrest if it is not possible for the employees to support their feet comfortably without one. It should be stressed that these are minimum requirements and the mere provision of one seat for every three members of staff would in fact be totally insufficient in a travel agency.

Floors, passages and stairs

These must be of sound construction, properly maintained and free from obstruction and from anything likely to cause staff to injure themselves. A substantial handhold or handrail should be provided on the open side(s) of a stairway. Where one side is open, safe and efficient means of preventing people from accidentally falling through the space must be provided.

Dangerous machinery

This must be securely fenced and adequately guarded against all foreseeable injuries. (It is doubtful that a travel agency would have such machinery.)

First aid

All premises covered by the Act must be equipped with an adequate first-aid box, which must be kept in an accessible place, and regularly checked. A separate box must be kept for every 150 employees. A member of staff, competent in first aid, must be in charge of the first-aid box.

The Act is enforced by local environmental health officers. They have powers of entry, search, inspection and interview. Contravention may lead to prosecution.

SUMMARY

(a) For the purposes of the Offices, Shops and Railway Premises Act 1963, a travel agency is an office.

(b) This Act makes provision for minimum working conditions for employees.

(c) Premises and their furnishings have to be clean.

(d) Each worker is entitled to a minimum amount of space.

(e) Premises must be heated, ventilated and lit according to minimum standards.

(f) Toilets and hot and cold running water – as well as a good supply of drinking water – must be available.

(g) Employees must have suitable places in which to hang coats, and seating of a safe and suitable design.

(h) Floors, passages and stairs must be kept free from obstruction; handrails must be provided on the open side of stairs.

(i) A first-aid box must be kept, in an accessible place.

♔ Health and Safety at Work etc. Act 1974

Because the aim of this Act is to provide a legislative framework to promote, stimulate and encourage high standards of health and safety at work, it is included here, although it is treated in more depth in Chapter 12, on employment law.

What is the duty?

There is a general duty imposed on employers to ensure, so far as is reasonably practicable, the health, safety and welfare of all their employees and other people such as passers-by, neighbours and customers.

To do this, employers must provide and maintain safe plant and machinery and systems of work, so far as it is reasonably practicable to. Employees must co-operate with the employer, or any other person on whom a duty under the Act is imposed, so far as is necessary to enable that duty or requirement to be performed or complied with.

Enforcement of the Act's provisions

Inspectors may enter premises, at any reasonable time, if they have reason to believe it is necessary for them to enter. They may bring on to premises any equipment they need and may take any measurements, photographs or recordings necessary for any investigation.

SUMMARY
(a) The Health and Safety at Work etc. Act 1974 contains provisions to encourage high standards of health and safety at work.

(b) The Act imposes a duty on employers to provide and maintain safe plant and machinery and systems of work.

(c) The Act imposes a duty on employees to co-operate with the employer to enable him or her to carry out the Act's provisions.

(d) Inspectors may enter premises to enforce the provisions of the Act.

SELF-ASSESSMENT QUESTIONS

State whether the following statements are correct or incorrect.

1. Planning permission is required if a material change is to be made in the use to which premises are to be put.

2. The Use Classes Order permits changes of use within specified classes without the need for planning permission.

3. A change of use from a café to a travel agency does not require planning permission.

4. A change of use from a betting shop to a travel agency does not require planning permission.

5. Alterations to the structure of an internal supporting wall do not require planning permission.

6. The painting of an advertisement on an outside wall of a travel agency does not require planning permission.

7. Illuminated signs in travel agency windows require planning permission.

8. The Secretary of State may appoint an inspector to determine appeals against decisions of planning authorities.

9. (a) The Occupiers' Liability Act 1957/Occupiers' Liability (Scotland) Act 1960 governs the liability of owners of commercial premises.
   (b) The Act imposes a duty to ensure that premises are safe.
   (c) No duty of care is owed to trespassers in England and Wales.
   (d) A greater degree of care is owed to children under the provisions of the Act.

10. The Defective Premises Act 1972, which places a duty on a landlord to repair and maintain premises let under a lease, gives anyone injured by defects in those premises the right to sue if the injury arose from the landlord's failure to repair.

11. The Offices, Shops and Railway Premises Act 1963 provides minimum working conditions for those employed in travel agencies.

12. There is no legal requirement to provide a first-aid box where less than five employees are working in the premises.

13. The Health and Safety at Work etc. Act 1974 provides a legislative framework to promote high standards of health and safety at work.

14. Employees are legally bound to co-operate with employers on matters of health and safety.

15. Health and safety inspectors may not enter premises unless they are accompanied by a policeman.

5 The Tour Operator and Travel Agent Relationship

AIMS The aim here is to consider the application of the law of agency to the relationship between the tour operator and the travel agent.

The legal status of the tour operator and travel agent

Understanding *legal status* means finding out what principles of law apply to travel agents and tour operators, a task which would be easy if legislation had been enacted to apply specifically to travel agents and tour operators. Such legislation would also provide definitions of the terms 'travel agent' and 'tour operator', thereby giving information on their legal status. In the United Kingdom the travel industry is self-regulating, there being in operation the voluntary code of conduct of the Association of British Travel Agents (ABTA), which contains definitions of travel agent and tour operator. Although the

 Package Travel, Package Holidays and Package Tour Regulations 1992 have specific application to the travel industry, they deal with 'organisers' and 'retailers' rather than 'tour operators' and 'travel agents'.

In order, then, to define their legal status we can describe what each does, then we can look at the legal basis of the relationship between the travel agent and tour operator.

Travel agents are described as *retailers* and *intermediaries*: retailers because they stock their premises with the products of tour operators (i.e. brochures containing package holidays), intermediaries because the customer, having selected a holiday, will indicate a choice to the agent who then books the holiday with the particular tour operator. Travel agents also sell plane tickets, make bookings at hotels and some organise their own package holidays (when they, therefore, act as tour operators).

Tour operators put the raw materials of a holiday together; in other words they organise all the elements of the holiday: the means of travel, accommodation, facilities, excursions. Customers buy this package for an all-inclusive price which is generally lower than had they booked the various components themselves. Some tour operators sell direct to the public, for example Saga.

The *law of agency* provides the legal basis for the relationship. In the business world very often businessmen or women have neither the time nor the expertise to perform all their tasks and so employ agents to act on their behalf. Agents use their technical or professional skill, for which a fee or commission is paid. In other words, the agent is employed by someone called the *principal* to use his or her expertise to negotiate contracts on the principal's behalf. There are, therefore, three parties involved: the principal, the agent and the person who wishes to enter into the contract with the principal. Thus, the agent is given legal power to alter the principal's legal relations with third parties. The law of agency does not apply, therefore, when Joan asks David to congratulate Fiona on passing her driving test.

The agency relationship comes into being because the principal and agent have agreed between themselves that the agent should use his or her expertise to perform certain jobs for the principal. The tour operator is the principal who employs the travel agent to contract with clients on his behalf. This relationship between the tour operator and the travel agent is evidenced by a contract: the agency agreement. This contract expressly appoints the travel agent to act as the agent of the tour operator and sell the holidays detailed in the tour operator's travel brochures. The travel agent acts as an agent because the third party, the client, having selected his or her holiday from the tour operator's brochures displayed in the travel agent's premises, then uses the travel agent to book the holiday with the tour operator.

SUMMARY

(a) Tour operators and travel agents who are members of ABTA are regulated by a voluntary code of conduct.

(b) Travel agents are retailers and intermediaries.

(c) Tour operators put the raw materials of a holiday together.

(d) The law of agency provides the legal basis for the relationship between the tour operator and travel agent.

(e) The principal employs the agent for his or her particular skills and expertise.

(f) The agent contracts with third parties on behalf of the principal.

(g) When the agent is appointed to act he or she is given authority by the principal to act for him or her.

(h) The tour operator is the principal who employs the travel agent to contract with the customer on his or her behalf.

(i) The agency agreement sets out the terms and conditions and scope of the travel agent's authority.

(j) The travel agent acts as an agent because the third party, having chosen his or her holiday, uses the travel agent to book the holiday with the tour operator.

Appointment of the travel agent

When the principal asks the agent to act for him or her, and the agent consents, the two parties are entering into a contract, which may be oral or written. While the law does not demand that the contracts should be in writing, if the agent is to be appointed for a period of time and has to perform complex acts for the principal, it is better to have a written agreement.

When the tour operator appoints someone to be an agent the agreement they draw up is called an agency agreement. In this situation the parties, the tour operator and travel agent, have expressly agreed to enter into an agency relationship which will be evidenced by the agency agreement, and in which each party will be described; for example: 'Billabong Tours Ltd, hereinafter called "The Operator", and Walsh & Mathilda Travel Agents, hereinafter called "The Agent" '.

What would be the situation if a tour operator gave a travel agent brochures, tickets or vouchers and the travel agent displayed the material and sold the tickets even though there is no written agency agreement? Here the agency relationship may be *implied*. We can say that the tour operator impliedly appointed that travel agent to act as his or her agent by providing the brochures and tickets and that the travel agent, by accepting them and selling the tickets, has consented to act. There is, therefore, a contract of agency created between them.

An unusual feature of the appointment of a travel agent is that one of the clauses in the agency agreement will usually read:

The operator appoints the agent to be a non-exclusive agent of the operator.

Non-exclusive agent

What is meant by this term 'non-exclusive'? It means that travel agents can sell their own holidays, make their own travel arrangements for customers or sell the package holidays of any other tour operator. Perhaps as a reaction to this, some tour operators may appoint only one travel agent in a particular locality. This is known as franchising.

SUMMARY

(a) The principal and the agent enter into a contract when the principal asks the agent to act and the agent consents.

(b) This contract does not have to be written.

(c) The tour operator and travel agent enter into an agency agreement which contains the terms and conditions.

(d) This is termed express appointment.

(e) The agency relationship may also be impliedly created as where a travel agent displays the tour operator's brochures and sells his or her tickets and vouchers.

(f) Travel agents are usually appointed as non-exclusive agents.

Authority of the travel agent

When there exists a contract between the travel agent and tour operator evidenced by the agency agreement, it will contain some statements detailing the scope of the agent's authority, for example:

> *The authority of the Agent to represent the operator shall be specifically limited to the authority expressly granted by this Agreement.*

Such statements describe the agent's *express actual authority*. The travel agent may also have *implied* actual authority to act for the tour operator because every agent has implied authority to do everything necessary to carry out the job of agent. Therefore, travel agents will have implied actual authority to process the holidays of the tour operator because that is one of the acts that this group of agents customarily performs.

Sometimes the principal may limit in some way, or withdraw altogether, the agent's authority. So, for example, a tour operator may withdraw a travel agent's authority to sell its holidays or tickets. If the tour operator has not asked for them to be removed and they are still on display in the travel agent's premises, the customer is not to know that the agent's authority to act for the particular tour operator has been withdrawn. What would happen if the customer chose a holiday from one of the brochures and the travel agent booked it with the tour operator? Would the tour operator be able to say that the travel agent had no authority to act in taking the booking? Would the customer have to book another holiday with another operator?

If the principal does not inform third parties of any limitation on, or withdrawal of, an agent's authority the law provides that the agent has ostensible or *apparent* authority to act for the principal. Therefore, the holiday booked by the travel agent would be valid and the tour operator would be bound by the contract which the travel agent had negotiated on his behalf.

If there is an emergency and an agent has to act outside the scope of his or her actual authority the law states that the agent has *presumed* authority. This would apply, for example, where a travel agent has been asked to supply another coach because the one sent by the tour operator has broken down.

SUMMARY   (a) The agency agreement contains clauses describing the scope of the agent's authority.

(b) Agents have express actual authority and implied actual authority.

(c) If the principal limits or withdraws the agent's authority and does not inform third parties of this then the agent may have ostensible authority to act.

(d) In an emergency, agents may have presumed authority to act for their principals.

Duties of the travel agent and tour operator

The main duties incumbent on the agent will be found in the agency agreement which will detail the acts which the travel agent is to perform for the tour operator, for example:

> *The Agent agrees to sell the holidays and other travel arrangements provided by the Operator at the Operator's advertised prices.*

This means that the travel agent is under a *contractual duty* to perform these acts to the best of his or her ability (on the matter of the advertised price, see Chapter 6 generally).

As a travel agent is a supplier of services there is a *statutory duty* to supply the service to the customer with reasonable skill and care (Supply of Goods and Services Act 1982, s.13 – in Scotland this is provided by the common law).

If the agent has agreed to perform certain acts for the principal he or she has to do them personally; in other words it is not possible to get someone else to do the job. However, *delegation* is allowed if this is customary in the trade or profession. Travel agents delegate; however, it is their duty to delegate to competent staff who have made a careful study of the tour operators' brochures and, thus, are able to give accurate information to customers (ABTA Code).

Principal and agent are also described as having a *fiduciary relationship*, that is, a relationship of trust. The agent's chief duty here is not to allow his or her personal interest to conflict with the interests of the principal. For the travel agent a possible area of conflict may develop over the question of travel insurance. A travel agent has the duty to the principal to persuade the customer to buy the tour operator's own insurance which is offered as an 'extra' part of the holiday package. There is a conflict of interests if the travel agent considers that the tour operator's own insurance cover is not the best value or does not suit the particular needs of a customer who has booked one of the tour operator's holidays. The travel agent may also seek to promote his or her own travel insurance from which he or she may get a higher commission. The travel agent has a fiduciary duty to the principal to persuade the customer to buy the tour operator's insurance cover, but he or she also owes the customer a duty of skill and care.

Duties are also imposed on the travel agent by the ABTA Code: there is a duty to act in accordance with the aims of the Code, and to act as intermediary in any dispute between the client and tour operator.

The principal has the duty to pay the agent if the work asked of him or her has been done. The travel agent is paid *commission* by the tour operator and an express clause in the agency agreement will set out the details. *Reimbursement of expenses* and *compensation against losses* incurred by the agent while acting on behalf of the principal are two more duties which the principal owes to the agent. There will be express clauses in the agency agreement dealing with these matters.

The ABTA Code imposes duties on tour operators in connection with booking conditions and minimum standards of brochures.

Rights of the travel agent and tour operator

The agent has a right of *lien*, which means that if the travel agent has in his or her possession property which belongs to the tour operator the travel agent may keep possession of that property as security for the settlement of any claims against the tour operator.

The principal may dismiss the agent without notice or payment of compensation if the agent has not done what he or she undertook to do; for example, if he or she has failed to promote adequately the packages of the tour operator.

Rights and obligations of the client *vis-à-vis* the travel agent and tour operator

It is the function of travel agents to create contracts between tour operators and third parties (clients). Once this has been done they drop out of the relationship, which means that they have no personal liability under that contract. It is the tour operators and third parties who acquire the rights and obligations under the contract. In order to escape personal liability, though, agents must disclose that they are acting as agents and name their principals. Therefore, it is necessary that travel agents disclose that they are acting on behalf of tour operators because clients may believe that they are contracting for the holiday with the travel agent. If the holiday they have contracted for is unsatisfactory then they look only to the travel agents for performance of the contract. The travel agents may find themselves being sued and becoming liable in damages to the clients. (It is usually clear from the brochure and the booking form that the client's contract is with the tour operator and not with the travel agent.)

Sometimes clients ask the advice of travel agents regarding their choice of holiday because they may have special needs. Here the travel agents' expert knowledge is relied upon by the clients. While the travel agents do not cease to be the agents of the tour operators, they may in these circumstances become personally liable if the holiday goes wrong. Travel agents also hold clients' deposits and these monies are held by them as agents for the clients until the tour operators confirm the holiday booking or until they have to account for these sums to the operators.

Clients, therefore, contract for their holidays with the tour operators and under that contract have the right to performance – that is, to get the holiday they have paid for and, if performance is unsatisfactory, the right to sue for damages.

The clients' obligations under the holiday contract are that they must pay the full price for their holidays and take the holidays they have paid for, in accordance with the rules set out in the booking conditions.

The EC Directive

It should be noted that the EC Directive on Package Travel, Package Holidays and Package Tours regulates the relationships between 'organisers', 'retailers' and 'consumers' in respect of 'packages'. These provisions are implemented in the UK by the Package Travel, Package Holidays and Package Tours Regulations 1992 and are discussed in Chapter 8. It is important to read that chapter when considering the relationship between a tour operator acting as an 'organiser' and a travel agent acting as a 'retailer' within the meaning of regulation 2(1).

SUMMARY   Before we go on to the assessment let us clarify the rights and obligations of tour operators, travel agents and clients:

(a) Agents are under a contractual duty to perform the tasks their principal asks them to do with skill and care.

(b) Agents are also under a statutory duty to do the job with reasonable skill and care.

(c) Agents cannot delegate performance, except if it is the custom of the trade or profession.

(d) Principal and agent have a relationship of trust, which means that the agent's personal interests must not conflict with those of the principal.

(e) Duties are imposed on agents by the ABTA Code.

(f) The principal has duties to his or her agent which means that the agent has the right to be paid, to be reimbursed and compensated.

(g) The ABTA Code imposes duties on tour operators.

(h) Agents have a right of lien.

(i) Once travel agents have completed their task the contract is between the tour operators and the clients.

(j) Agents must disclose their principals; otherwise they may become personally liable under the contract.

(k) Travel agents may become personally liable to clients if clients ask for and receive expert advice from them.

(l) The clients' obligations include payment of the full price of their holidays or a cancellation charge.

SELF-ASSESSMENT QUESTIONS

State whether the following statements are correct or incorrect.

1. Legal status means defining the terms 'tour operator' and 'travel agent'.

2. Travel agents cannot act as organisers of travel packages.

3. The legal basis for the relationship between tour operator and travel agent is the law of agency.

4. The principal employs the agent to act for him or her because the agent has expert skill and knowledge.

5. The agent makes contracts with third parties on behalf of the principal.

6. The principal and agent must draw up a formal written deed as the evidence of their relationship.

7. The agency agreement is the document in which the tour operator expressly appoints the travel agent as his or her agent.

8. The travel agent must be expressly appointed to act on behalf of the tour operator.

9. The agency agreement contains clauses describing what acts the travel agent has the authority to perform.

10. Travel agents may only perform those acts which are described in the agency agreement.

11. Withdrawal of an agent's authority to act means that any contract negotiated by the travel agent with a third party is automatically void.

12. The law sometimes presumes that agents have authority to act.

13. The agent has a contractual duty to act for his or her principal to the best of his or her ability.

14. Travel agents must perform personally those acts they have undertaken on the principal's behalf.

15. The principal and agent relationship is a fiduciary one.

16. The agent must not allow his or her personal interests to conflict with those of the principal.

17. The principal has no duties towards his or her agent.

18. If the travel agent does not disclose that he or she is acting for the tour operator he or she may become personally liable on the contract.

6 Consumer Protection Legislation and the Travel Industry

GLOSSARY **consumer** A person buying goods and services which are not used for business purposes.

surcharges Charges levied by tour operators in addition to the contract price. These are usually levied due to increases in fuel costs, current fluctuations, etc.

1992 regulations Package Travel, Package Holidays and Package Tours Regulations 1992.

AIM **To describe the legislation governing the trading practices of the travel industry and affording protection to the package holiday consumer.**

The legislation under consideration in this chapter has been designed to protect consumers against restrictive and unfair trade practices as well as to describe their rights and give them the means of redress. This is the concept of 'fair trading' which links consumer protection with competition policy with the aim of controlling practices and agreements which restrict trade, limits monopolies and prevents mergers which would lead to a concentration of economic power.

 The Package Travel, Package Holidays and Package Tours Regulations 1992 also provide protection to the package holiday consumer, and this is dealt with in Chapter 8.

The Fair Trading Act 1973

This Act was introduced chiefly to protect the economic interests of the consumer from unfair trading practices and provides for *three* things in order to achieve this:

(a) the appointment of a Director General of Fair Trading;

(b) setting up a Consumer Protection Advisory Committee;

(c) conferring new functions for the protection of consumers on the Director, the Secretary of State for Trade and Industry, and the Restrictive Practices Court.

Director General of Fair Trading

The Act creates the office of the Director General of Fair Trading who, in conjunction with the Office of Fair Trading (OFT), has to look after the interests of consumers and encourage competition between one business and another which is fair to both the businessperson and the consumer. This is to be achieved through improving trading standards and stamping out unfair trading practices. By what means is this to be done?

The Director has

(a) to keep under review the carrying on of commercial activities in the United Kingdom which relate to goods supplied ... or which relate to services supplied for consumers in the United Kingdom.

and

(b) to receive and collate evidence available in respect of (a) above.

Thus, it is the Director's duty, first, to be on the alert to detect commercial activities which may adversely affect the economic interests of consumers and to collect information about such activities. Organisations and individuals such as the Citizens' Advice Bureaux, local trading standards officers, Consumers' Association, MPs, the media and consumers themselves all supply him or her with valuable data.

Secondly, the Director has to put together this evidence about all commercial practices which may adversely affect consumer interests. He or she publishes a yearly report.

Thirdly, the Director has power to make recommendations to the Secretary of State for Trade and Industry about any action which, in his or her view, the Secretary of State or any other minister should take about any commercial activities which are harming consumer interests.

In order to stamp out unfair consumer trade practices the Director is given power to ban or regulate such activities and individual traders can be bought before the Restrictive Practices Court if they persist in courses of action which contravene civil or criminal laws.

The Act defines a 'consumer trade practice' as 'any practice which is for the time being carried on in connection with the supply of goods (whether by way of sale or otherwise) to consumers or in connection with the supply of services to consumers'.

Thus, the provisions of the Restrictive Practices Acts 1956 and 1965 are extended to cover services.

Then follow six groups of practices which cover everything to do with the way goods and services are sold, including:

(a) the terms or conditions on which goods and services are to be supplied;

(b) the way in which payment is to be made for goods or services;

(c) the manner in which terms and conditions are communicated to the consumer.

What can the Director do about unfair consumer trade practices?

Consumer Protection Advisory Committee

This is where the Consumer Protection Advisory Committee (CPAC) comes in. It was set up under the Act and consists of between 10 and 15 people, one or more coming from each of three groups: suppliers, local enforcement officers and consumers – all chosen as experts in their field. Other 'independent' members such as lawyers and accountants may also be appointed.

The Committee's primary function is to report on references made to it by the Director in respect of consumer trade practices which he or she believes to have certain adverse consequences on consumer interests. It also makes recommendations to the Secretary of State about any proposals for banning or regulating a consumer trade practice which the Director may put to it. If it agrees with the Director's proposals the Secretary of State can make an order to ban or otherwise control the trade practice in question. Subject to affirmative resolution of both Houses of Parliament, the order becomes law carrying the penalty of a fine, imprisonment, or both.

The consumer trade practices which the Director can refer to the CPAC are those which relate to the terms or conditions subject to which goods or services are supplied; the way in which consumers are informed of the terms or conditions; advertising, labelling or marking of goods and other forms of promotion of goods or services; methods of salesmanship and packaging of goods; and methods of demanding payment for goods and services.

The undesirable trade practices which the Director seeks to regulate are defined in the Act as those which mislead or confuse customers as to the nature, quality or quantity of goods or services; and those which withhold adequate information or put pressure on them to enter into a transaction.

Where traders or individual companies persist in a course of conduct detrimental to the interests of consumers by breaking the civil or criminal law, the Director has powers under the Act to take action. He or she may first try to obtain from the offender a satisfactory written assurance, or, if the assurance is given but not observed, the Director may bring proceedings before the Restrictive Practices Court in England or the sheriff court in Scotland. The court may then make an order against the trader. Any breach of this order amounts to a contempt of court, which could result in a fine or a prison sentence if it is committed by an individual. Alternatively, if the court thinks fit, it may accept instead an undertaking from the manufacturer or trader to refrain from the course of conduct about which the complaint has been made. In the exercise of the power the Director relies on the local trading standards officers who are also responsible for enforcing the Secretary of State's orders.

Monopolies and Mergers Commission

The other area in which the Director operates relates to surveillance and encouragement of competition, which means that in the case of monopolies he or she may hold preliminary inquiries where he or she believes that provisions of the Restrictive Practices Act apply and then refer to the Monopolies and Mergers Commission (MMC). The Director also has to publicise information and advice to consumers and encourage trade associations to prepare codes of practice.

In connection with these duties on 1 August 1984, the Director sent this reference to the MMC:

> *The Director General of Fair Trading hereby refers to the MMC the matter of the existence or possible existence of a complex monopoly situation in relation to the supply in the UK of agency services by travel agents for tour operators in relation to the marketing and supply of foreign package holidays.*

Under the Act a complex monopoly exists if one quarter of a product or service is supplied either by a single retailer or by two or more suppliers who have agreed to conduct their respective affairs to prevent competition.

The specific question the MMC had to consider was whether a complex monopoly situation existed in relation to the tour operators prohibiting travel agents from supplying their foreign holidays at a discount from the price prescribed by the tour operators in the brochures.

This reference was made to the Commission because three of the leading tour operators (Thomson, Horizon and Intasun) had taken steps to prevent Ilkeston Consumer Co-operative Society Ltd from offering vouchers in respect of holidays booked with their companies because they believed that Ilkeston Co-op was cross-subsidising its foreign package holiday business.

The inquiries of the MMC (published in its report of 1986) found this to be a mistaken belief on the part of the tour operators. The conclusion of the Commission in relation to the reference question was that, because a tour operator interfered with the way a travel agent induced customers to book holidays with it rather than another travel agent, the public interest was not served. The reason for this was that competition between travel agents was being adversely affected, innovation was being discouraged and customers were being deprived of services suited to their needs.

In order to remedy this situation the MMC recommended that the Director General of Fair Trading consult with ABTA on the question of making an addition to the Code of Practice so that travel agent members would be free to offer inducements. It was also recommended that the findings of the Commission be brought to the attention of ABTA members. Should these recommendations not be acted upon, it was further suggested that the Secretary of State take legislative action to ensure that travel agents are free to compete with one another in relation to inducements.

An order came into force on 31 July 1987 which had the effect of ensuring that

a travel agent is free to offer inducements to customers to buy foreign package holidays through him, rather than through another agent, provided that the inducement is made expressly on his own behalf.

As an illustration of the Director's duty to keep under review commercial activities affecting the economic interests of consumers, a survey to measure the effectiveness of the ABTA Code was undertaken and a report was compiled by the Office of Fair Trading and published in July 1988.

Consumers, travel agents and tour operators were all surveyed on matters such as satisfaction with the holiday, level of awareness of the ABTA Code, brochures, insurance, surcharges, representatives and complaints. All the surveys found a high level of problems and the OFT was disturbed to find that 'holidaymakers were not receiving the best possible service from the travel trade' (p. 21).

Some of the recommendations were that brochures should be more accurate, that ABTA should monitor members' brochures more closely, that tour operators should include information on health matters and noise levels at resorts, and that improved levels of compensation be offered where holidays were materially altered by the tour operators.

Further, the Director felt that tour operators should accept responsibility for *all* aspects of a package holiday they have provided regardless of who is providing a specific part. They also recommend that the tour operators' Code of Conduct be amended so that the tour operator accepts responsibility for the due performance of all parts of a package holiday. By and large these provisions have been implemented.

SUMMARY

(a) The Fair Trading Act 1973 creates a Director General of Fair Trading to oversee consumers' interests and encourage competition by eradicating unfair trading practices.

(b) The Act extends the provisions of the 1956 and 1965 Restrictive Practices Acts to cover services.

(c) The Director is helped by the CPAC, which reports on those consumer trade practices and traders referred to it by him or her.

(d) The Director has to encourage competition and may, then, refer monopolies to the MMC for investigation.

(e) The MMC has investigated the anti-discounting practices of tour operators.

(f) The MMC decided that there was a monopoly situation and made an order that travel agents could discount the tour operators' holidays.

(g) The effectiveness of the ABTA Codes had also been investigated by the Director who has recommended that brochures be more accurate and that tour operators be responsible for all aspects of the packages they provide.

♔ The Restrictive Practices Act 1976

It was in the nineteenth century that large numbers of trade associations were formed under which the members agreed, among other things, to fix minimum prices for goods and services. Such associations brought trade benefits to their members and imposed penalties on those traders who were not members. However, it was only after the Second World War, with changes in economic and social opinion, that pressure was put on the government to control restrictive practices and monopolies and to promote competition.

The Restrictive Practices Acts 1956 and 1965 provided some means of control in that under these Acts all agreements and arrangements between retailers and suppliers had to be *registered*. These Acts have been replaced by the 1976 Act.

Registration

A wide variety of restrictive agreements relating to the supply of goods and services which might be harmful to the public interest have to be registered and examined by the Restrictive Practices Court.

An agreement should be registered:

(a) if there are two or more parties to it carrying on business in Britain in the production, supply or processing of goods and services;

(b) if more than one party to it accepts restrictions in the form of some limitation on its freedom to make decisions; and

(c) the restrictions concern such matters as prices, conditions of sale, market sharing, or on which services are to be quoted, paid for and supplied.

The registration process involves, first, that the agreement be considered by the Director General of Fair Trading and, if registrable, placed on the public Register of Restrictive Agreements. Copies of the register are kept in London, Belfast and Edinburgh. The second step (which can be dispensed with if the Director so decides) is to have the agreement approved by the Restrictive Practices Court. This court consists of judges and lay members who have experience in industry, commerce or public affairs. It may sit anywhere in the United Kingdom to hold public examinations of restrictive agreements referred to it. The court has jurisdiction to declare whether or not any restrictive agreements are contrary to the public interest.

It is the parties to the agreement, or the trade association (such as ABTA), who have to show that the restrictions are not contrary to the public interest, which means they have to show that the agreement satisfies at least *one* of seven conditions laid down in the Act. Thus, ABTA had to register its articles of association, and codes of conduct.

If the court declares the restrictions to be against the public interest they are void and, thus, the parties cannot give effect to the agreement.

The Restrictive Practices Court has considered several ABTA restrictions such as the 'stabiliser', restrictions on the sale price of holidays sold by agents and restrictions concerning agents' staffing and premises.

Stabiliser

Under the exclusive dealing agreement (stabiliser) ABTA members selling through agents may not sell through non-ABTA travel agents. ABTA travel agents may not sell any foreign package holiday not organised by an ABTA member. Stabiliser does not affect domestic holidays and those in the Irish Republic. ABTA members may sell the foreign package holidays of the Bonded Coach Holidays section of the Bus and Coach Council and the cruises of the Passenger Steamships Association.

The court found in 1982 that stabiliser supported ABTA's measures for the financial protection of the public and that it was not against the public interest.

 The court also considered, in the same judgement, clause 2 of the Standard Agency Agreement which ABTA recommended to its members in October 1977. The clause read:

> *The agent agrees to sell holidays and other travel arrangements provided by the operator at the operator's advertised price or such other prices as may be advised in writing by the operator to the agent from time to time.*

The court found that the restriction to which this clause related was contrary to the public interest. In 1984 an order of the Restrictive Practices Court prohibited ABTA from including this clause in a standard agency agreement. Tour operators and travel agents remain legally free to use the clause by individual agreement.

In another hearing before the court ABTA's premises and staff requirements were modified in order to obtain the approval of the court.

SUMMARY (a) Any agreements between persons in business which restrict the supply of goods or services have to be registered.

(b) Registration involves, first, that the agreement is considered by the Director, who puts a copy on the Register of Restrictive Agreements. The second step is approval by the Restrictive Practices Court.

(c) The Restrictive Practices Court found that the stabiliser agreement protected the interests of consumers. It did not allow a clause in the standard agency agreement under which agents agreed to sell tour operators' holidays at the prices decided on by the tour operators.

ABTA and the Tour Operators' Study Group

ABTA is the main trade association concerned with the foreign package holiday industry. It was established in 1951 and represents both tour operators and travel agents. The two ABTA Codes (Travel Agents' Code of Conduct and the Tour Operators' Code of Conduct) were drawn up by ABTA in co-operation with the OFT. Under the Fair Trading Act 1973 it is one of the duties of the Director to encourage self-regulation by trade associations. The main aims of these associations are to maintain and encourage high standards of professionalism and to serve the public interest. ABTA's aims are:

> to ensure that the public receive the best possible service from travel agents; to maintain and enhance the reputation of the Association; to encourage initiative and enterprise and to ensure that the public interest predominates when considering standards of competitive trading between travel agents.

The Tour Operators' Study Group (TOSG) was set up in 1967 by the largest tour operators within ABTA. There are now 18 members, who between them control three-quarters of the market. It tackles current problems of the travel industry. One of its chief functions is the operation of the TOSG Travel Fund Ltd. Members of TOSG have to arrange a bond with a bank or insurance company before they are granted their annual Air Tour Organisers' Licence (ATOL) by the Civil Aviation Authority. A bond is an irrevocable financial guarantee provided by the bank or insurance company and it can be made available to the TOSG Travel Fund Ltd if a tour operator fails. The bond money is then used to enable passengers abroad to continue their holiday and to travel home again, and also to repay those who have booked and paid for holidays but have not been able to take them.

Since 1985 TOSG has taken on another role: that of sponsoring educational training trips for agency staff. According to an article in *Travel Agency*, January 1987, 'since 1985 TOSG has taken more than 1,200 staff on mega-educational trips to Spain, Malta and Tunisia'. Trips to destinations in Italy and places further abroad were also planned. The aim of such trips, in line with TOSG's philosophy of identifying and solving problems of the trade, is to promote better awareness and knowledge of what the host countries have to offer to the holidaymaker.

SUMMARY

(a) ABTA was set up in 1951 and regulates the business of tour operators and travel agents by means of Codes of Practice.

(b) TOSG was set up in 1967 by the tour operators with the aim of looking at current problems in the travel industry and suggesting solutions to them.

(c) It also operates the TOSG Travel Fund Ltd, from which funds are available if a TOSG member fails leaving holidaymakers stranded on foreign shores.

(d) TOSG plays a leading role in training agency staff.

⚜ Resale Prices Act 1976

Under the Restrictive Practices Act 1976 it is unlawful for suppliers (and trade associations) to impose conditions for the maintenance of minimum prices by threatening to withdraw supplies if those prices are not charged.

Any price-fixing agreements are subject to registration along with all other restrictive agreements, which means they have to be registered with the Director General of Fair Trading and authorised by the Restrictive Practices Court. Unless exempted by the court they are unlawful. However, resale price agreements have largely been replaced by a list of recommended prices. This leaves the retailer free to charge whatever price he or she likes, whether more or less than the recommended one, and thus has the effect of increasing price competition among retailers, which is good for the consumer.

⚜ Competition Act 1980

The provisions of the Act go hand in hand with those in the Restrictive Practices Act and Fair Trading Act. Under the Fair Trading Act the Director refers cases to the MMC for investigation if he or she considers that there is a monopoly in the hands of one company or group of interconnected companies. This MMC report may take a long time and may extend over the whole market because all aspects of the companies' behaviour in the monopoly have to be investigated.

However, with the Competition Act power is given to the Director to investigate particular companies and businesses whose practices distort or restrict competition. Therefore, the Act provides a simpler method of investigating practices of a particular business or company.

The investigation is carried out in two stages:

(a) First, the director can carry out a preliminary investigation to establish whether a particular course of conduct is an anti-competitive practice. If it is, he or she can refer it to the MMC for further investigation *or* accept an undertaking from the business or company. The Director has 12 weeks from the publishing of the report in which to negotiate this undertaking.

(b) Second, if a reference is made to the MMC it must, again within a limited period, decide if the practice is anti-competitive and, if it is, whether or not it is against the public interest.

Finally, if the Commission's report contains a decision that the practice is anti-competitive, the Secretary of State can ask the Director to obtain an undertaking from the business or company. The Secretary of State could also make an order which bans the practice or which would remedy or prevent its adverse effects.

Anti-competitive practices

The kinds of practice which would be considered anti-competitive under the Act are:

(a) those which do or could eliminate the competition a firm or company faces in a market in which it does business;

(b) practices which do or could prevent new competitors emerging, or restrict competition in a market by making it hard for existing competitors to expand;

(c) practices which distort competition between businesses because they affect the terms and conditions of supply in a market.

Under the Act the Secretary of State may refer questions to the MMC about public bodies, which includes nationalised industries which supply goods or services. (Under this section the Welsh Water Authority's charging policy and the efficiency of its service were investigated in a reference dated 7 September 1987.)

Thus, the tour operators may not prevent agents from competing among themselves, for example: the local travel agent discounts all of a tour operator's holidays to Spain by £20 and is warned by the tour operator that this is contrary to the agency agreement. The travel agent can report this to the OFT. The various other inducements offered by travel agents such as free travel insurance or sets of luggage would be viewed as positive competition and therefore good for the market.

♔ Trade Descriptions Act 1968

A man goes to a travel agent, selects a brochure published by a tour operator and, relying on statements in that brochure, books a holiday. When he gets to his holiday destination he finds that the statements in the brochure do not match up to the actual services, accommodation or facilities available so that he does not have the holiday for which he contracted. Section 14 of this Act has been designed to give such a person, in the course of a trade or business,

(a) to make a false statement about aspects of services, facilities or accommodation provided knowing that it is false, or

(b) recklessly to make a statement which is false.

The matters in respect of which false or misleading statements must not be made are listed in the section under these headings:

(a) 'the provision in the course of a trade or business of any services, accommodation or facilities' deals with false statements about the fact that services are provided – for example, the travel agent who agrees to supply holiday accommodation which he or she has no power to provide;

(b) 'the nature of any services, accommodation or facilities provided in the course of trade or business' applies to the quality of services – for example, a tour operator who advertises a trip by air but has already arranged that passengers be carried by sea and land commits an offence;

(c) 'the time at which, manner in which, or persons by whom accommodation, or facilities are provided': thus, the hotelier who entices guests with statements that a famous French chef works for him commits an offence if the 'French chef' is his cousin from Kirkudbright;

(d) 'the examination, approval or evaluation by any person of services, accommodation or facilities so provided': this would cover the person who described his establishment as 'a fine five-star hotel' when he had not been given this rating by the Automobile Association; or when a travel agent falsely claims to be a member of ABTA;

(e) 'the location and amenities of any accommodation so provided': here the over-optimistic tour operator is caught with his or her descriptions of the hotel in Spain which, when the traveller arrives, is miles from the required seaside and bears little resemblance to the photographs in the brochure.

Subsection (2) explains that 'false' means that the party making the statement intended to deceive the party hearing it or reading it; that 'a statement made regardless of whether it is true or false shall be deemed to be made recklessly, whether or not the person making it had reasons for believing that it might be false'.

Therefore, the offence created by the section is committed when a person in the course of a trade or business knowingly or recklessly makes a false statement about the matters in (a) to (e) above.

The term 'person' includes corporations, so that if an offence is committed by a body corporate the company's director and principal officers are jointly liable.

False statement

What does the Act mean when it says that an offence is committed when a person makes a statement which he or she knows to be false (s.14(1)(a))?

 A number of cases have discussed this question. In *Wings Ltd v Ellis* (1985)

the court had to consider whether Wings Ltd could be convicted of an offence under section 14(1)(a). Wings had discovered that there was a false statement in one of its brochures distributed to travel agents, the statement being that the accommodation in the Seashells Hotel, Sri Lanka, was air-conditioned. The company instructed its sales agent to inform all the travel agents that the hotel was not air-conditioned but cooled by ceiling fans. A customer booked a holiday at this hotel but was not told about the lack of air-conditioning, a fact he discovered only when he got to the hotel

The tour operator was charged with an offence under section 14(1)(a).

The House of Lords considered the wording of this section and held that a false statement was made by Wings, in the course of its business, when it was read by customers. The offence was committed because the tour operator knew that it was false to state that the hotel accommodation was air-conditioned. It was irrelevant that Wings was unaware of the falsity of the statement when it was published in the brochure.

It was said in the decision that the false statement about air-conditioning was one which continued to be made so long as the brochures remained in circulation without effective correction.

In *R v Sunair Holidays Ltd* (1973) the tour operator, Sunair, was charged with making, in its 1970 brochure, six false statements under section 14(1)(a) in relation to the Hotel Cadi. The hotel was described as being a comfortable hotel in the centre of the town and about 20 yards from the beach. There was a luxurious lounge which looked on to the sea, a bar, a swimming pool and a restaurant where English dishes were available as well as children's meals. There was also a night-club. Cots were available and push-chairs could be hired.

A customer read this brochure and booked a holiday for a fortnight beginning 27 May 1970. However, he and his family did not enjoy their holiday because there was no night-club or disco; the swimming pool could not be used because it leaked. The food comprised soup, steak, chops or chicken with chips and there were no children's meals, though they could eat an hour earlier than the adults. There were no push-chairs for hire at the hotel. The hotel-owners had undertaken improvements and additions during the winter of 1969–1970 which had been delayed; as a result, Sunair sent no customers until May 1970.

Sunair was charged with making six false statements, namely that the hotel had a swimming pool, that push-chairs could be hired at the hotel, that it had a night-club and disco which would be open every night, that children's cots were available and that good food with English dishes and children's meals were provided.

The lower court decided that Sunair had no case to answer in relation to the statement about the cots; however, it did convict the tour operator on the statements relating to the swimming pool, push-chairs and the food, and it acquitted the company on those relating to the night-club and disco.

Sunair appealed. The Court of Appeal, therefore, had to decide whether section 14 was limited to statements of fact, past and present (which was Sunair's contention), or whether it included assurances about the future. The court held that section 14(1) dealt with statements of which it could be said that they were, at the time when they were made, false. This description could only be applied to a statement of fact, past or present, because a statement that a fact exists now, or that it existed in the past, is either true or false at the time it was made. This cannot be said about a promise – it can only be kept or broken. Thus, section 14(1)(a) did not deal with promises as such, it was limited to statements of fact, past or present. Accordingly, the lower court's verdict on the statements relating to the swimming pool, push-chairs and food was overturned because these statements were promises. Sunair's appeal was allowed.

The court found in *Sunair Holidays Ltd v Dodd* (1970) that no offence under section 14(1)(a) had been committed. The tour operator had contracted with the hotel to provide accommodation which included terraces, and printed this statement in its brochure: 'all twin-bedded rooms had private bath, shower, w.c. and terrace'. Two couples booked holidays on the basis that their rooms would have a terrace but found, when they arrived at the hotel, that their rooms were without terraces and brought an action against the tour operator. The court held that no offence had been committed because at the time the statement was made the accommodation existed, so the statement was not false. What happened afterwards, that the holidaymakers were given rooms with no terraces, had no effect on the accuracy of the description when it was made.

This decision is important because it shows that an offence will not be committed simply because services, accommodation or facilities described in the statement have not been supplied. The services, accommodation and facilities existed when the statement was made and the tour operator intended to provide them.

Contrast this with *British Airways Board v Taylor* (1976), where a customer booked a return flight to Bermuda with BOAC and paid for it. Two weeks before he was due to fly out he received a letter confirming his reservation from BOAC. However, BOAC operated an over-booking policy and when the traveller arrived at the airport on the appointed day and time all the seats were filled and he was not allowed to board.

The House of Lords held: the statement in the letter was false in terms of section 14. The statement and the ticket were statements of fact that they would confirm the client's reservation. This statement was false because of BOAC's over-booking policy.

It was found, however, that British Airways were not criminally liable for the acts of the former BOAC.

Also, note *R v Clarksons Holidays* (1972), where statements were made about a hotel which had not then been built and was illustrated by an artist's drawing. It was held that the statements and the drawing were interpreted as representing statements of existing fact; therefore Clarksons was convicted.

False statement, recklessly made

 An offence is committed under section 14(1)(b) if a person recklessly makes a statement which is false. The meaning of recklessly for the purposes of section 14 was discussed in *MFI Warehouses Ltd v Nattrass* (1973). The company (MFI) sold wooden doors by mail order on 14 days' approval without pre-payment and a carriage fee of 25p per door. It also advertised sets of sliding door gear to go with these doors to enable them to be used as sliding doors. It was the company's intention to sell the sliding door gear with the doors, not as separate items, and at no extra carriage. The same 14-day period applied as with the doors.

The purchaser understood from the advertisement that the sliding door gear could be bought separately and ordered a set. He had to pay carriage on it, despite the fact that the advertisement stated 'carriage free', and he had to pay for it before despatch despite the '14 days' free approval' statement in the advertisement. The court convicted MFI of two offences under section 14(1). The company appealed and the Court of Appeal had to consider whether the statement in the advertisement had been made recklessly. The court found that the word 'reckless' had been given a special meaning by the draftsmen of the Act. The Act was designed to protect consumers; therefore Parliament had placed a positive obligation on advertisers to have regard as to whether their advertisements were true or false. Thus, if the prosecution can show that advertisers did not have regard to the truth or falsity of their advertisements they will have committed an offence even though they had no dishonest intention.

Accordingly, the appeal of MFI was dismissed.

Wings Ltd v Ellis also considered the meaning of 'reckless'. The court found here that not only had the tour operator made a false statement regarding the air-conditioning but that it also included in the brochure a photograph which was supposed to be of the Seashells Hotel but which was of another hotel. Was this a 'reckless' act?

The court decided that it was not necessary for the prosecution to prove that an employee of the tour operator responsible for the publication had been reckless; nor did the prosecution have to find that there was evidence on which to decide that the tour operator was reckless. However, it was necessary for the prosecution to prove recklessness on the part of a director or controlling manager because he or she represented the will of the company and therefore, controlled what the company did.

Accordingly, this decision defined clearly the standard required for 'reckless' within the meaning of the Act.

Defences

Section 24 deals with defences which may be put forward by the defendant (defender, in Scotland). It states that the defendant (defender) must prove that the commission of the offence was due to:

(a) a mistake;

(b) reliance on information supplied;

(c) act or default of another;

(d) an accident;

(e) some other cause,

and that he or she took all reasonable precautions and exercised all due diligence to avoid commission of such an offence by himself or herself or any other person under his or her control.

Subsection (2) states that if a person alleges the offence was due to the act or default of another, he or she will not be able to rely on that defence unless, seven clear days before the hearing, he or she has given notice in writing to the prosecutor containing information as to the identity of that other person.

If mistake is going to be accepted by the court it must have been made by the defendant (defender), not an employee of the tour operator or travel agent.

The most common defence is act or default of another. For example, a tour operator produced and distributed a brochure. Shortly after doing so the tour operator realised that the brochure contained an error indicating that a particular hotel had a swimming pool when in fact it merely had a paddling pool. The tour operator issued erratum slips to all travel agents urging them to draw this to their staff's attention and to the attention of customers booking this holiday. Sue, the travel agency manager of Contacts had received the erratum slips but failed to insert them in brochures, did not bring them to the attention of staff and did not inform customers booking that holiday. If the tour operator is charged with an offence under section 14 it could make use of the defence contained in section 24(1): the offence was due to the act or default of Sue. The tour operator had taken all reasonable precautions and exercised all due diligence to avoid commission of the offence. Sue could then be charged under section 14.

The defence of reliance on information supplied would be available to a travel agent who relied on information supplied to him or her by the tour operator. He or she would have to establish that he or she took all reasonable precautions and exercised all due diligence to avoid commission of the offence by himself or herself or any other person under his or her control, and that it was reasonable to rely on the information supplied. The agent may fail if the information contains an error which would be obvious to a diligent member of the trade or profession.

If the defendant (defender) pleads accident, he or she has to establish that the event was unexpected and if he or she exercised due diligence and took the proper standard of care the accident would not have been discovered.

If he or she relies upon some other cause beyond his or her control he or she has to prove that all reasonable precautions and due diligence were taken. This defence has been used where a machine, such as a computer, has unexpectedly malfunctioned.

However, these defences are available only if the defendant (defender) can show that he or she rook all reasonable precautions and exercised due diligence to avoid commission of the offence by himself or herself or by any other person under his or her control. Therefore, it will usually be sufficient for the tour operator or travel agent to establish that there is a good system of recruitment, training and supervision of staff, and of checking information in order to avoid misleading advice.

Penalties for contravention are:

(a) on summary conviction: a fine not exceeding £2,000 for each offence;

(b) on indictment: an unlimited fine and/or up to two years' imprisonment.

In *R v Thomson Holidays* (1974) the tour operator was convicted of making a false statement by issuing a brochure falsely stating that a hotel had a swimming pool. The operator was convicted in one local authority area for having committed an offence under section 14 and later was prosecuted in another area in respect of the same false statement. Thomson pleaded that it could not be charged more than once for the same offence.

The Court of Appeal held that a new statement is made on every occasion that an interested member of the public reads it in a brochure published by a company engaged in attracting custom.

Compensation

The Powers of the Criminal Courts Act 1973 and the Magistrates' Courts Act 1980, as amended by the Criminal Justice Act 1982, enable a court in England and Wales to make a compensation order following a successful criminal prosecution. The order requires the convicted person to pay compensation for any damage resulting from the offence. The measure of compensation is unlimited in the Crown Court, but is limited to £2,000 in the magistrates' court. The £2,000 refers to each offence; therefore a tour operator convicted of three offences may be required to pay compensation of £6,000.

In Scotland, under the Criminal Justice (Scotland) Act 1980, the court has the same power to make a compensation order. If the case is heard in the High Court of Justiciary or in the sheriff court, on indictment the measure of compensation is unlimited, but if it is heard in the sheriff court under summary procedure the sum is set from time to time by the Secretary of State.

Avoiding committing an offence

Tour operators and travel agents who are prosecuted under the Act attract adverse publicity; therefore, there are some practical steps that should be taken in order to avoid committing an offence.

(a) When preparing brochures, holiday advertisements and circulars care should be taken when making statements describing accommodation, facilities or services which can be physically checked – for example: that a hotel is a specific distance away from the beach. The tour operator must see to it that the services indicated in the brochure are available throughout the holiday period; thus if entertainments are available only in 'the high season' this should be stated. With regard to the price of the holiday, it must be clear what is and is not included.

(b) Advertisements in the agency window should be checked regularly and removed when the holidays, flights, etc. are no longer available. If these displays are regularly checked this can be used as a defence when a mistake has been made.

(c) The Tour Operators' Study Group has made these recommendations in relation to brochures:

    (i) amendment sheets, numbered and dated, should be printed so that they may be easily inserted into the travel agent's file copies and brochures;

    (ii) correction advice should be issued by tour operators as soon as possible;

    (iii) if a computer system is in operation, tour operators should have included any necessary amendments on individual invoices;

    (iv) any oral advice given to clients by travel agents should be carefully checked because false information about visas, vaccinations, availability of excursions, etc. may constitute an offence. The court will not accept as a defence: 'I was only trying to be helpful.'

SUMMARY The Trade Descriptions Act 1968 obviously has important implications for the travel industry; here are the main points:

(a) Section 14 makes it an offence for any person in business to make a false statement about the services, accommodation or facilities he or she provides, or make such a statement recklessly.

(b) 'False' means that the person who made the statement intended to deceive the person hearing or reading it.

(c) 'Reckless' means that the statement was made by the person without regard to its truth or falsity.

(d) False statements in brochures continue to be made so long as the brochures remain in circulation without effective correction.

(e) Section 14 is limited in its scope to statements of fact, past and present, which may be false.

(f) An offence under section 14 will not be committed simply because the services, etc. described in the brochure have not been supplied. If they existed when the statement was made the tour operator will not be convicted.

(g) If the prosecution can show that the person had no regard for the truth or falsity of his or her statement an offence will be committed.

(h) The person charged with the offence has to prove that he or she took all reasonable precautions and exercised due diligence and that the offence was due to a mistake, accident, or some cause beyond his or her control, or that he or she relied on information from another, if conviction is to be avoided.

(i) Penalties are a fine not exceeding £2,000 for each offence (summary procedure); unlimited fine and/or up to two years' imprisonment (on indictment).

The Consumer Protection Act 1987

Part III of this Act makes it a criminal offence to give customers a misleading price indication about goods, services, accommodation or facilities.

Section 11 of the Trade Descriptions Act 1968 made it an offence to apply to goods a false indication as to price, but did not make the same provision for services. An attempt was made to remedy this by the Price Marking (Bargain Offers) Order 1979 but it was difficult to enforce because of its obscure and ambiguous wording.

Part III of the Consumer Protection Act 1987 replaces section 11 of the Trade Descriptions Act 1968 and the Price Marking (Bargain Offers) Order 1979, and came into force on 1 September 1988.

The Act makes it an offence if a person, in the course of any business, gives by any means whatever to any consumers an indication which is misleading as to the price at which any goods, services, accommodation or facilities are available.

The trader will be guilty of this offence if, after he or she has given the price indication, it becomes misleading and consumers might reasonably be expected to rely on it at some time after it has become misleading. The trader has to show that he or she has taken all reasonable steps to prevent consumers from relying on the price indication. It will be immaterial whether the trader is acting on his or her behalf or on behalf of another or whether or not he or she is the person from whom the goods, services, accommodation or facilities are available, and whether the price indication has become misleading to all the consumers to whom it was given or only to some of them.

The 1992 Regulations also have provisions dealing with misleading price indications, and these are dealt with in Chapter 8.

Consumer

 Section 20(6) defines 'consumer' as a person who might wish to be provided with services or facilities or accommodation other than for the purposes of any business of his or hers. It also defines 'price' as the aggregate of the sums the consumer has to pay for goods, services, accommodation or facilities or the method used to determine this aggregate.

Section 20 has, therefore, special significance for tour operators because an offence will be committed even though the price indication was innocent when made but became misleading subsequently. Tour operators have to take all reasonable action to prevent consumers relying on the price indication which has become misleading. They may, therefore, try to protect themselves by inserting warnings about extra charges such as surcharges in their brochures. If inserted they should be obvious enough to the customer.

Misleading

 The Consumer Protection Act defines 'misleading': a price is misleading if:

(a) in fact it is more than the price given;

(b) if it is described as being available generally but is really only applicable in certain circumstances; for example, the air fare from London to Paris is given as £85, but to get a ticket at this price one must be a student;

(c) if the price includes other things for which an additional charge is in fact made; for example, the price of a holiday is given as '£298 which includes flight and hotel accommodation. There will be a coach at the airport to transport you to your hotel.' Customers are not aware from this that there is an additional charge for the transfer by coach.

It is not essential for the prosecutor to prove that anybody was actually misled. It is sufficient if the indication is potentially misleading.

The penalties are: on summary conviction a fine not exceeding £2,000; on conviction on indictment, an unlimited fine.

Defences

 The Act provides a number of defences: the most relevant of these for tour operators and travel agents are contained in section 24(3) and (4). These provide that the person who has been charged with an offence under section 20 will have a defence if:

(a) he or she can show that the price indication published in a book, newspaper, magazine, film, radio or television broadcast was not in an advertisement;

(b) that the price indication did not relate to the availability from him or her of goods, services, etc., that the price had been recommended to every person from whom the goods or services were indicated as being available and it was reasonable for the person who gave the indication to assume that everyone was following the recommendation.

The Act contains a general defence of 'due diligence', that is that the person charged can show that he or she has taken all reasonable steps and exercised due diligence to avoid committing the offence, and the third-party defence of 'act or default of another', or 'reliance on information provided by another'.

The burden of proof is on the defendant (defender).

Code of practice

The Act provides for the creation of a code of practice which aims at giving traders practical guidelines as to how to give price indications without contravening the Act.

There are several sections relating directly to the travel industry. Part 2 of the code deals with the actual price to the consumer, and under the heading 'Holiday and Travel Prices' it states that if the trader gives a number of prices to consumers so that they have a choice, for example, to pay more or less for a standard of accommodation, it has to be made clear in the brochure (or anywhere else) what the basic price is and what the consumer is getting for this. Then, clear details of additional charges are to be put close by these statements. Statements such as the right to increase prices after consumers have made their booking also have to be prominent and clear. If tickets for the theatre, sports, etc. are sold at a price higher than they would be if bought at the box office, this must be clearly shown.

Part 3 of the code deals with price indications which have become misleading after they have been given. If a price indication has become misleading, for example because a surcharge has to be made, tour operators who sell direct to the consumer have to make the correct price clear to anyone booking a holiday to which the charge relates; tour operators who sell through travel agents must communicate the correct information to those travel agents who stock their brochures, and be prepared to cancel any holiday bookings consumers have made on the basis of a misleading price indication. Travel agents, therefore, have the duty to see that the correct price indication is placed in the brochures as soon as it is received from the tour operator and that it is communicated to consumers before they book.

Surcharges

That the travel industry is particularly vulnerable under these provisions can be demonstrated in the matter of surcharges: tour operators who have not offered surcharge protection will have to apply to ABTA for permission to surcharge which may then, under the code and the provisions of the Act, leave them open to cancellation of holidays, at best, or prosecution (or both), at worst.

The rules governing surcharges in respect of regulated packages are discussed in Chapter 8.

SUMMARY

(a) It is an offence to give customers a misleading price indication about goods, services, etc.

(b) An offence will be committed if, after the trader gives the price indication, it becomes misleading and customers might reasonably be expected to rely on it.

(c) In order to avoid conviction the trader has to show that he or she took all reasonable steps to prevent consumers from relying on the price indication.

(d) Tour operators should be especially vigilant in relation to prices in brochures. If surcharges have to be made and there is no indication or warning about such extra charges they may be committing an offence.

(e) The prosecutor does not have to prove that anyone was misled by the price; it is sufficient that it is potentially misleading.

(f) A person charged with an offence will have a defence if he or she can prove that the price in the book, magazine, etc. was not in an advertisement or that the price did not relate to the availability of the goods, services, etc. from him or her.

(g) There is also the defence of due diligence and the third-party defence of act or default of another, or reliance on information provided by another.

(h) A code of practice aimed at giving traders some guidance about prices has been drawn up with several recommendations relating specifically to the travel industry, in particular referring to surcharges.

SELF-ASSESSMENT QUESTIONS

State whether the following statements are correct or incorrect.

1. The Fair Trading Act 1973 created the post of Director General of Fair Trading.

2. The Director's chief job is to look after consumers' economic interests by encouraging monopolies.

3. The Act is important because it extends the provisions of the Restrictive Practices Acts to include services.

4. The Director can use the Restrictive Practices Court in order to eliminate unfair consumer trade practices.

5. The Consumer Protection Advisory Committee receives complaints from consumers.

6. The Monopolies and Mergers Commission helps the Director to encourage competition.

7. It was common before the Second World War for traders to control prices and restrict competition.

8. The Restrictive Practices Court makes it necessary for any such restrictive agreement to be registered.

9. A restrictive agreement has to be entered into by all traders and retailers who are in the same business and a copy of the agreement must placed on the Register of Restrictive Agreements.

10. The Restrictive Practices Court examines those restrictive agreements which the Director refers to it in order to judge if they are contrary to the public interest.

11. The TOSG Travel Fund Ltd enables the TOSG to send ABTA members to foreign resorts for training sessions.

12. The Resale Prices Act 1976 allows suppliers of goods to fix minimum prices for goods.

13. The Competition Act 1980 gives power to the Director to investigate the trading practices of particular businesses which restrict competition.

14. The Competition Act would allow tour operators to prohibit travel agents from offering their customers free travel or insurance.

15. The Trade Descriptions Act 1968 makes it an offence for a person in business to make a false or reckless statement about services he or she is offering to consumers.

16. Section 14 of the Trade Descriptions Act 1968 imposes criminal liability on the tour operator rather than the travel agent.

17. An offence is committed whenever the tour operator fails to provide the services etc. as described in the brochure.

18. Section 14 is limited to statements of past and present facts and not future promises.

19. The Consumer Protection Act 1987 makes it a criminal offence to give misleading price information about goods, services, accommodation or facilities.

20. An offence is committed under the Act if the price indication was correct at the time it was given but has subsequently become incorrect.

21. No defences are provided by the Consumer Protection Act 1987.

7 The Law of Contract

GLOSSARY

consideration A contractual requirement in English law that the parties must have exchanged something of value.

contract A legally binding agreement between two or more persons.

exclusion clause A clause in a contract whereby one party seeks to avoid his or her liability to the other (e.g. 'The management cannot accept liability for items deposited in this cloakroom').

implied contract A contract made neither in writing nor orally (e.g. using a vending machine).

invitation to treat A call to others to make offers.

legal capacity The legal ability of a person to enter into a contract; certain persons, e.g. young children, lack legal capacity.

oral contract A contract created purely by word of mouth (also called a verbal contract).

patrimonial interest A contractual requirement in Scots law that one party has transferred something of value.

AIM In this chapter we consider the rules governing contracts. These rules apply to all of the contracts that a tour operator or travel agent enters into. There are, however, special rules governing 'package' arrangements made by tour operators and travel agents, and these are discussed in Chapter 8. In this chapter we discuss the rules of offer and acceptance, cancellation, the legal capacity of parties to enter into a contract, contractual conditions, the role of tickets and the rules of payment. We also consider the position where errors or misrepresentations have been made.

Introduction

We must distinguish the popular meaning of the word 'contract' from its legal meaning. People often consider a contract to be a formal, written document – and thus an employee may speak of having worked for an employer for many years 'without a contract'. It is a popular misconception. The law provides that most employees should be provided with a written statement of the main terms of their employment; it does not require that they be given a written contract (see Chapter 12).

To the lawyer a contract means an agreement that the law will enforce. It covers the whole range of agreements, from the very simple (e.g. buying a cup of coffee from a vending machine) to the very complex (e.g. contracts for building the Channel Tunnel). There are basic rules that apply to all types of contract. Some contracts, however, are so complex that although they are governed to some extent by these basic laws of contract, special rules have been developed for them (e.g. the Consumer Credit Act 1974, Companies Acts 1985 and 1989 and the Financial Services Act 1986).

As has been stated, there are new rules governing 'packages', contained in the 1992 Regulations. These mainly govern package holidays but may also cover other travel arrangements made by travel agents. These rules do not, however, replace the common law of contract, which continues to apply unless the Regulations specify otherwise.

Basic requirements of valid contract

The law of contract is concerned principally with promises which constitute part of an agreed exchange. It governs such questions as which agreements the law will enforce, what obligations are imposed by the agreement in question and what remedies are available if the obligations are not performed.

A contract may be defined as:

> *an agreement which creates or is intended to create a legal obligation between the parties to it (Jenks' Digest of English Civil Law).*

Thus the following conditions must be satisfied if a contract is to be enforceable:

(a) *There must have been an agreement.* The parties must have voluntarily consented to the agreement (i.e. one should not have forced the other to enter into it). There must be *consensus in idem* (i.e. the parties must have agreed on all material aspects of the contract – they must be 'of one mind'). There should have been no error or misrepresentation.

(b) *There must be at least two parties to the contract.* There must be at least two parties to the contract and they must have contractual capacity (i.e. the legal power to enter into the contract – small children do not have legal capacity to enter into complex transactions).

(c) *It must have been a legal obligation.* There must have been an intention to create a legally binding contract. Illegal and immoral obligations and mere social engagements are not enforceable in the courts.

The tour operator provides a package of travel and accommodation for an all-inclusive price paid by the customer. The contract is between the tour operator and the customer, and the travel agent acts as an intermediary. It is against the tour operator that the client must seek legal remedies in the event of a breach of the contract.

The client and the tour operator must have reached agreement. It must be clear what is and what is not included in the package holiday. Once the booking has been confirmed there is a legally binding contract between the tour operator and the client. The client must have had contractual capacity to enter into the contract. Most tour operators will not accept a booking from persons under 18 years old without the signed consent of a parent or guardian.

Travel agents generally act as agents for other parties (the 'principal') such as airlines, shipping companies and tour operators. The contract is between the client and the principal. Thus, the client's remedies for breach of contract etc. lie against the principal unless it can be shown that the travel agent mishandled the booking or was negligent in some way. It should be noted, however, that travel agents may create their own packages or make tailor-made arrangements for clients and in so doing have a direct contractual relationship with them.

Consideration

It is an essential requirement of English law that for a contract to be legally binding each party must have agreed to provide something of value to the other. This 'something of value' is known as 'consideration'. Consideration is the price paid by the plaintiff for the defendant's promise. Each side has altered its position in reliance on the other's promise.

When a customer books a package holiday and this booking has been confirmed, the contract may be legally binding even where he or she has not yet paid for it. The consideration given by the customer is the promise to pay the price for the holiday when required by the agreement to do so. The consideration given by the tour operator is the promise that the holiday is available.

English law does not require that the consideration should be adequate. 'Cut-price' holidays or extremely cheap holiday bargains do not fail the consideration test.

The requirement of consideration also applies in Northern Ireland. The doctrine of consideration does not apply in Scotland. Scots law recognises gratuitous contracts whereby only one party undertakes to perform an obligation with the other party having to do nothing (e.g. a free holiday). There must be patrimonial interest, however (i.e. material loss or gain, although this need not be mutual).

If any of these requirements are missing, the contract will not be enforced in the courts.

Form of contract

A contract may be created:

(a) orally – by word of mouth;

(b) in writing – by any form of writing, formal or informal;

(c) impliedly – from the conduct of the parties.

Most contracts do not need to be in writing at all so long as all the other essential requirements are present. Indeed, millions of contracts are entered into every day without being set out in formal writing. A contract, or parts of it, may be inferred from the conduct of the parties, trade custom, and any previous dealings between the parties.

When called upon to interpret whether or not a contract may be implied by the conduct of the parties the court will apply the *objective test* (i.e. it is construed from the outward conduct of the parties rather than what they claim they were thinking). Before the 1992 Regulations, there was no legal requirement that a package holiday contract had to be in writing. Most of the contracts a travel agent enters into (other than 'packages') do not require to be in writing, but in many cases it is preferable that they should be. The reason, apart from administrative convenience, is that they contain a clear record of what was agreed.

SUMMARY

(a) The following conditions must be satisfied if a contract is to be legally enforceable:
   (i)   there must have been agreement between the parties on all material aspects of the contract
   (ii) the parties must have intended to create a legally binding contract.
   (iii) there must be at least two parties in the contract and they must have contractual capacity.

(b) The package holiday contract is an agreement between the client and the tour operator: the travel agent is merely an intermediary.

(c) It is an essential requirement of English law that there must be consideration (i.e. both parties must have exchanged something of value). This also applies in Northern Ireland.

(d) In Scotland even gratuitous contracts are legally enforceable.

(e) Formerly, there was no legal requirement that a package holiday contract had to be in writing, but this was altered by the 1992 Regulations.

Offer and acceptance

For there to be a valid contract there must be an offer made by one party and an acceptance of that offer by the other party. There are certain essential requirements before there is a valid offer (i.e. one which is capable of acceptance):

(a) *The offer must be firm.* There must be a definite intention to adhere to the offer. Words such as 'I hope to be able', 'I am thinking of taking a holiday', 'I'll need to check with my wife first of all ...' do not indicate a commitment and do not therefore amount to an offer.

(b) *The offer must be certain.* It must be clear what it is that is being offered. An offer is not capable of acceptance if it is vague:

In order to constitute a valid contract the parties must so express themselves that their meaning can be determined with a reasonable degree of certainty. It is plain that unless this can be done, it would be impossible to hold that the contracting parties had the same intention. In other words the consensus ad idem would be a matter of mere conjecture (Viscount Maughan in the case of Scammel v Ouston (1941)).

There is an exception to this rule that an offer must be certain, however. The parties may agree to defer a decision on a particular matter until later, and so long as they have indicated how that matter is to be decided it will be legally enforceable. Thus, a tour company may arrange for clients to hear the Vienna Boys Choir sing at the Chapel Royal, with the exact seating arrangements to be allocated on arrival. This will be enforceable if the client agreed to those terms at the outset.

(c) *The offer must be communicated.* Generally, in package holiday contracts, the offer is communicated by the client completing a booking form which is then passed on to the tour operator by the travel agent.

An offer must not be confused with 'an invitation to treat' or 'an expression of willingness to negotiate' (i.e. where a party is merely inviting offers which he or she is then free to accept or reject).

Most advertisements are not made as offers but as an expression of willingness to negotiate, inviting the reader to request the holiday described – to make an offer which the tour operator may accept or reject (depending on availability etc.). The display of brochures in a travel agency or their issue by a 'direct-sell' tour operator amounts to an invitation to treat. It is the customer who makes the offer to buy the holiday, which the travel agent or tour operator can accept or reject.

The tour operator does not have to supply the holiday at the price indicated or at any price at all. However, the tour operator must be careful not to contravene the Consumer Protection Act 1987 which provides criminal penalties for misleading price indications (see Chapter 6).

The travel agent or tour operator may refuse bookings from anyone and does not have to give reasons for doing so. However, it is a criminal offence to refuse a booking from a customer on grounds of sex (Sex Discrimination Act 1975) or on grounds of race, colour, national or ethnic origin or nationality (Race Relations Act 1976). There are a few exceptions to this regulation, the most relevant of which is on grounds of decency or privacy (e.g. where there are only a limited number of places available in shared accommodation such as a dormitory). Religious discrimination is not unlawful and thus special pilgrimage tours, for example, can be restricted to particular religious denominations. *Note*: Fair Employment legislation in Northern Ireland, however, *see* Chapter 12.

It is preferable that the tour operator requires bookings to be made by the client on the appropriate booking form. In completing the form and in allowing the travel agent to process it the client is making a firm offer. It is important that the travel agent checks that the booking form has been fully completed, thus ensuring that it is clear what it is that the client is booking.

2.6 Booking Procedure

Travel agents shall ensure that booking procedures are complied with in every detail and in accordance with any relevant agency agreement. All booking references shall be shown (ABTA Travel Agents' Code of Conduct).

The booking made by the client amounts to an offer to the tour operator. It is communicated by completion of the booking form which is then processed by the travel agent. If the travel agent fails to process the booking properly or to communicate essential information which the client wanted drawn to the tour operator's attention (e.g. special needs), the travel agent may be held directly liable to the client.

An acceptance logically concludes a contract. The tour operator accepts the booking made by the client by confirmation of it. There are certain essential requirements for that acceptance to be valid.

(a) *The acceptance must be communicated to the offeror*. The acceptance is not effective until it is communicated to the offeror. Mere mental assent is insufficient. The communication can be by word of mouth (e.g. over the telephone), by letter, telex, telegram, facsimile (fax) or by recorded message. Whatever method is used, the tour operator must ensure that confirmation of the booking is communicated to the client.

The law recognises that acceptance may be implied from conduct. If the client receives tickets, for example, from the tour operator this may amount to an implied acceptance of the booking even though no letter of confirmation is received.

If the acceptance is sent through the post, the contract is binding as at the date of posting, not the date of receipt by the client. This rule may be altered, however, by the tour operator in the booking conditions.

(b) *The acceptance must meet the offer*. The tour operator must confirm the offer made by the client. It must be the same holiday the client requested.

(c) *The acceptance must be unqualified*. If the confirmation indicates that the tour operator cannot provide a holiday identical to that requested by the client but can provide an alternative flight/hotel/tour, this is not an acceptance but a counter-offer which may be accepted or rejected by the client.

Most tour operators provide in the booking conditions that the client must accept a suitable alternative and in that case the client is not entitled to turn down a reasonable alternative provided by the tour operator.

The client may withdraw an offer to purchase the holiday at any time before the booking has been confirmed. He or she must notify the tour operator before confirmation is sent. The booking is automatically withdrawn on the death, insanity or bankruptcy of the client if this occurs before confirmation has been sent.

Generally, once confirmation is sent the tour operator cannot cancel the holiday. If the tour operator does so he or she may be liable to the client for damages for breach of contract. If confirmation has been posted to the client or communicated to the travel agent, the tour operator can cancel the holiday at any time up until the client has received confirmation or has been notified of it by the travel agent.

These rules in respect of bookings, cancellations and alternative arrangements clauses are those provided by common law. In practice the rules will be those contained in the booking conditions and, if appropriate, must comply with the 1992 Regulations.

SUMMARY

(a) In order for there to be a valid contract there must be an offer made by one party which is accepted by the other party.

(b) The client makes the offer by completing a booking form.

(c) The tour operator accepts the offer by confirming the booking.

(d) The booking must be:
  (i) firm – the client is not merely considering whether to purchase the holiday;
  (ii) certain – it is clear which holiday the client has chosen;
  (iii) communicated – the booking form must be sent to the tour operator.

(e) Displays of brochures and other advertising material are an 'invitation to treat'.

(f) It is the client who makes the offer, which the tour operator can accept or reject.

(g) The tour operator must ensure that confirmation has been passed on to the travel agent for communication to the client.

(h) The travel agent must ensure that confirmation has been communicated to the client.

(i) The confirmation must be of the same holiday which the client offered to purchase.

(j) If the confirmation alters any of the important details (flight/dates/hotel/board, etc.) requested in the booking, it amounts to a counter-offer which the client can accept or reject.

(k) The client may have agreed 'suitable alternative arrangements'.

(1) Unless the booking conditions provide special rules relating to cancellations, the client may cancel the booking at any time before confirmation has been sent. The tour operator may cancel at any time before the client has received confirmation.

Contractual capacity

For a contract to be valid, the parties to it must be legally capable of entering into the contract. Certain categories of people (e.g. young children and the insane) have no contractual capacity and others (e.g. the intoxicated) have limited capacity. It is therefore important to consider who can validly make a booking.

Adults/groups

All persons over the age of 18, unless incapacitated by intoxication or insanity, can enter into a holiday contract. A person may make a booking on his or her own behalf and/or on behalf of others. That person may be acting as an agent for a group of people. In that case most booking forms require the person making the booking to acknowledge that he or she has authority to act on behalf of the group. If a member of the group fails to pay for the holiday the person making the booking is liable for the fee. This is also the case where a married person makes a booking on behalf of the other spouse and family.

Children

English law refers to persons under the age of 18 as 'minors'. Minors have a limited capacity to enter into contracts and it is for this reason that most tour operators require clients under the age of 18 to obtain the consent of a parent or guardian. A minor who holds himself or herself out to be of full age would be legally obliged to pay for the holiday unless it was obvious that the client was under 18 years old.

 In Scotland the rules are contained in the Age of Legal Capacity (Scotland) Act 1991. Persons under the age of 16 have no legal capacity to contract. Contracts are entered into on their behalf by a parent or guardian. Persons over 16 have full contractual capacity. A contract entered into by a person aged 16 or 17 which is shown to be to his or her serious detriment may be set aside by a court. Persons who have reached their 16th birthday may marry in Scotland without parental consent.

Insane persons

A person who is incapable of understanding a contract due to insanity is not legally bound by it. Such a person would be bound by a holiday contract, however, if the travel agent did not know and had no reason to suspect that the client was suffering from insanity. In Scotland the booking would not be valid notwithstanding the fact that the travel agent was unaware of the client's insanity.

Intoxicated persons

A booking made by an intoxicated person is legally binding unless the client was so intoxicated as to be incapable of understanding the holiday contract. In that case the holiday contract will be considered invalid only if he or she seeks to have it set aside immediately on becoming sober.

SUMMARY   The main points to remember here are:

(a) For a contract to be considered legally binding both parties must have contractual capacity.

(b) A person may make a booking on behalf of others as their agent. Most booking forms require that person to acknowledge that he or she has authority to act on their behalf.

(c) In English law, persons under the age of 18 have only a limited contractual capacity and thus most tour operators require them to obtain the consent of a parent or guardian to make a booking.

(d) In Scotland a person who has reached his or her 16th birthday has the capacity to enter into a holiday contract without a parent or guardian's consent.

(e) A contract with a person who is insane is not legally binding on him or her unless the other party knew or ought reasonably to have known that he or she was insane. In Scotland the contract is not binding under any circumstances.

(f) Intoxicated persons are bound by their contracts unless they can prove that they were so intoxicated as to be beyond understanding.

Terms and conditions

It is an essential requirement for a contract to be legally binding that the parties have reached agreement. The parties make their agreement orally, impliedly or in writing, or partly in writing and partly orally. These terms of the agreement which they have set out, whether in writing, orally or a mixture of the two, are known as express terms.

English law divides express terms into conditions and warranties. Conditions are the most important terms of the contract which form its main purpose. If a condition is broken the injured party may cancel the contract and claim damages. Warranties are the less important terms of the contract. If a warranty is broken the injured party cannot cancel but can claim damages. This distinction between conditions and warranties is becoming increasingly blurred.

Scots law does not make a rigid distinction between conditions and warranties. A party can cancel the contract only if there has been a material (important) breach by the other party. If the breach is minor the injured party cannot cancel the contract but can claim damages.

Certain terms of a contract are so obvious that it goes without saying that they form part of a contract. These are labelled implied terms.

Example

Harry booked a holiday with Cheap Holidays Ltd which included 14 nights' accommodation at a hotel in Malaga. When he arrived he was amazed to discover that his room did not have a bed. The hotelier offered to hire him a bed for 1600 pesetas (approximately £10) per night.

The holiday representative was unhelpful and told him that he would have to pay or sleep on the floor. On his return he claimed a refund of £140. The tour operator pointed out that there was no mention of beds in the brochure.

The reasonable person would argue that it is implied that when a holidaymaker books a room he or she is entitled to be provided with a bed as part of the price.

In the package holiday contract the express terms of the agreement between the tour operator and client are usually set out in the booking conditions. It is important that the tour operator should ensure that the client's attention is drawn to the booking conditions and that these are made part of the contract between them. The tour operator will usually require the client to sign a statement on the booking form acknowledging that he or she has read, and agrees to be bound by, the booking conditions. The travel agent also has a duty under the ABTA Code of Conduct to draw the client's attention to the booking conditions.

The Regulations require detailed information to be provided to the client before the contract is entered into. In addition, once the booking has been confirmed, the client must be provided with specified information, in writing.

SUMMARY   The main points about booking conditions and tickets are:

(a) An agreement may be made orally, impliedly, in writing or partly orally and partly in writing.

(b) Express terms of a contract are those set out orally, in writing or in a mixture of the two.

(c) If either party breaches an important term of the contract the other may cancel and claim damages.

(d) A breach of a minor term allows the other party only to claim damages, not to cancel the contract.

(e) Certain terms (e.g. that a hotel bedroom should have a bed) are so obvious that they are automatically implied as part of the contract.

(f) Generally, the main terms of the package holiday contract are those set out in the booking conditions.

(g) It is important for the tour operator that the client should acknowledge that he or she has read and agrees to be bound by the booking conditions.

Tickets

Generally speaking, a ticket is not a written contract. A travel ticket is a voucher; it is evidence of the right to travel in the manner indicated. The traveller must retain the ticket and present it when required to do so. It must be made clear to the client that the document he or she is being handed is a ticket and that he or she is required to take care of it. The travel agent or tour operator is not required to replace or refund lost, expired, unendorsed or unused tickets.

Most airline, ferry, rail and coach tickets refer to by-laws or conditions subject to which the passenger is being carried. The ticket may contain those conditions, but more frequently it will refer the holder to conditions or by-laws contained elsewhere. Passengers are bound by those conditions or by-laws if they were clearly referred to on the ticket. It does not matter that they did not read them – they will still be bound by them if they are of a kind which could reasonably be expected to apply to such a contract of carriage.

The Unfair Contract Terms Act 1977

Many business organisations use standard forms of written contract. Apart from administrative convenience, these standard contracts are used to ensure that the contract is 'watertight' and that the rights and obligations of the parties may be clearly identified should a dispute arise. Tour operators use standard booking conditions.

Exclusion clauses

A term may be inserted into a contract which purports to exclude or to limit financially one party's liability for breach of contract, misrepresentation or negligence. Tour operators frequently include booking conditions which exclude liability for the acts and omissions of airlines, hoteliers, etc.; which exclude liability for delays of less than *x* hours; which permit them to provide 'suitable alternatives'; etc. Such terms and conditions are usually referred to as 'exclusion clauses'.

Historically, the courts have sought to control such clauses. For example, in *Anglo-Continental Holidays Ltd v Typaldos Lines (London) Ltd* a group of Jewish schoolchildren were booked on a cruise. The cruise was to include a two-day stop at Haifa, enabling them to visit Jerusalem and Galilee. A week before departure they were informed that they would be travelling on a ship of inferior quality to that originally booked and that they would be stopping at Haifa for only eight hours, not giving them enough time to visit Galilee. The shipowners relied on a clause in the handbook which indicated 'steamers, sailing, rates and itineraries are subject to change without prior notice'.

Lord Denning stated:

> *The change from the 22,000 ton Atlantica (with two swimming pools and lots of accommodation) to this small old crate (as one of the witnesses called the Angelika) was itself substantial departure. But most important of all was the shortened time at Haifa. The climax of the trip for these Jewish boys and girls was two days at Haifa, whereas they were only to have eight hours. The defendants cannot excuse it by reliance on the clause.*

The aim of the Unfair Contract Terms Act 1977 is to control such exclusion clauses. Most of the provisions of the Act apply only to business liability. The Act would apply to travel agents and tour operators relying on such clauses. Protection is afforded to a person 'who deals as a consumer'; thus the Act provides protection for the ordinary client but it may not provide the same degree of protection for business clients.

The Unfair Contract Terms Act makes certain provisions of a contract void.

Negligence

Liability for death or personal injury resulting from negligence cannot be excluded or restricted by any contract provision or notice. A term excluding liability for other matters will be effective in so far as it satisfies the 'reasonableness' test. A coach operator which excludes liability for loss or damage to luggage which is not properly labelled or secured could reasonably rely on the clause.

Contract

Where one party to a contract deals as a consumer on the other's written standard terms of business, here as against that party, the other cannot, unless the reasonableness test is satisfied, rely on a contract term which:

(a) excludes or restricts any liability in respect of a breach of contract; or

(b) purports to entitle him or her to render a contractual performance substantially different from that which was reasonably expected of him or her, or to render no performance at all.

This provision is of considerable importance when considering variations, cancellations, delays and surcharge clauses. Such clauses will be effective only if they pass the 'reasonableness test'.

The reasonableness test requires that the term must have been a fair and reasonable one to have been included in such a contract. The burden of proving that the term was fair and reasonable lies with the party relying upon it (i.e. in the case of the holiday contract that burden lies with the tour operator). The court may take into consideration the availability of insurance to cover these matters.

Note: The Regulations contain provisions governing exclusion clauses in respect of regulated packages.

SUMMARY A brief summary of the implications of this Act is:

(a) Most businesses rely on standard form contracts to ensure that the rights and obligations of the parties are clearly identified at the outset.

(b) Most tour operators rely on standard booking conditions.

(c) Terms in contracts which aim to exclude or restrict the liability of the business for certain matters are known as 'exclusion clauses'.

(d) Exclusion clauses are subject to the provisions of the Unfair Contract Terms Act 1977.

(e) Variations, cancellations, delays and surcharge clauses are governed by the provisions of the Act and, where appropriate, by the Regulations.

(f) The tour operator cannot exclude or restrict liability for the death or injury of the client caused by its negligence.

(g) Clauses or terms excluding or restricting liability for loss of luggage or breach of contract will be enforced only if they are fair and reasonable.

♛ The Supply of Goods and Services Act 1982

Parliament may, in furtherance of a policy of consumer protection, state certain terms in an Act of Parliament which are to be implied in all contracts of a particular type (e.g. Sections 12–15 of the Sale of Goods Act 1979, which require that goods sold in the course of a business must meet certain standards).

Although there have been a number of Acts of Parliament setting out implied terms relating to goods, the implied terms relating to services were those provided by the common law (i.e. determined by the courts). The National Consumer Council argued in its report *Services Please* that most consumers were not aware of their rights in respect of services and that a codification of these rights in an Act of Parliament would clarify them and draw them to public attention.

The Supply of Goods and Services Act 1982 sets out certain implied terms in relation to services. The Act does not apply to Scotland but there are similar provisions in the Scottish law.

Section 13 is the most relevant provision of the Act for tour operators and travel agents. The section provides that:

> *In a contract for the supply of a service, where the supplier is acting in the course of a business, there is an implied term that the supplier will carry out the service with reasonable care and skill.*

The tour operator/travel agent must exercise the skill and care of a competent tour operator/travel agent. The court may consider the ABTA Code of Conduct in determining whether a particular tour operator or travel agent has met that standard.

Errors and misrepresentations

Some types of error made in forming contracts will make the final contract invalid. Errors that invalidate a contract are errors in fact and not in judgement. The law of contract does not help those who have paid too much for a holiday or who cannot cope with the heat and yet booked a package holiday to Corfu in the middle of August. These are errors of judgement and the contract is still valid.

We must distinguish between errors in fact and errors in law. If the tour operator or client is mistaken about his or her legal rights or obligations it does not affect the validity of the holiday contract.

If the parties to the holiday contract have contracted on the basis of a mistaken set of facts the contract may be void or at least voidable. If the misunderstanding was so fundamental to the contract there is no contract at all. A contract will be rendered void if both parties are mistaken as to the existence of the subject-matter of the contract at the time the contract was made (e.g. if the client has booked accommodation at a particular hotel which, unknown to both parties, has been destroyed by fire).

The requirement that the mistake must be fundamental means that very few holiday contracts are rendered void by errors. It could be argued by the client that where such errors arise the tour operator or travel agent has failed to

exercise the degree of care and skill required by section 13 of the Supply of

Goods and Services Act 1982 and by the Codes of Conduct. Furthermore, such errors are less likely to arise where the package is regulated and the client has been provided with the information required.

Far more successful claims have been made against tour operators and travel agents for misrepresentation than for error. A misrepresentation is a false statement of existing or past verifiable fact. It induces a person to enter into a contract. The statement may be verbal, written, a signal, facial expression or a gesture. The statement must be one of fact not law. Mere statements of opinion, so long as that opinion is honestly held, are not to be taken as statements of fact. Statements of future intention (e.g. that a swimming pool will be built at a hotel) are not statements of existing fact.

There are three types of actionable misrepresentation:

Fraudulent misrepresentation

This is a deliberately made untrue statement or a half-truth. It is also fraudulent misrepresentation to make a statement without belief in its truth, or recklessly, not caring whether it is true or false. If such a statement is made and it induces the client to choose a particular holiday he or she would be entitled to cancel that holiday and claim damages.

Negligent misrepresentation

The party making the misrepresentation did so carelessly. The Misrepresentation Act 1967 provides that the injured party can have the contract set aside and claim damages unless the party making the misrepresentation can prove that he or she reasonably believed in the truth of what he or she said and was not, therefore, negligent. This remedy was introduced in Scotland by the Law Reform (Miscellaneous Provisions) (Scotland) Act 1985.

Innocent misrepresentation

The party making the misrepresentation honestly believed it to be true. The injured party can have the contract set aside or claim damages under the Misrepresentation Act 1967. In Scotland there is no entitlement to damages for innocent misrepresentation.

SUMMARY   This section was important so let us sum up:

(a) An error of judgement will not invalidate a contract.

(b) A contract is legally binding notwithstanding the fact that one of the parties is mistaken about its legal rights and obligations under it.

(c) If a fundamental mistake has been made and both parties are at cross-purposes, the contract is not valid.

(d) A misrepresentation is a false statement of existing or past verifiable fact which induces another party to enter into a contract.

(e) A fraudulent misrepresentation entitles the injured party to cancel the contract and claim damages.

(f) A negligent misrepresentation entitles the injured party to cancel the contract and claim damages.

(g) An innocent misrepresentation entitles the injured party to cancel the contract or claim damages.

(h) There is no claim for damages for innocent misrepresentation in Scotland.

Rules of payment

The client must pay for the holiday and other services provided by the travel agent and/or tour operator when required by the contract to do so. The travel agent has a duty to the tour operator to take reasonable steps to ensure that the client pays all monies due under the contract.

The travel agent is entitled to demand payment for the exact sum in current and legal tender, but most are willing to give change.

Current legal tender includes Bank of England notes of any amount; the £1 coin (any amount); bronze coins up to 20p in total; silver or cupro-nickel coins over 10p up to £10; cupro-nickel or silver coins of 10p or less up to £5. Scottish banknotes are not legal tender in England but most reasonable travel agents will accept them.

The travel agent or tour operator is not bound to accept a cheque. Acceptance of a cheque is conditional on it being honoured. It is a criminal offence to issue a cheque in the knowledge that there are insufficient funds to meet it or that there is no overdraft facility to support it. It is also an offence to issue a cheque with the intention of 'stopping it' without justification. If a bank guarantee card is used, the travel agent must endorse the cheque card number on the reverse of the cheque, not the customer, otherwise the guarantee is not valid.

Now, go on to the assessment.

SELF-ASSESSMENT QUESTIONS

State whether the following statements are correct or incorrect.

1. Generally, the package holiday contract is one between the tour operator and the client; the travel agent is merely an intermediary.

2. The tour operator should make clear what is and what is not included in the package holiday.

3. The holiday contract is not legally binding until the client has paid for the holiday.

4. It is an essential legal requirement that the client must have paid a reasonable price for the holiday.

5. Package holiday contracts must be created in writing if they are to be legally binding.

6. It is essential that the tour operator and client have agreed on all material aspects of the holiday contract, otherwise the contract is not binding.

7. The display of brochures is an 'invitation to treat' not an offer to sell the holidays contained in them.

8. It is illegal to arrange special religious tours restricted to one particular denomination.

9. It is the client who makes the offer to purchase the holiday by submitting a completed booking form.

10. A tour operator is legally entitled to reject bookings from groups of single English males under 21 years old.

11. The tour operator must ensure that confirmation of the holiday has been communicated to the client.

12. It is illegal to sell a foreign inclusive holiday to a person under the age of 18 without the consent of a parent or guardian.

13. The sale of a package holiday to an intoxicated person is automatically void.

14. The express terms of a contract are those which are set out in writing.

15. It is important to ensure that the client has signed a written acknowledgement that he or she has read the booking conditions and agrees to be bound by them.

16. A travel ticket is a voucher evidencing the right to travel in the manner indicated on it.

17. If a client loses a ticket the travel agent is bound to replace it if it has not been used.

18. Most tour operators provide standard booking conditions.

19. Booking conditions which enable the tour operator to provide suitable alternative accommodation to that booked by the client are rendered invalid by the Unfair Contract Terms Act 1977.

20. The travel agent has a duty of reasonable care and skill in processing the client's booking.

21. A client who has booked a holiday in Benidorm because the name suggests a restful, peaceful place is legally entitled to a refund on discovering that it is a busy, lively commercial resort.

22. A client who books a package holiday at a particular hotel because the brochure indicated that an Olympic size swimming pool was being built there, would be entitled to sue the tour operator for damages for negligent misrepresentation if the pool was not completed by the time he or she took the holiday.

23. The travel agent has a duty to the tour operator to take reasonable steps to obtain payment for the holiday from the client.

24. Acceptance of a cheque is conditional on it being honoured.

8 The Package Travel, Package Holidays and Package Tours Regulations 1992

GLOSSARY   **ABTA** Association of British Travel Agents.

DTI Department of Trade and Industry.

EC Directive This sets out provisions which are to be implemented by member states within a set time limit. The method by which the Directive is implemented is left to the individual state.

rescission Where one party to a contract is in breach of an important provision the other is entitled to withdraw from the contract.

regulation Delegated legislation made by a Minister of the Crown under authority laid down in an Act of Parliament.

AIM   It is the aim of this chapter to consider the application of the provisions of the Package Travel, Package Holidays and Package Tours Regulations 1992 to the package holiday contract.

Introduction

 The EC Directive on Package Travel, Package Holidays and Package Tours was adopted on 13 June 1990. The aim was to harmonise the rules governing packages throughout the Community. Member states were required to introduce measures to implement the Directive and these measures were to come into force before 31 December 1992.

The provisions of the Directive do not replace national laws, except where those laws conflict with its provisions. Thus the law described in other chapters of this book will also apply to package holidays (as well as package travel and package tours) except where it is consistent with the provisions discussed below.

The Directive was implemented in the UK by means of regulations made under section 2(2) of the European Communities Act 1972. The Package Travel, Package Holidays and Package Tours Regulations 1992 came into force on 31 December 1992.

Definitions and application of the Regulations

It is important at the outset to consider the definitions provided by the Regulations. These definitions are contained in Regulation 2:

> ' *"Brochure" means any brochure in which packages are offered for sale*'

It does not apply to purely promotional material, provided that specific packages are not described in that material.

> ' *"Contract" means the agreement linking the consumer to the organiser or to the retailer, or to both as the case may be*'

In the majority of cases, the consumer's contract is with the tour operator ('the organiser').

> ' *"The Directive" means the Council Directive 90/314/EC on package travel, package holidays and package tours.*'

These are other Directives which also apply to the travel industry.

> ' *"Offer" includes an invitation to treat whether by means of advertising or otherwise, and cognate expressions shall be construed accordingly.*'

The meaning of an 'invitation to treat' is explained in Chapter 5. In Scotland it is referred to as 'an expression of willingness to do business'.

> ' *"Organiser" means the person who, otherwise than occasionally, organises packages and sells or offers them for sale, whether directly or through a retailer*'.

The EC Directive on Package Travel, Package Holidays and Package Tours does not use the terms 'tour operator' or 'travel agent' as this gives rise to linguistic difficulties and wide difference of practice between member states. Furthermore, the scope of the Directive covers more than package holidays and thus, the definitions of the parties involved had to reflect that. Tour operators are clearly 'organisers', but that term also covers those who, other than occasionally, organise and sell packages. It may apply for example to educational establishments and religious bodies, which organise package study tours or religious pilgrimages. The definitions do not define 'occasionally' and it may therefore be some time before the courts define to what extent the Regulations apply to other bodies. It should be noted that the definition covers travel agents who put together packages:

' *"the other party to the contract" means the party, other than the consumer, to the contract, that is the organiser or the retailer, or both, as the case may be.'*

In the majority of cases, it refers to the tour operator.

' *"Package" means the pre-arranged combination of at least two of the following components when sold or offered for sale at an inclusive price and when the service covers a period of more than twenty-four hours or includes overnight accommodation:*

(a) transport;

(b) accommodation;

(c) other tourist services not ancillary to transport or accommodation and accounting for a significant proportion of the package;

and

(d) the submission of separate accounts for different components shall not cause the arrangements to be other than a package;

(e) the fact that a combination is arranged at the request of the consumer and in accordance with his specific instructions (whether modified or not) shall not of itself cause it to be treated as other than pre-arranged.'

The definition is not confined to package holidays and could cover business and conference travel, for example. The provision of a weekend break at a hotel which included theatre tickets would come within the scope of the Regulations even though transport was not provided.

The definition specifically includes 'tailor made' packages.

Where transport is one of the elements it must be a significant part of the package. Thus, it would be unlikely that a hotel which provides a courtesy coach to the local airport would be considered as providing a package. Likewise, accommodation which is incidental to transport (e.g. a cabin or a sleeping compartment on a train) would not be considered a separate element unless it formed an important touristic element (e.g. a cabin on a cruise ship or sleeping accommodation on a luxury train).

The other 'tourist services' must come as an important part of the package. It excludes business or educational services and the mere provision of a facility, *see* Chapter 6).

'Retailer' means the person who sells or offers for sale the package put together by the organiser.

In most package holiday contracts the travel agent is the retailer.

 'Consumer' is defined in Regulation 2(2) as:

'In the definition of "contract" (stated above), "consumer" means the person who takes or agrees to take the package ("the principal contractor") and elsewhere in these Regulations "consumer" means, as the contract requires,

principal contractor, any person on whose behalf the principal contractor agrees to purchase the package ("the other beneficiaries") or any person to whom the principal contractor or any of the other beneficiaries transfers the package ("the transferee").'

It appears that this includes business consumers and is therefore broader than the usual definition given in consumer protection legislation (*see* Chapter 6).

The Regulations apply to packages sold or offered for sale in the United Kingdom. Regulations 4–15 apply to packages sold or offered for sale on or after 31 December 1992. Regulations 16–22 apply to contracts which, in whole or part, remain to be performed on 31 December 1992.

SUMMARY

(a) The Package Travel, Package Holidays and Package Tours Regulations 1992 came into force on 31 December 1992.

(b) The Regulations do not replace existing law except in so far as it is inconsistent with the provisions of the Regulations.

(c) Regulation 2 contains important definitions.

(d) The Regulations refer to 'organiser' and 'retailer' rather than 'tour operator' and 'travel agent'.

(e) A travel agent who puts together packages will be considered an 'organiser'.

(f) The definition of a 'package' covers more than package holidays and may include business travel arrangements.

(g) 'Tailor made' packages are covered by the Regulations.

(h) Business clients may be considered as 'consumers' under the Regulations.

(i) The Regulations apply to packages sold or offered for sale in the UK.

Brochures and advertising

 Regulation 4(1) provides:

'No organiser or retailer shall supply to a consumer any descriptive matter concerning a package, the price of a package or any other conditions applying to the contract which contains any misleading information.'

In Chapter 6 we have already discussed the provisions of the Trade Descriptions Act 1968 and the Consumer Protection Act 1987 and these provisions continue to apply to packages. However, whereas section 14 of the 1968 Act deals with 'false' statements Regulation 4 deals with 'misleading' information and is thus a wider prohibition. Regulation 4(2) provides the consumer with a right to compensation for any loss which he suffers as a result of relying on the misleading information.

Regulation 5(1) contains provisions dealing with brochures. There is no legal requirement to provide a brochure but where one is provided it must contain in a 'legible, comprehensive and accurate manner' the price and adequate information about the matters specified in Schedule 1:

> '1. *The destination and the means, characteristics and categories of transport used.*
>
> 2. *The type of accommodation, its location, category or degree of comfort and its main features and where the accommodation is to be provided in a member state, its approval or tourist classification under the rules of that member state.*
>
> 3. *The meals which are included in the package.*
>
> 4. *The itinerary.*
>
> 5. *General information about passports and visa requirements which apply for British citizens and health formalities required for the journey or stay.*
>
> 6. *Either the monetary amount or the percentage of the price which is to be paid on account and the timetable for payment of the balance.*
>
> 7. *Whether a minimum number of persons is required for the package to take place and, if so, the deadline for informing the consumer in the event of cancellation.*
>
> 8. *The arrangements (if any) which apply if consumers are delayed at the outward or homeward points of departure.*
>
> 9. *The arrangements for security for money paid over and for the repatriation of the consumer in the event of insolvency.*'

Points to note about the matters specified in Schedule 1:

(a) The reference to 'characteristics and categories of transport used' is a reference to the means of transport and class of travel and not a reference, for example, to the type of aircraft used.

(b) Classification of accommodation situated outside the EC is not required.

(c) The 'meal plan' is a reference to the number or frequency of meals provided.

(d) The information required in respect of passports, visas and health is 'general information' but is more than a mere referral to the appropriate embassy.

Regulation 5(3) makes it a criminal offence for an organiser to issue a brochure which contravenes the requirements of Regulation 5(1).

Regulation 5(2) and (3) provides that it a criminal offence for a retailer to supply to a consumer a brochure which he knows or has reasonable cause to know does not comply with Regulation 5(1). Travel agents may, therefore, require tour operators to guarantee that the information contained in their brochures complies with the Regulations.

Regulation 6 makes the particulars contained in the brochure, including those required by Regulation 5(1), implied warranties and thus legally binding. This does not apply, however:

(a) to the information required by paragraph 9 of Schedule 1 (financial security details);

(b) where the organiser and consumer agree, after the contract has been made, that some or all of the particulars in the brochure will not form part of the contract.

The tour operator may expressly reserve the right in the brochure to make changes to the particulars contained in it, provided that these changes have been clearly communicated to the consumer before the contract is made.

SUMMARY

(a) Regulation 4 provides that descriptive material concerning a package and supplied by the organiser or retailer to the consumer must not contain misleading information.

(b) A consumer who relied on the misleading information is entitled to compensation.

(c) Brochures must contain legible, comprehensive and accurate information concerning the price and, where relevant, the information specified in Schedule 1.

(d) It is also a criminal offence for an organiser to supply a brochure in contravention of these provisions.

(e) It is also an offence for a retailer to supply a brochure which he or she knows or ought reasonably to have known contravenes Regulation 5(1).

(f) The particulars in the brochure are legally binding on the organiser (except in the circumstances specified in Regulation 5(2) and (3).

Provision of information

Regulation 7 requires the organiser to provide the consumer with:

(a) general information on passport and visa requirements applicable to British citizens and the periods for obtaining them;

(**b**) information on health formalities required for the journey or stay;

(**c**) information on the arrangements for security for the money paid over (where applicable) and for the repatriation of the consumer in the event of insolvency.

The information must be provided in writing or 'in some other appropriate form' before the contract is concluded. An organiser who fails to provide this information is guilty of an offence.

Regulation 8 requires 'the other party to the contract' to supply the consumer with certain specified information in good time before the start of the journey. In most cases, the organiser will be the 'other party to the contract'. In determining what is and what is not 'in good time' regard must be had to the length of time between the consumer making the booking and the date of departure for the holiday. In the initial draft of Regulation 8 it specified that the information had to be given 'in good time' 'whether before or after the contract has been made'. This latter reference has been removed and the time of the contract becoming legally binding is no longer relevant for this provision.

As in the case of Regulation 7, the information must be given in writing 'or in some other appropriate form'. It is preferable that it should be given in writing whether or not also in some other appropriate form. It would also be useful to require the consumer to sign an acknowledgement that he or she had received the information specified, perhaps at the time of collecting the tickets.

The information to be provided is contained in Regulation 8(2):

(a) 'the times and places of intermediate stops and transport connections and particulars of the place to be occupied by the traveller (for example, cabin or berth on ship, sleeper compartment on train).'

The previous draft referred to 'particulars of the type of accommodation allocated to the consumer for the journey'.

Although the Regulation does not so specify, the DTI, in their commentary, have indicated that they regard the reference to 'intermediate stops' as those which significantly affect the nature of the holiday. It would not therefore include a coffee break, for example.

(b) 'the name, address and telephone number—
    (i)   of the representative of the other party to the contract in the locality where the consumer is to stay or, if there is no such representative
    (ii) of an agency in that locality on whose assistance a consumer in difficulty would be able to call, or, if there is no such representative or agency
    (iii) a telephone number or other information which will enable the consumer to contact the other party to the contract during the stay.

(c) 'in the case of a journey or stay abroad by a child under the age of 16 on the day when the journey or stay is due to start, information enabling direct contact to be made with the child or the person responsible at the place where he is to stay'.

The draft Regulation referred to 'a journey or stay outside the United Kingdom'. The new reference to 'abroad' is more confusing. Is Northern Ireland 'abroad'? Does a child travelling from Londonderry to Donegal go 'abroad'? What about trips to the Isle of Man and the Channel Islands (which are outside the United Kingdom)?

This provision would not apply to a child accompanying a parent, guardian or other adult who is not acting on a professional basis. It would apply to school trips and children participating in trips organised by voluntary bodies but making use of a 'package' organised by a tour operator or other 'organiser'.

(d) 'except where the consumer is required as a term of the contract to take out an insurance policy to cover the cost of cancellation by the consumer or the cost of assistance including repatriation, in the event of accident or illness, information about an insurance policy which the consumer may, if he wishes, take out in respect of the risk of those costs being incurred'.

Regulation 9 requires the organiser to ensure that the contract contains at least the elements specified in Schedule 2, depending on the particular package, i.e.

(a) the travel destination(s) and, where periods of stay are involved, the relevant periods, with dates;

(b) the means, characteristics and categories of transport to be used, and the dates, times and points of departure and return;

(c) where the package includes accommodation, its location, its tourist category or degree of comfort, its main features and where accommodation is to be provided in a member state, its compliance with the rules of that member state;

(d) the meals which are included in the package;

(e) whether a minimum of persons is required for the package to take place and if so, the deadline for informing the consumer in the event of cancellation;

(f) the itinerary;

(g) visits, excursions or other services which are included in the total price agreed for the package;

(h) the name and address of the organiser, the retailer and where appropriate the insurer;

(i) the price of the package, if the price may be revised in accordance with the term which may be included under Regulation 11, an indication of the possibility of such price revisions, and an indication of any dues, taxes or fees chargeable for certain services (landing, embarkation or disembarkation fees at ports and airports and tourist taxes, where such costs are not included in the package);

(j) the payment schedule and method of payment;

(k) special requirements which the consumer has communicated to the organiser or retailer when making the booking and which both have accepted;

(l) the periods within which the consumer must make any complaint about the failure to perform or the inadequate performance of the contract.

The terms of the contract must be communicated to the consumer before the contract is made and he must be provided with a written copy of the terms. The requirement to communicate the information in advance does not apply, however, in the case of a late booking where the interval is so short that it would be impracticable. It is an implied condition of the contract that the organiser will comply with the requirements of Regulation 9. In Scotland, it is an implied term, which if breached, justifies rescission of the contract.

SUMMARY

(a) Regulation 7 requires the organiser to provide the consumer with information on passports, visas, health and financial security arrangements before the contract is concluded.

(b) Breach of Regulation 7 is a criminal offence.

(c) Regulation 8 provides that the organiser must supply the consumer with specified information in good time before the start of the journey. This information relates to travel arrangements, contact numbers and insurance.

(d) Regulation 9 and Schedule 2 set out certain essential elements to be contained in the contract, depending on the nature of the particular package.

(e) The terms of the contract must be communicated to the consumer before the contract is made and he or she must be provided with a written copy.

Transfer of booking

 Regulation 10(1) provides an implied term in the contract entitling the consumer to transfer his or her booking to another person ('the transferee') if he or she is prevented from proceeding with the package. This represents a considerable change from previous practice. Regulation 28 provides that this term is implied irrespective of the law governing the contract. It applies whatever the booking conditions provide and cannot be excluded.

The original draft of the Directive was amended to permit an administration charge to be imposed for making the transfer and this is contained in Regulation 10. In order to avail him or herself of this remedy, the tour operator should ensure that it is made clear at the outset and preferably contained in the booking conditions.

The consumer must have been 'prevented from proceeding with the package'. There must have been some substantial reason such as illness, illness or death of a close relative, jury service or the requirements of an employer. A mere change of mind is insufficient. The consumer must give reasonable notice before the departure date of his or her intention to transfer. The transferee must satisfy any conditions applicable to the package (e.g. as regards age or fitness). The consumer and the transferee are jointly and severally liable for the price of the package and for the extra costs arising from the transfer.

Price revision

 Regulation 11 provides that contract terms permitting price revision are automatically void unless they provide for decreases in price as well as increases and satisfy the requirements of Regulation 11(2), i.e.

(a) The term must state precisely how the revised price is to be calculated.

(b) Price revisions must solely relate to variations in:

   (i) transport costs, including the cost of fuel;

   (ii) dues, taxes or fees chargeable for services such as landing taxes or embarkation or disembarkation fees at ports and airports;

   (iii) exchange rates applied to a particular package.

The original draft was stated more positively, permitting surcharges. The new wording stresses that such clauses are void, but with exceptions. The regulation does not prevent a tour operator from giving a 'no surcharge guarantee' or from providing that only some of these factors will give rise to price revisions. Increases for other factors will be void and unenforceable but this does not affect the enforceability of the rest of the contract.

 Regulation 11(2)(c) prohibits increases within a period of less than 30 days prior to departure. Any clause permitting an increase within the 30 day period is void and of no effect. Organisers are required to absorb increases of up to 2% but no upper limit is put on the increase which may be imposed. A significant increase may, however, entitle the consumer to cancel under Regulation 12.

The provisions of Regulation 11 reflect the existing provisions of the ABTA Code, although they are less onerous.

Alterations to the terms of the contract

Regulation 12 provides that where the tour operator is 'constrained' to significantly alter any of the essential terms of the contract, he must notify the consumer as quickly as possible. A significant price increase is given as an example of an 'essential term'. The DTI have indicated that the information contained in Schedule 1 would also be considered as essential terms. It may be useful for the tour operator to specify in the booking conditions what would be considered as essential terms and what is 'significant alteration' to those terms. It should be pointed out, however, that the Unfair Contract Terms Act 1977 will apply to such clauses and the test in this regard and in regard to what is 'as quickly as possible' is an objective rather than subjective one.

The original draft referred to the organiser being 'compelled' to make alterations. Its replacement by 'constrained' indicates that it should be due to factors outside the tour operator's control.

Where significant alterations have been made the consumer may cancel without penalty or accept a rider to the contract stating the alteration(s) and the impact on the price. The consumer must notify the retailer or organiser as soon as possible; an unreasonable delay would deprive him or her of the benefits of this regulation.

This implied term cannot be varied or excluded from the booking conditions.

Cancellation

This is dealt with by Regulation 13. It deals with cancellations by the consumer due to significant alterations made by the tour operator (Regulation 12) or where the tour operator is constrained to cancel the package before the departure date. It does not apply where the tour operator has cancelled the package due to the fault of the consumer.

Regulation 13 provides the following implied terms:

(a) that the consumer is entitled, where the organiser is able to provide it, to take a substitute package, and where that package is of a lower quality than that originally booked, to be paid the difference in price or to have all monies which he or she has paid under the contract to be repaid to him or her;

(b) the consumer is entitled to be compensated for non-performance of the contract except where the package was cancelled because the minimum number required was not reached or where the package was cancelled due to unusual and unforeseeable circumstances beyond the control of the organiser.

The choice of what to do in the event of cancellation by the organiser is entirely up to the consumer. He or she is not obliged to accept a substitute package offered by the organiser, even if this is of higher quality to that originally booked. Whether he or she is entitled to be repaid insurance premiums is open to question. It may be argued that he or she is entitled where the contract required him or her to take out the insurance policy.

The original draft referred to compensation for breach of contract. However, technically, there may be no breach of contract, particularly where the consumer has agreed to repayment of all monies due and thus this has been replaced by 'non-performance'. The draft also referred to the consumer's entitlement to compensation 'without prejudice' to his or her rights with regard to substitute packages or repayment. This has been removed and it is not clear whether the consumer may still claim compensation notwithstanding that a substitute has been offered or money repaid.

 Article 4 (6) of the Directive provides that no compensation is payable in the event of 'force majeure' and this is defined as:

> *'Unusual and unforeseeable circumstances beyond the control of the party by whom it is pleaded, the consequences of which could not have been avoided even if all due care had been exercised'.*

Although 'force majeure' is not mentioned in the Regulations (the term is not applicable in Scotland) the definition is. It does not include overbooking. It should be noted that even where unusual and unforeseeable circumstances arise the tour operator will have to provide compensation if the consequences of those circumstance could have been avoided.

Significant proportion of the services not provided

 Regulation 14 applies where, after departure, a significant proportion of the services contracted for are not supplied or the organiser becomes aware that they will not be supplied. It requires the tour operator to make suitable alternative arrangements, at no extra cost to the consumer, and provide compensation for the difference between the services supplied and those contracted for. Where the organiser is unable to make alternative arrangements or the consumer has reasonable grounds for rejecting them, he or she must arrange for the consumer to be transported back to the point of departure or to a place agreed by the consumer. The transport should be equivalent to that contracted for.

As to what is and what is not a 'significant proportion of the services' contracted for is a question of fact dependant on the particular contract. No mention is made of 'force majeure' and thus it would appear that the organiser must meet this obligation notwithstanding that the failure was due to factors over which he or she had no control. This provision is an implied term and cannot be varied or excluded.

The DTI have indicated that the level of compensation should not be confined to the proportion of the cost of services not provided but may include compensation for disappointment and inconvenience. (*Note: Jarvis v Swans Tours Ltd* [1973], discussed in Chapter 9.)

SUMMARY

(a) Regulation 10 entitles the consumer to transfer his or her booking if prevented from proceeding with the package.

(b) The transferee must satisfy all the conditions applicable to the package.

(c) The price laid down in the contract must not be revised unless the contract expressly provides for increases and decreases and states precisely how the revised price is to be calculated.

(d) Price revisions are only permitted in respect of the matters specified in Regulation 11.

(e) No price increases are permitted within 30 days of departure.

(f) The organiser must notify the consumer of any material alterations to the terms of the contract as quickly as possible.

(g) In the event of material alterations, the consumer may cancel without penalty or accept a note to the contract specifying the alterations and the impact on price.

(h) Regulation 13 provides that where the consumer cancels due to material alterations being made to the arrangements or where the organiser cancels (other than due to the consumer's fault), the consumer is entitled to a substitute package of equal or higher quality, a refund of the difference if the substitute is of lower quality, or to be repaid where no substitute is available or the consumer does not wish to accept it.

(i) Regulation 13 also entitles the consumer to compensation unless the organiser cancelled due to the minimum number specified for the package not being reached or due to 'force majeure'.

(j) If after departure, a significant proportion of the package is not provided or is unlikely to be provided, the organiser must make suitable alternative arrangements and, where necessary, compensate the consumer.

(k) Where suitable alternative arrangements are not possible, or where the consumer rejects them with good reason, the organiser must transport the consumer back to the point of departure at no extra cost and, if necessary, compensate him or her.

Liability

The organiser is liable to the consumer for the proper performance of the contract irrespective of whether the component services are to be performed by him or her or by other parties. This is provided by Regulation 15. The organiser may, in turn, have recourse against the actual supplier of the service. The organiser is liable to compensate the consumer for damage caused to him or her by the failure to perform the contract or improper performance of the contract. There is no liability where the failure or improper performance was neither due to the fault of the organiser or other supplier of services because:

(a) the failure which occurred in the performance of the contract was the fault of the consumer;

(b) the failure was attributable to a third party unconnected with the provision of the services contracted for and was unforeseen and unavoidable;

(c) the failure was due to unusual and unforeseeable circumstances beyond the control of the organiser, the consequences of which could not have been avoided even if all due care had been exercised;

(d) the failure was due to an event which the organiser or the supplier of services, even with all due care, could not foresee or forestall.

In relation to defence (b) above, the third party must be wholly unconnected with the package. Providers of tours which are offered in connection with a package will not therefore be considered 'third parties' even where they make an additional charge for the tour or excursion.

As to what is and what is not 'foreseeable' and 'avoidable' is a question of fact in the particular circumstances. Air-traffic control delays may be foreseeable but unavoidable. The requirement to exercise 'all due care' means that the organiser must take all practical steps necessary, irrespective of the cost.

The organiser may include terms in the contract providing for a reasonable limitation of liability, other than for death or personal injury. The organiser can also benefit from the limitations on liability contained in international conventions which govern the relevant services. (These conventions are discussed in Chapter 10.) Subject to these permitted limitations, the organiser cannot exclude liability under Regulation 17 by a term in the contract.

Regulation 15 also provides the following implied terms:

(a) that the organiser will give prompt assistance to the consumer in the event of any failure in the performance of the contract not due to the consumer's fault;

(b) the organiser, or his or her representative, will make prompt efforts to find appropriate solutions where he or she has received a complaint from the consumer about a defect in the performance of the contract.

The contract must clearly and explicitly require the consumer to notify the supplier and the organiser immediately of any defect in the service provided. This must be communicated by the consumer at the earliest opportunity and should be in writing 'or any other appropriate form'.

SUMMARY

(a) The organiser is liable for the proper performance of the contract.

(b) Even though the component services are provided by other suppliers, the organiser is liable for them.

(c) The consumer is entitled to compensation for non-performance or improper performance of the contract.

(d) Regulation 15(2) contains a number of defences available to the organiser.

(e) Exclusion of liability is not permitted.

(f) Limitation of liability, other than for death or personal injury, is permitted, provided that it is fair and reasonable.

(g) The organiser may make use of limitations of liability contained in the appropriate international conventions.

(h) The organiser has duties to assist the consumer where defects occur to find appropriate solutions.

(i) The consumer must notify the supplier and the organiser of any defects at the earliest opportunity.

Financial security

 Regulation 16 provides that the organiser must provide sufficient evidence of security for the refund of money paid over and for the repatriation of the consumer in the event of insolvency. This is an ongoing obligation and the organiser should be able to provide such evidence at all times. The Regulation does not specify how the organiser is to meet this requirement, but there are a number of ways in which this may be done. Bonding is the most common method used in the UK and this is discussed below.

 Under the provisions of Regulation 16(2), the organiser must have in force one of the following arrangements unless the package is covered by the equivalent arrangements of another member state or where the package is one in respect of which he or she is required to hold a licence under the Civil Aviation (Air Travel Organisers Licensing) Regulations 1972 (see Chapter 6):

 (a) bonding (Regulation 17);

(b) bonding where the approved body has a reserve fund or insurance (Regulation 18);

(c) insurance (Regulation 19);

(d) monies in trust (Regulation 20);

(e) monies in trust where the organiser is acting otherwise than in the course of a business (Regulation 21);

It is a criminal offence to fail to comply with Regulation 16. The bonding requirements under the ATOL system are considered by the DTI to be sufficient to exempt licence holders from the requirements of Regulation 16(2).

Summary of the Options Available under Regulations 17–21

(a) Bonding (Regulation 17)

The organiser must obtain a bond from a bank or insurance company whereby the latter binds itself to pay to an approved body, of which the organiser is a member, a sum to cover the cost of insolvency. The bond must not be less than 25% of the organiser's annual turnover. In theory, any organisation can apply to be an 'approved body' but in practice it will most likely be a trade association. The approved body is responsible for calling in the bond and distributing the funds to consumers in the event of insolvency.

(b) Bonding where approved body has a reserve fund or insurance (Regulation 18)

This is a similar system to (a) above; however, as the approved body has a reserve fund or insurance, the bond is for not less than 10% of the organiser's annual turnover (rather than 25%). The regulations do not prescribe how the reserve fund is to be created. It may come from membership fees, from insurance, or from a levy imposed on packages sold.

(c) Insurance (Regulation 19)

The organiser obtains insurance from an authorised insurer to provide for repayment of monies paid by consumers in the event of the organiser's insolvency. The insurer must be authorised by the DTI to operate the scheme.

(d) Monies in trust (Regulation 20)

Money paid over by the consumer under a package contract is held by a person acting as a trustee for the consumer until the contract has been fully performed. There are no regulations laid down regarding the appointment of the trustee or who may be appointed. Neither are there any specified requirements that the trustee should be an independent person, although the general law of trusts applies.

(e) Monies in trust where the organiser is not acting in the course of a business (Regulation 2)

This does not apply to tour operators or travel agents

Criminal Sanctions and Enforcement

The rules governing enforcement of Regulations 5, 7, 8, 16 and 22 are contained in Schedule 3. In England and Wales, local weights and measures authorities (in practice, 'trading standards departments') are responsible for enforcement and for prosecutions. In Scotland, weights and measures authorities are responsible for investigations etc. but prosecutions are conducted by the Procurator Fiscal. In Northern Ireland, the Department of Economic Development is responsible for enforcement.

It is a defence for the defendant (defender in Scotland) to show that he or she took all reasonable steps and exercised all due diligence to avoid committing an offence. Where in relying on this defence the organiser alleges that the commission of the offence was due to an act or default of another or due to reliance on information given by another he or she must give the prosecutor written notice, seven clear days before the hearing (trial in Scotland), of information as to the identity of that other person. He or she must also show that it was reasonable for him or her to rely on the information which was supplied to him or her:

> ' ... *having regard in particular—*
> (a) to the steps which he took, and those which he might reasonably have taken, for the purpose of verifying the information, and
> (b) to whether he had any reason to disbelieve the information'.

Regulation 25 contains the standard by-pass provision to enable proceedings to be taken against the 'other person' notified to the prosecutor. This may be used whether or not the prosecutor takes proceedings against the original defendant. The Regulation also provides for prosecution of officers who may be considered to be of sufficient seniority as to be part of the 'controlling mind of the company'.

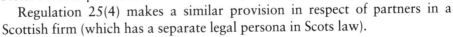 *Note: Tesco Supermarkets Ltd v Nattrass* (1972), discussed in Chapter 6.

 Regulation 25(4) makes a similar provision in respect of partners in a Scottish firm (which has a separate legal persona in Scots law).

SELF-ASSESSMENT QUESTIONS

State whether the following statements are correct or incorrect.

1. The aim of the EC Directive on Package Travel, Package Holidays and Package Tours was to harmonise the rules governing packages throughout the European Community

2. The Directive was implemented in the UK by the Package Travel, Package Holidays and Package Tours Regulations 1992.

3. The regulations replace the existing law governing package holiday contracts.

4. The regulations only apply to foreign inclusive package holidays sold or offered for sale in the UK.

5. The package must include transport and one of the following:

   (a) accommodation;

   (b) other tourist services not ancillary to transport and accommodation and accounting for a significant proportion of the package.

6. The Regulations refer to 'organisers' and 'retailers' rather than 'tour operators' and 'travel agents'.

7. In certain circumstances a travel agent may be considered an 'organiser' under the Regulations.

8. Tailor-made packages are excluded from the Regulations.

9. It is an offence for a retailer to supply a brochure which he or she ought reasonably to have known contains misleading information.

10. The particulars contained in a brochure are legally binding on the organiser.

11. Regulation 7 requires the organiser to provide the consumer with information on passports, visas, health formalities and financial security arrangements in good time before departure.

12. The organiser must provide the consumer with a written copy of the terms of the contract.

13. Schedule 2 contains certain essential elements to be included in the contract, depending on the nature of the package.

14. The consumer is automatically entitled to transfer his or her booking without giving a reason for doing so.

15. An administrative charge may be imposed for processing the transfer of a booking.

16. No price increases are permitted within 20 days of departure.

17. The consumer is entitled to compensation where the package is cancelled due to failure to reach the minimum number specified as being required for the package to go ahead.

18. The organiser is liable for defects in performance of the services contained in the package unless the defect was the fault of an independent supplier.

19. The organiser may make use of limitations of liability contained in relevant international conventions.

20. The consumer has a duty to notify the supplier and organiser of any defect in a service contained in the package at the earliest opportunity.

21. The organiser must provide sufficient evidence of security for the refund of money paid over and for repatriation of the client in the event of insolvency.

22. The bond to be paid to an approved body with a reserve fund or insurance must not be less than 25% of the organiser's annual turnover.

23. In England and Wales, the regulations are enforced and prosecutions conducted by the DTI.

24. In Scotland, infringements are investigated by the local weights and measures authorities.

25. In Northern Ireland, the Department of Economic Development is responsible for enforcement.

9 Settlement of Disputes

GLOSSARY **Act of Sederunt** A rule made by the Court of Session in Scotland to regulate procedure in the civil courts.

arbitration The settlement of a dispute between two parties by a third party in a semi-judicial manner.

conciliation Attempt by an independent person to seek an amicable solution without recourse to arbitration or the courts.

costs The lawyers' fees involved in litigation. In Scotland these are referred to as expenses.

damages A sum of money awarded by a court as compensation in a civil case.

force majeure Events totally beyond the control of the parties to the contract (e.g. adverse weather conditions). In Scotland this term is not used but is covered by the term 'Act of God' or by 'impossibility of performance'.

frustrated contract A contract which cannot be performed because of some event which makes it impossible or renders it illegal or so radically alters the circumstances that it would change the nature of the contract.

litigation The pursuit of a remedy to a dispute through the civil courts.

AIM It is the aim of this chapter to consider the legal position when disputes arise and the legal remedies available.

Cancellation and frustration

An offer met by an unqualified acceptance creates a legally binding contract. In the case of a package holiday contract, the contract is legally binding on both parties once the booking has been accepted (i.e. 'confirmation' has been given). The general rule is that an offeror may withdraw an offer at any time before it has been accepted by the offeree. For this to be effective, however, the offeror must notify the offeree *before* the latter has communicated acceptance. In the situation where a tour operator confirms a booking by post, the client would be too late in withdrawing the booking if confirmation has already been posted to him or her, even though he or she has not yet received it.

Offers do not last for ever. Clients may state that they require to know within a specified time whether the tour operator can confirm a booking, failing which they are no longer interested in purchasing that particular holiday. Most clients do not specify a time limit, however, and therefore their offer to purchase the holiday remains open for a reasonable time. If the tour operator or travel agent does not deal with the booking promptly, customers may be entitled to assume that it has not been accepted and could withdraw from the booking.

These rules of withdrawal of booking or cancellation by either party may be altered by the booking conditions relating to a particular holiday. Those booking conditions will only apply in so far as they have been reasonably drawn to the attention of the customer and are fair and reasonable. In making the booking, customers are usually required to sign an acknowledgement that they have read, and agree to be bound by, the booking conditions.

Most tour operators' booking conditions permit clients to cancel their holidays but impose cancellation charges. The nearer the cancellation is to the date of departure, the greater the charge. The booking conditions may also entitle the tour operator to cancel the holiday in certain circumstances. In those circumstances the client is entitled to a full refund of all monies paid. An exception to that rule applies where the cancellation by the tour operator arose from the failure of the client to perform his or her obligations (i.e. to pay the outstanding balance when required by the booking conditions to do so). In that case the client may forfeit any deposit paid. Tour operators generally require clients to accept 'suitable alternative' arrangements when the tour operator is unable to provide the holiday specified. If this provision was clearly drawn to a client's attention and the alternative arrangements would be considered as a 'suitable alternative' in the circumstances by a reasonable bystander, the client would not be entitled to cancel the holiday. What is a 'suitable alternative' is a question of fact and must be judged according to the circumstances of the case.

The rules governing package holidays that are regulated by the Directive are described in Chapter 8. The client is entitled to cancel where he or she has been notified by the tour operator that it has been necessary to make significant alterations to the holiday. Alternatively, the client may accept a substitute package. If the substitute is of a lower standard than that booked, the tour operator must refund the difference. The client does not have to accept a substitute and can demand a refund of all monies paid under the contract. The requirement that a suitable alternative must be accepted is unenforceable under a regulated package.

If the tour operator cancels the package before the client's departure, the rules governing substitute packages also apply. In addition, the client is entitled to be compensated unless:

(a) cancellation was due to the minimum number specified in the booking conditions as being required for the package not being reached;

(b) cancellation was due to unusual and unforeseen circumstances beyond the control of the tour operator, the consequences of which could not have been avoided even if all due care had been exercised. This does not include overbooking.

☆ The ABTA Tour Operators' Code of Conduct provides

Booking conditions shall clearly indicate the tour operator's general policy both in the event of his cancelling and in the event of his altering a tour, holiday or other travel arrangements.

4.5. Cancellation of Tours, Holiday, or other Travel Arrangements by Tour Operators.

(i) A tour operator shall not cancel a tour, holiday or other travel arrangements after the date when payment of the balance of the price becomes due unless it is necessary to do so as a result of hostilities, political unrest or other circumstances amounting to force majeure, or unless the client defaults in payment of such balance.

(ii) If a tour operator for reasons other than hostilities, political unrest or other circumstances amounting to force majeure, cancels a holiday, tour or other travel arrangements on or before the date when payment of the balance of the price becomes due, he shall inform agents and direct clients as soon as possible, and shall offer clients the choice of an alternative holiday of at least comparable standard if available, or of a prompt and full refund of all money paid. Any such refunds shall be sent to agents within 10 clear days and to direct clients within 14 days.

(iii) If a tour operator has to cancel a tour, holiday or other travel arrangements as a result of hostilities, political unrest or other circumstances amounting to force majeure, he shall inform agents and direct clients without delay and shall offer clients the choice of an alternative holiday of comparable standard, if available, or a prompt and full refund of all money paid. Any such refunds shall be sent to agents within 10 clear days and to direct clients within 14 clear days.

These provisions of the Code apply where they are not inconsistent with the provisions of the Directive.

A contract may be considered 'frustrated' if, without the fault of either party, some event occurs which renders further performance an impossibility, renders it illegal or so radically alters the circumstances that the contract becomes something quite different from that originally intended. Most tour operators provide terms in the booking conditions to deal with such circumstances and the provisions of the Directive, indicated above, state the obligations of the tour operator when this arises.

Delays in departures on a tour, holiday or other travel arrangements caused by weather conditions, technical problems to transport, strikes and industrial action have been generally considered to be outside tour operators' control. Some tour operators nevertheless provide compensation in such circumstances for delays exceeding 12 hours. Delays exceeding 24 hours may be considered as frustrating the contract and entitling the client to cancel and obtain a refund of all monies paid. The test as to whether or not these would be considered outside the tour operator's control is whether they are unusual and unforeseeable, the consequences of which could not be avoided even though all due care had been exercised.

SUMMARY (a) The package holiday contract is binding on both parties once the booking has been confirmed.

(b) The client may withdraw from the booking at any time before confirmation has been communicated to him or her.

(c) The booking conditions will usually contain rules regarding cancellation of the holiday by the client or by the tour operator.

(d) These conditions are binding on the client in so far as they are fair and reasonable and have been brought to his or her attention.

(e) Most tour operators' booking conditions contain a schedule of cancellation charges.

(f) The booking conditions may require the client to accept suitable alternative arrangements and in such circumstances the client is not entitled to cancel the holiday where such arrangements have been made.

(g) The rules governing cancellation and suitable alternatives in the case of regulated packages are discussed in Chapter 8.

(h) The client is entitled to cancel the holiday where material (important) alterations have been made to his or her holiday.

(i) The ABTA Tour Operators' Code of Conduct contains detailed rules governing the tour operator's obligations when cancelling holiday arrangements, but these are subject to the provisions of the Directive.

(j) A holiday contract is 'frustrated' if, without the fault of either party, an event occurs which makes provision of the holiday impossible or substantially different from that originally intended.

Conciliation and arbitration

It is obviously preferable that disputes between travel agents or tour operators and their clients should be settled amicably and without recourse to the courts. For both parties litigation can be a costly and lengthy process with the added disadvantage for the tour operator or travel agent of the adverse publicity which may arise if the court finds against them.

  The ABTA Travel Agents' Code of Conduct provides:

2.10. Disputes

(i) In the event of a dispute with a client, travel agents shall make every effort to reach an amicable and speedy solution.

(ii) Travel agents shall make every reasonable effort to deal with complaints of a minor and general character with a view to avoiding recourse to principals. When

complaints are of such a nature that reference to the principal is necessary, a travel agent shall use his best endeavours acting as an intermediary to bring about a satisfactory conclusion.

The ABTA Tour Operators' Code of Conduct states:

4.9. Complaints and Correspondence from the Association

(i) Complaints shall be dealt with promptly and efficiently and in the event of a dispute with a client every effort shall be made to settle the matter amicably and as quickly as possible.

(ii) All correspondence from the Association about complaints and compliance with the Articles of Association and this Code shall be dealt with promptly and efficiently.

Conciliation and arbitration service

ABTA provides a conciliation and arbitration service for settling disputes between members and their clients. The service is voluntary and does not prevent the client from raising a civil action in the courts. The conciliation service is provided where there has been a breakdown in communication or a serious disagreement between the tour operator and client. The service is provided by ABTA officers. If the attempt at conciliation fails or the client is dissatisfied with the outcome, he or she may either raise a civil action in the courts or make use of the arbitration service.

ABTA tour operators are required to provide a term in the booking conditions entitling the client to refer any dispute which has not been settled amicably, or where conciliation has failed, to the ABTA Arbitration Scheme. The scheme has been specially devised by the Chartered Institute of Arbitrators for ABTA and the arbitration is conducted by a member of the Institute. Clients are not bound to make use of this service but once they have agreed to do so they must agree to be bound by the arbitrator's decision.

The scheme provides a simple and inexpensive method of arbitration on the basis of documents alone. Applications are made on the prescribed form and must be submitted within nine months of the date of return from the holiday. A longer period for submission may be permitted in special circumstances. Customers pay a small fee for themselves and additional small sums for other members of their party. Their liability for the expenses of the arbitration is restricted to double the amount of the registration fee. The parties are not required to attend a hearing. The decision of the arbitrator is final.

The arbitration scheme does not apply to claims for an amount greater than £1,500 per person or £7,500 per booking form. No claims can be made which are solely or mainly in respect of physical injury or illness or the consequences of such injury or illness.

SUMMARY

(a) The ABTA Travel Agents' Code of Conduct requires travel agents to use their best endeavours to deal with complaints of a minor and general nature.

(b) If reference of a dispute to a principal is necessary the travel agent should use his or her best endeavours acting as an intermediary to bring about a satisfactory conclusion.

(c) The ABTA Tour Operators' Code of Conduct requires them to deal with complaints promptly and efficiently and to use every effort to seek an amicable solution.

(d) ABTA provides a conciliation service to give help and impartial guidance to resolve disputes between members and their clients.

(e) If the attempt at conciliation fails, the client may have recourse to the ABTA Arbitration Scheme.

(f) The scheme provides a simple and inexpensive method of arbitration based on documents alone.

(g) The scheme is voluntary but once the client has agreed to make use of it he or she is bound by the arbitrator's decision.

(h) The maximum claim that may be made under the scheme is £1,500 per person or £7,500 per booking form.

(i) No claim can be made solely or mainly in respect of physical injury or illness.

Litigation

Most holiday booking conditions provide that the package holiday contract is to be construed according to English law and is subject to the *jurisdiction* of the English courts. Most holidaymakers' claims are brought in the county court. If the sum is for £1,000 or less it will automatically be dealt with under the county court arbitration procedure. This procedure is informal and inexpensive. Claimants pay a small sum, based on the amount of their claim, to cover the court's costs but they do not have to pay the defendant's legal costs if they lose. This procedure is, therefore, very attractive to the holidaymaker but less attractive to tour operators or travel agents who are required to meet their own legal costs even if they win the case. The aim is to keep the procedure simple and to deter lawyers from appearing to represent their clients. Lawyers are not banned, however, and most tour operators and travel agents choose to be legally represented because of the possible consequences of adverse publicity if they lose the case.

The proceedings under the county court arbitration scheme begin by the claimant taking out a summons and this is then served on the defendant. The defendant must then inform the court, within 14 days of the date of service, whether he or she intends to defend the case. If he or she fails to notify the court within 14 days, the plaintiff can have judgement against him or her and the court will fix the amount of damages. If notice of intention to defend is given, the district judge will hold a preliminary discussion with the parties to get them to reach agreement on as many facts as possible and to advise them as to what to do to prepare for the arbitration. Many simple claims are settled at this point. If not, the case goes on to the arbitration itself. The process is fairly short with most arbitrations taking 30 minutes or less. The district judge then makes an award which is binding on the parties unless it can be established that he or she acted contrary to natural justice or made an error in law. If, prior to the arbitration, it becomes clear that the case involves difficult questions of law or evidence, it may be referred back for trial before another judge.

The disadvantage of the county court arbitration scheme for travel agents and tour operators can be demonstrated by the case of *Chilton v Saga Holidays* (1986). Following a disappointing holiday, Mr Chilton brought a claim under the county court arbitration scheme against Saga Holidays. The company was represented by a solicitor who wanted to cross-examine Mr Chilton about his evidence. The registrar (today it would be a district judge) refused, insisting that any questions that the solicitor wished to put to Mr Chilton must be put through him. The registrar then rephrased the question and put it to Mr Chilton. Mr Chilton was successful in his claim against Saga. Saga challenged the decision in the Court of Appeal on the grounds of natural justice. The court held that the registrar should not have refused Saga's solicitor the opportunity to cross-examine Mr Chilton.

Most holiday cases are dealt with under this scheme and there is concern that the *Chilton* case is evidence of the possible bias of the arbitration scheme in favour of the plaintiff consumer who is not legally represented.

In Scotland claims for less than £1,000 will usually be dealt with under the 'summary cause' procedure in the sheriff court. This also provides a simple procedure which is relatively informal. The pursuer serves a summons on the defender in the form prescribed by Act of Sederunt. At any stage the parties may make a joint motion to have the case treated as an 'ordinary cause'. The case may be treated as an ordinary cause on a motion of one of the parties if the sheriff is of the opinion that the importance or difficulty of the case merits it. The advantage of the summary cause procedure is that the court expenses are on a lower scale and the more formal pleading requirements of an ordinary cause are not required. No formal record of the evidence is kept.

Larger or more complex claims may be brought in the county court under the ordinary procedure. That procedure is still simpler, speedier and less costly than in the High Court. In order to discourage minor cases from being conducted in the High Court, the successful party in a case which could have been dealt with in the county court may not be awarded costs or may only be awarded costs on the county court scale. Larger or more complex claims in Scotland may be brought by raising an action under the ordinary procedure in the sheriff court or by raising an action in the Outer House of the Court of Session.

SUMMARY

(a) Most holidaymakers' claims are brought in the county court.

(b) Claims for less than £1,000 are automatically dealt with under the county court arbitration scheme.

(c) The main advantages are that the procedure is speedy, informal and relatively inexpensive.

(d) The main disadvantage for tour operators and travel agents is that, even if successful, they are not awarded legal costs.

(e) Larger claims or more complex cases are dealt with under the ordinary procedure in the county court or are raised in the High Court.

(f) In Scotland, claims for less than £1,000 are usually dealt with under the 'summary cause' procedure in the sheriff court.

(g) More complex cases or larger claims in Scotland are dealt with under the ordinary procedure in the sheriff court or by raising an action in the Outer House of the Court of Session.

Damages

Damages are a remedy provided by the common law to provide financial compensation where there has been a breach of contract. It is the aim of the court, in awarding damages, to place the party who has suffered the loss as a result of the breach as nearly as possible in the same position as he or she would have been in if the breach had not occurred.

Contractual damages are a compensation for a loss suffered as a result of a breach of contract. They are not intended as a punishment for the party who failed to perform obligations under the contract. It is immaterial to assess any profit which was made by the party in breach as a result of the breach. In determining the measure of damages, the court does not consider the defendant's (defender's) ability to pay. The motive of the party in breach is also irrelevant.

It is possible for a plaintiff to claim against two or more persons jointly and severally for damages where there are closely connected breaches of duty, one of which is a breach of contract to him or her. Thus, a claim arising from a package holiday contract may be made against the tour operator and the travel agent, jointly and severally.

In assessing the measure of damages, the court will not award compensation for any damage which is too remote. In determining what is and what is not considered too remote, we must consider the decision in the important case of *Hadley v Baxendale* (1854). In that case the court held that damage is not too remote if it is *such as may fairly and reasonably be considered either as arising naturally, i.e. according to the usual course of things from the breach itself, or such as may reasonably be supposed to have been in the contemplation of both parties at the time they made the contract, as the probable result of the breach.*

The rule laid down in *Hadley v Baxendale* may be summarised as follows: damages may be awarded

(a) for any loss 'naturally arising' from the breach of contract – general damages; and

(b) for any loss which was 'in the contemplation of both parties ... as the probable result of the breach' – special damages.

In holiday cases general damages would be awarded for the ordinary expenses which the client incurred as a result of the tour operator's breach of contract or misrepresentations. These may include such items as bus and taxi fares, cost of extra meals caused by delays and other 'out of pocket' expenses. In addition, as a result of the landmark decision in *Jarvis v Swan Tours Ltd* (1973) the client may also seek damages for inconvenience, discomfort, disappointment, distress and upset at not being provided with the holiday in accordance with the contract.

In this case Mr Jarvis had booked a skiing holiday at Morlialp in Switzerland. The price of the holiday was £63. In booking the holiday, Mr Jarvis had relied upon the descriptions contained in the defendant's brochure. The brochure described the holiday as a house party. It indicated that there would be excellent skiing, a yodeller evening, a bar, afternoon tea and cakes. It stated that the atmosphere at the hotel was one of 'gemutlichkeit'.

On arrival at Morlialp, Mr Jarvis discovered that there were only 13 guests at the hotel during the first week. During the second week he was the only guest. 'Afternoon tea' comprised crisps and dried nutcake. The entertainments fell far short of the promised standard. The Court of Appeal held that the measure of damages should not be limited to the price of the holiday but should also take into account the frustration, mental distress and disappointment experienced by Mr Jarvis due to the loss of enjoyment of his holiday caused by the breach of contract.

In the case of *Jackson v Horizon Holidays* (1975), following a 'disastrous holiday', the Court of Appeal held that Mr Jackson was entitled to claim not only for his own frustration, disappointment and loss of enjoyment but also for that suffered by his wife and children who accompanied him on the holiday. Damages have been awarded in *Askey v Intasun North Ltd* and *Levine v Metropolitan Travel* for a 'thoroughly upsetting' holiday and for 'assault on feelings'.

Plaintiffs also recover special damages for the particular losses which they suffered if they can establish that the tour operator was aware of any special circumstances at the time that the contract was entered into. The question arises as to whether the knowledge of the travel agent is deemed to be the knowledge of the tour operator for whom he or she is acting. A client who informs a travel agent of his or her special circumstances or special needs may be entitled to assume that the travel agent has notified the tour operator. If the contract is broken and these special needs have not been taken into account, the client may be entitled to special damages.

In *Taylor v International Travel Services* (1984) the plaintiff claimed for a concert fee which his wife had lost due to alterations in the holiday arrangements. The court awarded special damages for the loss of the concert fee as the plaintiff had informed the tour operator in advance that his wife had been invited to perform at the concert.

In *Kemp v Intasun* (1987) Mrs Kemp claimed for special damages for the asthma attack suffered by her husband due to the conditions in the replacement accommodation to which the tour operator had sent them. Mrs Kemp had mentioned to the travel agent at the time of making the booking that her husband suffered from bronchitis and emphysema, but this was not included in the booking arrangements. The Court of Appeal dismissed the claim for special damages arising from Mr Kemp's condition on the grounds that this information was only given to the travel agent in a casual conversation and was not therefore sufficiently within the tour operator's knowledge to give rise to contractual consequences.

It must be noted that the decision in *Kemp v Intasun* may have been different if Mrs Kemp had given more formal notice of her husband's condition (e.g. by a statement on the booking form).

In *Jacobs v Thomson Travel* (1986) Mr Jacobs had booked a holiday which included accommodation at a five-star hotel in Israel. He cancelled the holiday when he heard, the day before departure, that he could not stay at the hotel which he had booked. He had been offered an inferior hotel as an alternative. The court awarded general damages to Mr Jacobs and his family but took into account the fact that he had had a holiday in Israel in May and that he and his family frequently took foreign holidays. The court refused his claim for special damages for the fact that he had to celebrate Passover at home on the grounds that he had not told the tour operator that he was religious and that Passover was important to him.

If the client incurred losses in a foreign currency, the plaintiff may be entitled to claim damages in that currency. This may be very important when there are major fluctuations between the value of sterling and the value of the currency of the country of destination.

The party claiming damages must have taken reasonable steps to have minimised his or her loss. What is and what is not reasonable is a question of fact in the particular circumstances. A client informed of a two-hour delay to a flight could reasonably be expected to accept the delay and perhaps claim a nominal sum for inconvenience. It would be unreasonable for him or her to abandon the holiday altogether. However, a 24-hour delay on a 'weekend break' holiday would justify cancellation. The client would be entitled to claim any reasonable expenses incurred in minimising his or her loss.

SUMMARY

(a) Damages provide financial compensation where there has been a breach of contract.

(b) Damages are compensation for a loss suffered as a result of the breach, not a punishment of the party who has failed to carry out contractual obligations.

(c) The defendant's motive or ability to pay is irrelevant in assessing damages.

(d) The loss must not have been too remote.

(e) Damages may be divided into general damages and special damages.

(f) General damages are awarded for losses which are the natural result of the breach of contract.

(g) Special damages are awarded for losses which the parties, at the time of entering into the contract, expected would be the probable result of the breach.

(h) Damages may be awarded for inconvenience, disappointment, distress and upset at the loss of enjoyment incurred as a result of the breach.

(i) The plaintiff holidaymaker may also claim damages for the other members of his or her group.

(j) The party claiming damages must have taken reasonable steps to have minimised any loss.

SELF-ASSESSMENT QUESTIONS

State whether the following statements are correct or incorrect.

1. In the case of a package holiday contract, the contract is legally binding on both parties once the booking has been accepted (i.e. 'confirmation' has been given).

2. Booking conditions usually contain rules relating to cancellation of holidays.

3. The ABTA Tour Operators' Code of Conduct provides that a tour operator is not permitted to cancel a holiday after the date when the balance of the price of the holiday is due for payment.

4. A package holiday contract will be deemed 'frustrated' if the tour operator's employee has mistakenly confirmed a booking for a client when there were no more places available on the tour.

5. A delay of more than 24 hours to a departure time due to technical difficulties in an aircraft not owned by the tour operator would generally be considered to have frustrated the contract.

6. The Directive contains rules governing cancellation and suitable alternative arrangements.

7. The ABTA conciliation service is provided by members of the Chartered Institute of Arbitrators.

8. Package holidaymakers involved in a dispute with an ABTA tour operator are required to pursue their claim through the ABTA Arbitration Scheme.

9. If a client is dissatisfied with the outcome of the arbitration, he or she may appeal to the county court (the sheriff court in Scotland).

10. The maximum claim that may be made under the ABTA Arbitration Scheme is £1,500 per person or £7,500 per booking form.

11. Holidaymakers' claims for less than £1,000 are automatically dealt with under the county court arbitration scheme (in England, Wales and Northern Ireland).

12. The main disadvantage of the county court arbitration scheme for travel agents and tour operators is that legal costs are not awarded even if they are successful.

13. The county court arbitration procedure is conducted by a member of the Chartered Institute of Arbitrators.

14. In Scotland, claims for less than £1,000 are usually dealt with under the 'ordinary' procedure in the sheriff court.

15. Damages are a form of financial compensation awarded when there has been a breach of contract.

16. A dissatisfied holidaymaker may sue a travel agent and tour operator jointly and severally.

17. General damages are awarded for any loss incurred which was the natural result of the breach of contract.

18. Damages may be awarded for loss of employment, even where the client has not suffered any 'out of pocket expenses'.

19. The courts do not award special damages arising from aggravated loss due to the client's physical infirmities which he or she already suffered from before going on holiday.

20. The party claiming damages must have taken reasonable steps to minimise his or her loss.

21. Damages can only be awarded in British currency in the British courts.

10 Carriage of Passengers and Their Luggage

Convention An international treaty drawn up at a conference of sovereign states to regulate matters between them, which then has to be incorporated into their national law. This is done, first, by those attending the conference who sign the convention. The second stage is ratification or adoption by individual nations, and the final stage is arrived at when the convention is put into force by these states through enacting legislation, e.g. the Warsaw Convention 1929 was brought into force in the UK by the Carriage by Air Act 1932.

Poincaré or Convention Franc This was the unit of valuation used in the Warsaw Convention 1929 and was based on the French franc, whose value was pegged to the price of gold. This fact made it easy for countries to convert the Convention Franc through the price of gold to their national currencies. Poincaré was the French administrator of the time who stabilised the French franc by tying it to the price of gold.

Special Drawing Rights Also abbreviated to SDRs – they are a new unit of monetary value created by the International Monetary Fund to replace the Poincaré or Convention Franc because the price of gold was no longer stable. This unit of value was introduced by the Montreal Protocol 1975.

Protocol In the context of this chapter it is an addendum to the Warsaw Convention 1929.

AIM In this chapter we explain the legal rules relating to the contract of carriage together with the relationship between the carrier and the travel agent, and the special international rules that apply to both the contract of carriage and the roles of the agent and the carrier.

Introduction

The original function of travel agents was to act as agents for shipping and railway companies in selling tickets to members of the public. Modern-day travel agents continue to sell tickets for the scheduled services of shipping companies and railway companies, as well as for airlines, ferry companies and coach operators. In doing so the travel agent clearly acts as agent for the carrier (or 'principal'). The legal rights and obligations of travel agents in the situation *vis-à-vis* the carrier and also *vis-à-vis* the client are those provided by the law of agency, discussed in Chapter 5. In so far as there are special rules governing the agent's role in respect of carriers, they are set out in the section on international conventions, below.

Travel agents and tour operators make use of scheduled transport in constructing a package holiday. More frequently, tour operators charter transport services from airlines, coach companies, etc. Their rights and obligations *vis-à-vis* the carrier and the package holiday client are discussed in 'Delays', below.

Contract of Carriage

It is important to identify what is involved in the contract of carriage. In this section we consider the rights and duties of the carrier towards the passenger.

'Carriers' are persons who carry passengers or goods otherwise than for their own purposes or for or in connection with their own trade or business. It does not matter whether the carriage is gratuitous or for payment. Those who use the services of the carrier do so by acquiring a ticket, which may be issued by the carrier, the travel agent or the tour operator. The role of the ticket is discussed below.

If the passenger is injured in an accident, he or she can claim damages from the carrier, provided that he or she can prove that the carrier (or an employee) was negligent and that this caused the accident. The claim may be based on the contract that exists between the passenger and the carrier, or it may be based on the law of tort (delict, in Scotland). The claim may be for damages for breach of contract or for negligence. In practice it does not matter under which head it is made.

In the case of a non-fare-paying passenger (e.g. one who has a free pass, or a child under a certain age), the claim would require to be made under the law of tort (delict), as there is no contract between passenger and carrier.

The standard of care discussed in this section is laid down by common law. In certain cases it has been amended by statutory provisions giving effect to international conventions on carriage of passengers and their luggage, and these too are discussed.

Carriers do not guarantee the safety of passengers – their duty is to take reasonable care to carry passengers safely. The standard of care is of a very high degree, however. Their responsibility is not confined to employees but extends to all persons connected with the carriage. They are liable for any defects in the vehicle, train, vessel or aircraft which would be apparent on reasonable inspection. There must be a periodical inspection and examination. The carrier must comply with all statutory provisions in respect of the vehicle etc.

The degree of care that must be taken by the carrier depends on the particular circumstances of the case. The precautions that must be taken when there is heavy fog or a snow blizzard must be greater than those required on a clear, dry day.

Carriers are under a duty to provide reasonable accommodation for passengers. They are in breach of that duty where a passenger is injured due to overcrowding. It is not negligence for carriers to permit drunken passengers aboard, but once they do so, they are under a duty to protect other passengers from annoyance or injury. Airlines are prohibited by law from permitting drunkenness on aircraft.

Carriers are bound to carry reasonable amounts of passengers' ordinary personal luggage without extra charge. The quantity may be fixed by advance notice given by the carrier or by a provision in the contract. Carriers are liable for the safe custody of a passenger's luggage unless retained under the passenger's sole charge and the loss is caused wholly or partly by the passenger's negligence. Liability arises as soon as the luggage has been handed over to the carrier, an employee or agent. Carriers' employees are under no duty to receive luggage sooner than a reasonable period before departure. Liability continues until the luggage is handed back to the passenger at the end of the journey.

SUMMARY

(a) Certain duties are imposed on the carrier of passengers, whether or not they are paying for the carriage.

(b) The carrier has a duty to take reasonable care for passengers' safety.

(c) A carrier's standard of care is of a high degree.

(d) An injured passenger may claim for breach of contract or for negligence under the law of tort/delict.

(e) The liabilities of carriers have been amended by certain international conventions adopted into United Kingdom law by Acts of Parliament.

(f) The carrier is bound to accept reasonable amounts of passengers' personal luggage.

(g) The carrier is liable for the safe custody of passengers' luggage.

Conditions of Carriage

The rights and obligations of carriers and passengers are usually set out in conditions of carriage. At common law carriers could avoid all their obligations by having exclusion clauses in their conditions of carriage. Their ability to avoid liability for the safety of passengers by using such clauses is now virtually abolished by statutes dealing with particular contracts of carriage, and by the provisions of the Unfair Contract Terms Act 1977. The common law principles on contractual conditions dealing with other matters still apply.

For carriers to rely upon conditions of carriage, they must incorporate them into the contract between them and the passengers, who must be given notice of the conditions. Most tickets contain a reference to conditions of carriage that are stated elsewhere. This reference may be on the front or back of the ticket. The question arises as to whether this is sufficient notice to incorporate those conditions into the contract of carriage between carrier and passenger.

Passengers are bound by the conditions of carriage if they have received notice of them. The problem is that most people never look at the ticket, let alone check the conditions of carriage referred to in it. Carriers must establish that passengers knew that there was writing or printing on the ticket and that this contained the conditions or – more probably – referred to them.

SUMMARY The legal position may therefore be summarised as follows:

(a) Most carriers set out their rights and obligations in respect of passengers and their luggage in conditions of carriage.

(b) The conditions will form part of the contract only if the passenger has received proper notice of them.

(c) The ticket usually refers to the conditions of carriage.

(d) If the passenger knew or ought to have known that the ticket contained a reference to the conditions, he or she is bound by them.

(e) If the passenger did *not* know that the ticket contained such a reference, he or she is not bound by the conditions.

(f) The conditions may attempt to limit the carrier's liability for the safety of passengers and their luggage.

(g) Such exclusion clauses are subject to the provisions of the Unfair Contract Terms Act 1977 (see Chapter 7).

Delays

Most carriers reserve the right to alter timetables and delay the departure or arrival of the various modes of transport. They do not guarantee that passengers will reach their destination by a specified time.

 In the case of *Great Western Railway Co. v Lowenfield* (1982) it was recognised that a passenger may be entitled to claim damages for inconvenience and discomfort caused by a carrier where the departure time is brought forward without notifying the passenger.

Most carriers exclude liability for delays and in most cases this would be upheld by the courts. The general rule is that in a contract for carriage by land or by sea there is no obligation to be on time unless the contract specifically indicates otherwise. Railway, coach and ferry operators contract only to use due diligence to reach the destination in time, and cannot be held liable for unavoidable delays, such as those due to flooding or freak weather conditions.

The tour operator–carrier relationship

The tour operator is the travel company that makes contracts with the carrier: the airline, shipping company, or whoever performs the contract of carriage so entered into.

When the tour operator engages the carrier to transport clients, the carrier is not usually the 'employee' of the tour operator; more often than not it will be an 'independent contractor'. There is an important difference at common law between the two, based on the doctrine of vicarious liability. Under this, employers are liable to third parties for the civil wrongs (torts/delicts) committed by their employees in the course of their employment. Therefore, if the carrier is an independent contractor the tour operator is not liable to third parties for any civil wrongs the carrier commits – unless he or she authorises the carrier to commit them. This can be seen from the case of *Ackroyd's Air Travel Ltd v DPP* (1950).

 Under section 23 of the Civil Aviation Act 1946 it was unlawful for 'any person other than the three corporations [BEA, BOAC and British South African Airways] ... to carry passengers or goods by air for hire or reward upon any scheduled journey between two places at least one of which is in the UK'. 'Scheduled journey' was defined in section 23(2) as:

> *one of a series of journeys which are undertaken between the same places and which together amount to a systematic service operated in such a manner that the benefits thereof are available to members of the public from time to time seeking to take advantage of it.*

 The facts of the *Ackroyd* case were that Mercury Airways Ltd, a South African company, had operated an air service between Cape Town and the United Kingdom until prohibited from doing so by an Order in Council. Thereafter its flights terminated in Paris. However, the company entered into an oral agreement with Ackroyd's whereby Ackroyd's arranged air travel between London and Paris for passengers who wished to travel by Mercury. Ackroyd's, as Mercury's agent, also made reservations for those wishing to travel in aircraft between Paris and South Africa. Ackroyd's made a plane available to anyone who wished to travel to Paris to connect with a Mercury flight to Cape Town.

The court held that this arrangement came within the definition of 'scheduled journey' in section 23(2), and Ackroyd's was convicted of aiding and abetting the offence.

The tour operator would also be vicariously liable in a situation where he or she provided his or her own coach in which to transport passengers from city centre to airport and the coach crashed as a result of the driver's negligence. The operator would not, however, be vicariously liable had he or she booked seats for its clients on a scheduled city centre/airport bus service because the bus company is an independent contractor. Having said this, even if the carrier is an independent contractor, the tour operator must act with care in selecting that carrier. This means that the reputation and competence of the carrier to carry the tour operator's clients should be established. If a tour operator receives a number of complaints from passengers about a particular carrier and neither passes on the information nor gives instructions on how best to avoid a recurrence, he or she will be liable. If a tour operator has been informed of a handicapped person's special needs and he or she has agreed to provide for these, he or she will be liable to the passenger for any distress or inconvenience suffered if those needs have not been passed on to the carrier.

Apart from these specific instances, the tour operator has very little control over carriers such as British Rail, European or other rail networks, ferry companies or airlines. They supply their own vehicles, ships or aircraft and are therefore responsible for maintaining them in a safe condition. These carriers are engaged in a quite different business from the tour operator: it is specialist work, free from the tour operator's supervision.

Statutes place liability on the carrier rather than the tour operator and we shall now examine this statutory liability and the limits placed upon it.

The Warsaw Convention 1929

General background to the Convention

The Warsaw Conference was held in October 1929, when 30 states met to discuss the regulation of international air transport. Out of the conference came the Warsaw Convention, signed on 12 October 1929. Its aim was to balance the interests of users and carriers: users of air transport had to be protected; at the same time the carriers' profitability and financial security had to be ensured. This aim was to be achieved through *international* co-operation.

The organisation of navigation and air transport services has always been controlled at national level by sovereign states. They enact legislation to control the functioning of air transport and, if necessary, bring it into line with international standards. Administrative bodies control the industry. For exam- ple, in the United Kingdom the Civil Aviation Act 1971 established the Civil Aviation Authority, which unified all the existing bodies. The Civil Aviation Act 1982 deals further with the function, constitution and objectives of the Authority. It deals also with aerodromes, and the design, construction and maintenance of aircraft.

In the United States the Civil Aeronautics Board (CAB) is a federal commission, independent from other transport bodies.

In France the administration of civil aviation is entrusted to the Department of Transport. Indeed, in most European countries, and in South America, Africa and Asia, the supervision of civil aviation is under that Department.

In all these countries there are laws governing the administration of civil aviation, and these bodies must apply them. In the United Kingdom the Carriage by Air Act 1932 regulates civil aviation; it also incorporates the Warsaw Convention into national law. In 1961 and 1962 amendments to the Convention were included, bringing the Act up to date. In France, since 1955, the Code de l'Aviation Civile includes all the legislative and regulatory decrees relating to civil aviation; in the United States the Federal Aviation Act 1958 is the main source.

In addition to these specific pieces of legislation, there are many rules of the general law that apply. For example, commercial law governs the legal relationship between users and carriers; insurance law can be applied to the question of liability; principles of civil or common law influence the contract of carriage and the question of liability.

Prior to the First World War it had been recognised that uniform international regulation of civil aviation was necessary. Governments realised, however, that the sovereignty states have over their territories and airspace would make such regulation difficult. After the war the air transport industry developed rapidly, the enormous advantages for passengers, goods and mail were realised, and hand in hand with the development came regulation: stricter domestic regulation by sovereign states to keep air transport under control. Thus the political climate was right for international co-operation; the main area needing it was liability: the liability of the international air carrier under the contract of international carriage. The Warsaw Convention took on the task.

Objectives and amendments

The Convention established the limit of liability at 125,000 Poincaré gold francs for each person (approximately £6,816). The amount quickly became inadequate, and several amendments and supplementary provisions were implemented.

The Hague Protocol 1955

This simplified the way in which tickets and transport documents were issued. It also amended the provisions relating to liability for wilful misconduct. The ceiling for compensation was doubled, to 250,000 Poincaré gold francs (approximately £13,633).

The Guadalajara Convention 1961

This amended the Warsaw Convention by dealing with the status of the contracting carrier and the actual carrier, there being no definitions in the Convention. By Article 1(b) a 'contracting carrier' is a person 'who as a principal makes an agreement for carriage governed by the Warsaw Convention with a passenger or consignor or with a person acting on behalf of the passenger or consignor'. By Article 1(c), 'actual carrier' *means a person, other than the contracting carrier, who, by virtue of authority from the contracting carrier, performs the whole or part of the carriage contemplated in Article 1(b), but who is not, with respect to that article, a successive carrier within the meaning of the Warsaw Convention. Such authority is presumed in the absence of proof to the contrary.*

The Montreal Agreement 1966

This came into being because the United States was dissatisfied with the limits of liability on international carriers. It is an agreement, not an international treaty, between US airlines and international airlines which fly into the US. The Agreement applies to those airlines that are signatories to it, and provides that they may enter into a special contract with the passengers. This contract allows, first, the parties to it to raise the limits of liability to US$ 75,000 (legal fees and costs included) or US$ 58,000 (legal fees and costs excluded). Second, carriers agreed not to invoke the defence in Article 20(1) of the Warsaw Convention, which allowed them to avoid liability if they could prove that they had taken all necessary steps to avoid the damage, or that it was impossible for them to do so.

The Guatemala Protocol 1971

Produced on 8 March 1971, this Protocol increased protection for users of aircraft. It was no longer necessary for the user to prove fault on the part of the air carrier, who became strictly liable for any accident in the course of air transport operations. The liability limit was further raised, to 1,500,000 Poincaré gold francs (approximately US$60,000), and was to be revised after five and ten years.

The Montreal Additional Protocol 1975

Most importantly, this Protocol dealt with the problem of the monetary unit for liability purposes: the Poincaré franc was linked to the gold standard, and during the preceding seven years the value of gold had fluctuated wildly. The International Monetary Fund (IMF) created a new unit based on the combined currencies of the 16 states in the Western Bloc, called the Special Drawing Right (SDR). The intention was to adopt this unit as it was independent of gold values. But as the socialist states were not members of the IMF the idea had to be dropped and a monetary unit based on gold (65.5 milligrams of millesimal fineness 900) was retained, but reference to the Poincaré franc was excluded.

To date only a handful of countries have adopted the Guatemala Protocol and the Montreal Additional Protocol. Neither is therefore in force as they require to be ratified by 30 countries before becoming effective.

General scope and principal definitions

The Warsaw Convention deals with transport by *aircraft*. This is interpreted to mean the type of aircraft that depends on the support and reaction of air for its locomotion. These aircraft are used to transport persons, baggage and goods *internationally* (Article 1, paragraph 2); such international carriage must result in remuneration for the carrier.

The Convention states that the air carrier is liable to the passenger when damage occurs on board the aircraft or in the course of any operation of embarking or disembarking during the *duration of the carriage* (these words are not defined, it being left to the courts to do this). The courts of most signatory states have taken the view that these words mean 'the time during which the user is under the control of the carrier'.

The parties to a contract of international carriage are the *user*, defined by the Convention as the person 'other than the carrier and comprises passengers, consignors and consignees of goods' (crew members and stowaways do *not* come into this category and are therefore outside the scope of the Convention), and the *carrier*, who was not defined in the Convention but has since been defined, as described above, in the Guadalajara Convention 1961.

Are travel agents included in the definition of 'contracting carrier'? Basically, no: a travel agent does not conclude a contract of carriage for goods or people, as a principal – he or she acts on behalf of the airline. Provided he or she acts as an agent he or she will *not* come within the scope of the Convention. The travel forms that holidaymakers complete make it clear that the travel agent acts only as an intermediary. However, a travel agent who issues tickets in his or her own name *will* be acting as a contracting carrier and be bound by the Convention.

Goods

The Convention deals with two kinds of goods: baggage and cargo. Baggage includes small personal baggage – all items necessary for a particular journey. Cargo covers any item of whatever kind which is not mail, passengers' baggage or items belonging to the carrier.

Documents

If the carrier is to gain the protection of the Convention he or she must comply with rules relating to the issue of transport documents. Passenger tickets must be clearly printed with information relating to the place of departure and destination, the name and address of the carrier and a statement that the carriage is subject to the liability rules of the Convention. To ensure these details are readable the Montreal Agreement fixed the type of character at ten points. The Guatemala Protocol stated that any other means which would preserve a record of the information required on tickets could be substituted for the delivery of a ticket, thus making way for computer cards. Baggage checks, like the ticket, have been simplified by the Guatemala Protocol so that they too may be produced by machines. Any defect in the machine places responsibility on the carrier.

Every carrier of goods has the right to require that the consignor makes out an air waybill. This document is handed over usually with the goods to the carrier. This also has now undergone change. The Montreal Amendments of 1975 settled it that the parties to the contract of carriage may replace the air waybill with a receipt for the goods in those cases where the information required under the Convention can be shown in some other way, thus allowing the process to be controlled by computer.

The air waybill, like the bill of lading in maritime law, is regarded as a negotiable instrument. It may therefore be used as a document of credit; it may be sold.

The principal ideas of the Convention

What are the carrier's obligations? He or she undertakes to carry the passenger or goods safely to his/their destination along with baggage belonging to the passenger.

What are the user's rights? That he or she and/or his or her goods will arrive safely, without undue delay and in good condition at the destination.

The main obligation, therefore, under the contract of carriage is placed on the carrier by the Warsaw Convention. It was, thus, considered fair to place limits upon this liability of the carrier. Two questions, then, must be examined: What is the nature of this liability? What limits have been placed on it by the Convention and successive amendments?

Under the Convention liability was based on presumed fault and was created by Articles 17, 18 and 19. Article 25 states:

(1) The carrier shall not be entitled to avail himself of the provisions of this Convention which exclude or limit his liability, if the damage is caused by his wilful misconduct or by such default on his part as, in accordance with the law of the Court seised of the case, is considered to be equivalent to wilful misconduct.

(2) Similarly the carrier shall not be entitled to avail himself of the said provisions, if the damage is caused as aforesaid by any agent of the carrier acting within the scope of his employment.

Misconduct was not defined in the Convention, leaving the courts to define its nature. However, it became recognised that it would be more just for litigants if the notion of the presumption of liability were revised. Following the lead given by the Montreal Agreement, the Guatemala Protocol adopted the principle of strict liability for passengers and baggage. This involved redrafting Article 17 of the Convention, which now reads:

1. The carrier is liable for damage sustained in case of death or personal injury of a passenger upon condition only that the event which caused the death or injury took place on board the aircraft or in the course of any of the operations of embarking or disembarking. However, the carrier is not liable if the death or injury resulted solely from the state of health of the passenger.

2. The carrier is liable for damage sustained in case of destruction or loss of, or damage to, baggage upon condition only that the event which caused the destruction, loss or damage took place on board the aircraft or in the course of any of the operations of embarking or disembarking or during any period within which the baggage was in charge of the carrier. However, the carrier is not liable if the damage resulted solely from the inherent defect, quality or vice of the baggage.

The Montreal Protocol No. 4 1975 extends strict liability to cargo. This protocol also redrafted Article 20 so that it now states that the carrier is liable for delay of passengers and their baggage, and for damage caused to cargo by delays. Presumed fault is retained here, however, because the carrier will escape liability, if he or she can prove he or she has taken all necessary steps to prevent the delay or the damage.

Article 22 of the Convention sets the limit on the carrier's liability. Today, following on from successive amendments and the Additional Montreal Protocols Nos. 1, 2, 3 of September 1975 the maximum amount of liability towards passengers is expressed as Special Drawing Rights. These are monetary units that have been defined by the International Monetary Fund and can be more easily converted into the currencies of member nations than can the gold francs. Protocol No. 3 states the limit to be 100,000 SDRs for passengers. The liability of the carrier in respect of damage to cargo is limited to 17 SDRs per kilogram of registered cargo, and for baggage which remains with the passenger, 1,000 SDRs. Liability for delay is specifically dealt with by the Guatemala Protocol. Article VIII revises Article 22 of the Convention in part and states:

(b) in the case of delay in the carriage of persons the liability of the carrier for each passenger is limited to sixty-two thousand five hundred francs [which converts into 4,150 SDRs];

(c) in the carriage of baggage the liability of the carrier in the case of destruction, loss, damage or delay is limited to fifteen thousand francs [which converts into 1,000 SDRs] for each passenger.

The carrier will not be able to rely on these limitations of his liability if the damage is caused by his or her 'wilful misconduct' (Article 25). There was no definition of 'wilful misconduct' and this was remedied by Article XIII of the Hague Protocol, so that the new version of Article 25 reads:

The limits of liability specified in Article 22 shall not apply if it is proved that the damage resulted from an act or omission of the carrier, his servants or agents done with intent to cause damage or recklessly and with knowledge that damage would probably result; provided that in the case of such an act or omission of a servant or agent, it is also proved that he was acting within the scope of his employment.

With the adoption of the idea of strict liability by the Guatemala Protocol (following the lead given by the Montreal Agreement in 1966), Article 25 as stated above does not apply for passengers because the ceiling of compensation was increased on the condition that it could not be exceeded under any circumstances. The Montreal Agreement No. 4 adopts strict liability in respect of cargo.

Articles 20 and 21 of the Convention respectively allow the carrier the right to use the defences of having taken all the necessary steps and the contributory negligence of the passenger.

The Warsaw Convention today

1989 was the 60th anniversary of the signing of the Convention. In the intervening years it continued to evolve; numerous court cases have resulted from it. The applicability and nature of the limitation of liability continue to be the main causes of legal argument. There are also proposals for a new standard and compensation plan in the USA. Italy has enacted new legislation: the Italian Constitutional Court declared Article 22(1) of the Convention unconstitutional because the limits relating to bodily injury/death for passengers were too low under Italian law. This led to a new law of 7 July 1988 which set new limits of SDR 100,000 which are binding on all Italian airlines operating from/to Italy. The airline is obliged to obtain insurance coverage up to SDR 100,000 per passenger.

The Athens Convention 1974

The Convention relating to the Carriage of Passengers and Their Luggage by Sea 1974, usually referred to as the Athens Convention 1974, was incorporated into the law of the United Kingdom by section 14 of the Merchant Shipping Act 1979. The section also brought into force a Protocol to the Convention, of 19 November 1976.

What is the aim of this Convention?

The Convention imposes basic liability on the carrier and performing carrier for the death of or personal injury to a passenger and for loss or damage to luggage caused by their fault or neglect or the fault or neglect of their servants or agents. The Convention sets limits on this liability to certain prescribed sums.

The application of the Convention

The Athens Convention applies to the *international* carriage by sea of passengers and their luggage for remuneration. It applies to carriage by ship, which includes ferries but not hovercraft, and it applies to international journeys. It does not apply when the carriage by sea is part of a mixed mode of transport, for example air and sea. The main provisions of the Convention deal with definitions, liability and limitations on that liability.

Definitions

Article 1 gives the following definitions:

carrier: *a person by or on behalf of whom a contract of carriage has been concluded, whether the carriage is actually performed by him or by a performing carrier.*

performing carrier: *a person other than the carrier, being the owner, charterer or operator of a ship, who actually performs the whole or part of the carriage.*

contract of carriage: *a contract made by or on behalf of a carrier for the carriage by sea of a passenger or of a passenger and his luggage.*

ship: *a seagoing vessel, excluding an air-cushion vehicle.*

passenger: *any person carried in a ship under a contract of carriage, or, who, with the consent of the carrier, is accompanying a vehicle or live animals which are covered by a contract for the carriage of goods not covered by the Convention.*

luggage: *any article or vehicle carried by the carrier under a contract of carriage. This excludes articles and vehicles under a charter party, bill of lading or other contract concerned with the carriage of goods, and live animals.*

cabin luggage: *luggage which the passenger has in his cabin or in his vehicle.*

carriage: *covers these periods:*

(a) in relation to the passenger and his cabin luggage, the period they are on board the ship or in embarking and disembarking. It does not include that time when the passenger is in a marine terminal, quay or other port installation.

(b) in relation to cabin luggage the period in which the passenger is in a marine terminal, quay or other installation, if the luggage has been taken over by the carrier.

(c) in relation to other luggage the period from when it is taken over by the carrier till it is re-delivered.

international carriage: *carriage where the departure and destination are situated in two different States, or in a single State if, there is an intermediate port of call in another State.*

Liability

The carrier is liable for damage to a passenger resulting from death or personal injury and for the loss of or damage to his or her luggage. This liability arises if the incident which caused the damage happened in the course of the carriage *and* it was due to the fault or neglect of the carrier, his or her servants (employees) or agents acting within the scope of their employment. The claimant (passenger) must prove two matters:

(a) that the incident which caused the loss or damage occurred in the course of the carriage;

(b) the extent of loss or damage.

The fault or neglect of the carrier, or of his or her servants or agents, is presumed if the death of or personal injury to a passenger, or the loss of or damage to cabin luggage, arose from or in connection with a shipwreck, collision, stranding, explosion or fire, or defect in the ship. If a passenger's other luggage is lost or damaged, fault or neglect of the carrier is presumed also. In this case the burden of proof lies with the carrier, i.e. he or she has to prove that the death or injury, loss or damage, was *not* due to the shipwreck, collision, etc. Article 6 states that if the carrier proves that the death of or personal injury to a passenger or the loss of or damage to his or her luggage was caused or contributed to by the fault or neglect of the passenger, the court which is hearing the case may relieve the carrier of the whole or part of his or her liability.

If the contract of carriage is to be performed in part by a 'performing carrier', the Convention states that liability for the entire carriage remains with the 'carrier', although the 'performing carrier' is subject to the provisions of the Convention for that part of the contract of carriage performed by him or her. Therefore, carrier and the performing carrier are liable for the death or personal injury to a passenger and for the loss of or damage to luggage caused by their fault or neglect or that of their servants or agents. The carrier is made vicariously liable for the negligence of the performing carrier, but where both carrier and performing carrier are in breach of their duty their liability is 'joint and several'. This means that each is liable with the other for the loss.

There is no liability for valuables such as money, gold, silverware, jewellery, works of art, etc., unless they have been deposited with the carrier for safe-keeping.

Limitations on liability

In respect of personal injury or death of a passenger, Article 7 limits the liability of the carrier to 700,000 francs per passenger.

The liability of the carrier for the loss of or damage to cabin luggage is not to exceed 12,500 francs per passenger, per carriage, and for the loss of or damage to vehicles including all luggage carried in or on a vehicle, it is not to exceed 50,000 francs per vehicle, per carriage. Liability for loss of or damage to any other luggage is not to exceed 18,000 francs per passenger, per carriage (Article 8).

The carrier and the passenger may agree, expressly in writing, to higher limits of liability than those described in Articles 7 and 8. However, the carrier loses the right to benefit from these limitations on liability if it is proved that 'the damage resulted from an act or omission of the carrier done with the intent to cause such damage, or recklessly and with knowledge that such damage would probably result' (Article 13).

The Protocol to the Convention, of 19 November 1979, modifies Articles 7, 8 and 9 of the Convention:

(a) In Article 7 the words '46,666 units of account' are substituted for the words '700,000 francs'.

(b) In Article 8 the words '1,200 units of account' are substituted for the words '18,000 francs'.

(c) Article 9 is modified in that the unit of account, which referred to a unit consisting of 65.5 milligrams of gold of millesimal fineness 900, is now the Special Drawing Right as defined by the IMF. The amounts set out in Articles 7 and 8 are to be converted into the national currency of the state in which the court hearing the case is situated.

The effect, therefore, of the Protocol is that it replaces the gold franc by a unit of account as the measure of liability, each unit of account being a Special Drawing Right as defined by the IMF.

Convention for the International Carriage of Passengers and Luggage by Rail 1961

This Convention lays down provisions relating to the extent of the railway's liability for personal injury to passengers and for loss of, or damage to, articles they might have with them. Section 1 of the Carriage by Railway Act 1972 brings the Convention into the law of the United Kingdom.

The Convention states that the damage caused to passengers and their luggage must arise out of an accident occurring in the territory of a state that is a party to it. The Convention does not apply to damage arising in the course of carriage by road or ship. However, where the railway vehicles are carried by ferry the Convention applies in respect of damage resulting from the death of, or personal injury to, passengers and for damage to, or loss of, any articles the passengers may have with them. The damage or loss must be caused by an accident arising out of the operation of the railway which happens while the passengers are in, entering or alighting from railway vehicles. The state on whose territory the accident occurs is 'the state whose flag is flown by the ferry'.

The Convention then describes the extent of liability of the railway (which the Convention refers to as the 'responsible railway', i.e. the one, according to the list of names in the Convention, which operates the line on which the accident occurs). Thus, the railway will be liable for damage resulting from the death of, or personal injury or 'any other bodily or mental harm' to, passengers. This harm must have been caused by an accident arising from the operation of the railway and happening while the passengers were in, entering or alighting from a train. Liability extends also to damage to, or total or partial loss of, any articles (including animals) the passengers might have had with them. The railway is also liable for the actions of its employees and of any other persons it employs to perform carriage for which it is responsible.

The amount of damages payable on the death of a passenger includes the cost of transport of the body, and burial or cremation. All persons dependent on the deceased for support and maintenance have the right to be indemnified by the railway for their loss. When a passenger has suffered personal injury or other 'bodily or mental harm' the damages include any necessary expenses such as the cost of medical treatment and transport, and a sum to compensate the person for loss due to total or partial incapacity to work. This last amount will also include a sum for any increased expenditure on his or her personal requirements arising because of the injury.

Compensation for such injuries as mental pain, suffering and disfigurement are determined by the national law. The Convention states that 'national law' means the law of the state on whose territory the accident occurs.

Limits are placed on the railway's liability for the death of or personal injury to passengers and for damage to, or loss of, their luggage.

(a)   In relation to the death of, or personal injury to, a passenger the amount of damages is determined by national law. However, if the national law lays down a limitation of liability of less than 200,000 francs, the Convention provides that this will be overridden by a limitation of liability of 200,000 francs per passenger. This amount may be paid either as a lump sum or as an annuity.

(b)   When the railway is liable to pay compensation for damage to, or total or partial loss of, articles that passengers who were injured had with them, up to 2,000 francs per passenger may be claimed. Article 21 of the Convention states that the 'franc' relates to the gold franc weighing 10/31 of a gram and being of millesimal fineness 900.

The Convention states certain conditions under which a railway will be wholly or partly relieved of liability:

(a)   if the accident has been caused by circumstances not connected with the operation of the railway and which the railway, despite having taken all reasonable care, could not avoid;

(b)   if the accident is due to a passenger's wrongful act or neglect, or behaviour on his or her part that does not conform to that of other passengers;

(c)   if the accident is due to a third party's behaviour which the railway, despite taking all reasonable care, could not avoid.

The railway is not liable under the Convention for damage caused by a nuclear accident; liability rests with the operator of the nuclear installation.

The railway cannot exclude or limit its liability. The Convention renders void any term in the contract of carriage by which the railway purports to exempt itself from liability or to reverse the burden of proof it has or to lower the limits of liability.

A claimant loses the right of action by failing to give notice of the accident to the railway against which the claim will be made. First, notice must be given within three months of the person becoming aware of the damage. Then, if the claim is for personal injury, any court action must be brought within three years of the accident. If the claim is for a passenger's death, it must be brought within three years of the passenger's death or five years of the accident, whichever is the earlier.

The International Convention for the Carriage of Passengers and Luggage by Road 1974

This Convention covers the extent of a road carrier's liability for personal injury caused to passengers by an accident arising from the carriage, and happening while the passengers were inside, entering or alighting from the vehicle. Liability is also placed on the carrier for loss of, or damage to, luggage.

'Carrier' is defined in the Convention as:

> *any person who, in the course of trade or business undertakes under an individual or collective contract of carriage to carry one or more passengers and their luggage, whether or not he performs the carriage himself.*

'Passenger' is defined as:

> *any person who in the performance of a contract of carriage made by him or on his behalf, is carried either for reward or gratuitously by a carrier.*

'Vehicle' means 'any motor vehicle used in the performance of a contract of carriage and intended for the carriage of persons'.

 The Convention was brought into United Kingdom law by section 1 of the Carriage of Passengers by Road Act 1974.

What is the scope of application of the Convention's provisions?

The Convention applies to each contract for the carriage of passengers and their luggage in vehicles by road. The carriage must be *international*, that is, it must take place in the territory of more than one state and the point of departure or destination must be in the territory of a state that is party to the Convention. Even if the carriage by road is interrupted and another mode of transport used, the Convention applies to *those portions of the carriage which are performed by road*, even if they are not international as described above. This is subject to the proviso that the carriage by road is not ancillary to the other mode of transport. The Convention applies where the vehicle itself is carried over part of the journey by another mode of transport.

The loss or damage must be caused by an incident connected with the carriage by the vehicle and occur while the passengers are inside it or entering or alighting from it.

What is the liability of the carrier?

The carrier will be liable for loss or damage resulting from 'the death or wounding of, or for any other bodily or mental injury caused to a passenger'. The death or personal injury must have resulted from:

(a) an accident connected with the carriage and happening while the passenger was in the vehicle or entering or alighting from it; or

(b) the loading or unloading of luggage.

The carrier is liable for loss or damage resulting from the total or partial loss of luggage. Responsibility runs from the time the luggage is handed to the carrier until it is delivered. The carrier is also liable for any damage that may be caused to passengers by the breach of his or her obligation to issue a ticket and a luggage registration voucher. The ticket must show the name and address of the carrier and contain a statement that the contract is subject to the provisions of the Convention. The voucher must indicate the number and nature of the pieces of luggage handed into the carrier's care. If it is not combined with the ticket, it too must state the name and address of the carrier and contain the statement concerning the Convention. The carrier is also liable for the acts and omissions of his or her agents and employees and for anyone else whose services he or she uses. This liability arises only if such persons are acting in the scope of their employment.

The Convention places limits on the carrier's liability:

(a) In relation to loss or damage resulting from death or personal injury of a passenger, the 'total damages' are limited to 250,000 francs per person 'in respect of the same occurrence'. This amount is exclusive of 'legal or other costs incurred by parties asserting their rights'. However, where there is more than one claimant, e.g. a family booking, and the total of their claims exceeds this stated limit, the claims will be reduced pro rata. A higher limit may be agreed between the parties to the contract.

(b) In the case of compensation for loss (partial or total) of luggage, or damage to it, the passenger may claim an amount equal to the loss or damage, but limited to 500 francs per piece of luggage and 2,000 francs per passenger.

(c) An amount may also be claimed in respect of the similar loss of any personal item carried or worn by the passenger. Here, the limit is 1,000 francs per passenger.

The amounts in (b) and (c) above are also exclusive of legal or other costs incurred. The franc referred to is the same as that for the Rail Convention 1961, discussed in the preceding section.

The Convention details some special circumstances that may wholly or partly relieve the carrier of liability:

(a) if the accident that resulted in the death of, or personal injury to, a passenger was caused in circumstances which a carrier, doing all that was reasonable in the situation, could not have avoided;

(b) if the loss or damage resulted from the wrongful act or neglect of the passenger, or from the passenger not behaving like the majority of passengers;

(c) if the loss or damage to luggage resulted from an inherent defect in that luggage or from circumstances which the carrier, acting in a careful and diligent way, could not have avoided;

(d) if the loss or damage is caused by a nuclear incident, the operator of the nuclear installation is liable for it.

The Convention states that the carrier will not be relieved of liability, for personal injury or damage to luggage, by reason of the physical or mental failing of the driver, any defect in or malfunctioning of the vehicle, or from any wrongful act or neglect on the part of the persons from whom the carrier may have hired the vehicle. Further, in circumstances where the carrier would normally be liable, but where a third party has contributed to the loss or damage by his or her acts or omissions, the carrier will be liable for the whole loss or damage – but without prejudice to any right of action the carrier may have against that third party.

Finally, if the loss or damage results from wilful misconduct or gross negligence by the carrier or his or her employees and agents, the carrier will not be entitled to take advantage of the provisions in the Convention that exclude liability, wholly or in part, or that limit the amount of compensation payable.

The carrier cannot insert in the contract of carriage a term that directly or indirectly derogates from these provisions of the Convention. Any such clause is void.

An action for damages arising out of the death of or injury to a passenger must be brought within three years from the date when the person suffering the loss or damage knew, or should have known, of it. In any event, no such claim may be brought more than five years after the accident. Actions for damages for loss of luggage must be brought within one year of the date on which the vehicle arrived or should have arrived at the passenger's destination.

SUMMARY
(a) Most carriers reserve the right to alter timetables and delay departure times.

(b) The tour operator makes the contract of carriage with the carrier.

(c) The tour operator has little control over the carrier.

(d) Statutes place liability on the carrier rather than on the tour operator.

(e) There are a number of international conventions that place liability on the carrier for death or personal injury caused to passengers and loss of or damage to their luggage.

(f) These conventions place limits on the carrier's liability.

SELF-ASSESSMENT QUESTIONS

State whether the following statements are correct or incorrect.

1. A fee-paying passenger who has been injured in an accident caused by the carrier may claim against the carrier for breach of contract or for negligence under the law of tort (delict, in Scotland).

2. A non-fare-paying passenger has no claim whatsoever against a negligent carrier who causes him or her injury.

3. The carrier must guarantee the safety of passengers.

4. The standard of care owed by the carrier to his or her passengers is of a very high degree.

5. The carrier may be held liable where a passenger is injured due to overcrowding on a vehicle, vessel or craft.

6. It is negligence on the part of a coach operator to permit a drunken passenger on board.

7. The carrier's liability for passengers' luggage is incurred as soon as the passengers hand over their luggage to the carrier, his or her employee or agent.

8. Provisions in conditions of carriage limiting the carrier's liability for the passenger's safety are subject to the provisions of the Unfair Contract Terms Act 1977.

9. A passenger will be bound by the carrier's conditions of carriage if he or she knew they were referred to on the ticket, even though he or she did not read the ticket.

10. British Rail has a legal duty to ensure that passengers reach their destination on time.

11. The tour operator is vicariously liable for the civil wrongs of the carrier.

12. The aim of the Warsaw Convention was to protect travellers by paying compensation for death or injury and to ensure that airlines were financially sound.

13. Before long it became necessary to amend this Convention because the initial limits on airlines' liability were too low.

14. Travel agents come within the scope of this Convention because they act as agents.

15. Under this Convention the liability of the carrier was based on presumed fault, which meant that the carrier had to show that the harm or loss did not arise because of wilful misconduct on his or her part.

16. This Convention also deals with liability for delay to passengers and their luggage.

17. The Guatemala Protocol of 1971 changed the basis of liability from presumed fault to strict liability.

18. Because the liability of the carrier is described as 'strict' no defences are available to carriers.

19. The Athens Convention regulates carriage of passengers and luggage by sea.

20. This Convention has not yet been brought into the law of the United Kingdom.

21. Persons who suffer injury or loss when travelling under an international contract of carriage by rail are not covered by an international convention.

22. Passengers travelling under an international contract of carriage by road will be covered by the 1974 Road Convention even if the road journey is interrupted by a ferry or rail journey.

11 Insurance

The Insurance Contract

A contract of insurance is subject to all the principles of the law of contract. Most tour operators include holiday insurance policies as part of their holiday package. The policy offered, however, may not satisfy the customer's needs, and he or she may be well advised to take out a separate policy. The insurance contained as part of the package may be only outlined in the brochure and the exclusions may be indicated only briefly or perhaps omitted altogether. In most cases the customer does not receive a copy of the master policy unless specifically requested.

The customer therefore enters into a separate contract with the insurer. The travel agent should then pay over to the insurer the premiums paid by the traveller. The contract of insurance is concluded when the customer pays the premium to the travel agent.

The Principle of Utmost Good Faith

Both parties, the insured and the insurer, have the duty to disclose all material facts before the contract of insurance is concluded. The reason for this is that insurance contracts belong to that category of contracts described as '*uberrimae fidei*' (of utmost good faith).

Parties to other kinds of contracts have no such duty of disclosure as they are said to contract 'at arm's length', i.e. it is for them to decide what information they require before entering into the contract. If they fail to ask for material information, this will not of itself invalidate the contract. This principle of full disclosure of material facts applies equally to the insurer and the insured, although in practice it is more likely to apply to the insured. However, the decision in *Banque Keyser Ullman SA v Skandia Insurance Co.* (1987) shows that the courts will apply the duty of full disclosure to the insurer.

What is this duty?

The insured has to disclose all material facts to the insurer prior to the conclusion of the contract. Failure to do this means that the insurer has the right to treat the insurance contract as void, that is, that it never existed. The insurer must inform the 'insured' of this fact within a reasonable time of becoming aware of the non-disclosure. The duty arises each time a new contract is concluded, in particular when a contract of insurance (except life insurance) is renewed.

The duty of disclosure applies to facts only, not opinion. In matters regarding the health of the insured, for example, if he or she does not know some specific facts, because he or she is not an expert in medical science, he or she can only give an opinion. He or she would not be guilty of non-disclosure of material facts. However, if that same insured had had to consult a specialist doctor he or she would be guilty of non-disclosure of a material fact if he or she omitted to disclose this, even although he or she may not have been in the possession of any medical facts.

It does not matter that the insured did not know he or she was under a duty to disclose; innocent non-disclosure is just as actionable as concealment or negligent non-disclosure. The insured can disclose only those material facts of which he or she is actually aware.

What is a material fact?

A fact is material if it is one which would influence the judgement of a reasonable insurer in deciding whether or not to accept the risk or what premium to charge.

Some categories of facts are always material. These facts relate to physical danger to the life or property, or the liability of the insured. Examples are the state of health or the fact that the insured is in a high-risk occupation or pursues a risky hobby such as potholing in relation to life insurance, or a bad accident record in relation to liability insurance.

The principle of *uberrimae fidei* applies to holiday insurance contracts. Because the insurance policy is often 'part' of the holiday package, however, the customer may not realise the importance of this duty of disclosure. If, for example, the customer wished to cancel the holiday because a recurring illness such as back trouble or a heart condition flared up, the insurance company could disallow the claim, if it could be shown that the illness existed when the policy was taken out but had not been disclosed on the insurance form.

The holiday brochure generally does not give the customer much information about what is being bought. Some brochures may say that the applicant has a duty of disclosure and give some space for the inclusion of any details. In others there is no space. Some policies appear to waive this duty to disclose by stating:'there are no exclusions applying to pre-existing medical conditions'.

It is, therefore, important that the travel agent be aware of these facts and draw the customer's attention to this. The travel agent should make sure that the customer has disclosed all facts which could be relevant, particularly in relation to his or her own health and any members of the family who are taking the holiday, or for any possibly dangerous activity the customer might engage in, either before or during the holiday.

Insurable Interest

It is one of the basic requirements of an insurance contract that the person who is named as the policyholder must have an insurable interest in the subject matter of the insurance, that is, to the life or property or liability to which he or she might be exposed. If no insurable interest is held the policy will be void or illegal or unenforceable.

When the policyholder enters into the contract of insurance he or she is insuring himself or herself, and spouse and children (if any) against the loss of their lives while on holiday. To claim under the policy an insurable interest has to be shown. This means a pecuniary or financial interest. Thus, the insured must show that he would suffer financially by the loss of a legal right on the death of the insured. Insurable interest is presumed where the life insured is one's own or a spouse's. Children under the age of 18 have an insurable interest in the lives of their parents as they would suffer financially from the loss of their support. The holiday insurance contract also insures against the loss of baggage and personal belongings, and the principle of insurable interest would generally apply.

Indemnity

The holiday insurance policy covers the insured in the event that personal belongings are stolen, lost or damaged while on holiday. The insurer guarantees that the customer will be indemnified against loss. The policy also covers claims made by other people if the customer, or his or her family, accidentally injures them or damages their property. This cover includes legal costs relating to the claim.

The question is how this loss is to be measured or assessed.

In relation to goods (movable property) the measure of what the insured has lost will usually be the market value of the property that was lost at the time of the loss: what it will cost the insured to obtain equivalent items. Thus, it is the item's value at the time of the loss that is recoverable. However, it is common for policies to undertake to pay replacement value instead of market value. The amount recoverable under third-party liability clauses is simply the amount of the insured's liability. However, whether it is property insurance or liability insurance, the insured cannot recover more than the amount specified in the policy. A maximum will be expressly stated in the policy. This is 'the sum insured'.

Holiday insurance policies vary considerably and the customer is well advised to shop around for the policy that suits his or her needs. There will usually be a limit of between £500 and £1,000 recoverable for personal belongings. There will also be a limit (mostly around £200) on what the insurance company will pay out for a single item, pair or set. Some policies have a limit for the total amount of valuables such as jewellery and watches, ranging from £150 up to £400.

The travel agent should be prepared to draw the customer's attention to these limits and point out that the cover, that is, the sum insured, may be too low. For example, an engagement ring, wedding ring, watch and a pair of ear-rings or a camera could be worth more than the total limit for valuables or individually be worth more than the single-item limit. If this is the case the travel agent should recommend that the customer look at his or her home contents insurance policy. The special 'all risks' part of the policy allows the insured to include valuables like cameras and jewellery. The customer would have to check to see whether the particular home contents policy provided cover for foreign travel.

In relation to personal liability cover, again, the holiday insurance policy will have a limit. Most policies now have a limit of £1,000,000, which is considered adequate. The customer should check with the travel agent whether this cover is provided if he or she is driving a car, moped or motor cycle, or piloting a boat or plane. It may not cover claims made by a member of the customer's own family, or a claim made in a court outside the United Kingdom.

Subrogation

The main points to note about subrogation are the following.

(a) The insured cannot make a profit from the loss.

(b) Any profit made is accountable for to the insurer.

(c) The insurer who has indemnified the insured may step into the shoes of the insured (that is, be 'subrogated') and in his or her name pursue any right of action available to the insured which may diminish the loss insured against.

(d) The insurer will have the right to sue a third party for damages in tort (delict, in Scotland) or for breach of contract. The third party's liability arises in respect of the event for which the insured has recovered from the insurer.

The two most important aspects of the doctrine of subrogation are that the insured cannot make a profit from the loss and the insurer has the right to sue a third party for damages or for breach of contract. Each of these two points will now be examined more closely.

There are three limitations on the rule that the insured cannot profit from the loss. First, the duty to account to the insurer arises only when there has been full indemnification. The idea of subrogation is that the insured must not be unjustly enriched and this can happen only if more than full compensation for the loss is received.

Second, the fact that the insured has received a gift following on from the loss may not necessarily mean that this gift will have to be taken into account. If the insured receives a gift which is intended to mitigate the loss, the rule is that account has to be made to the insurer for the amount of the gift. Only if the insured can show that a gift was given as extra compensation over and above any insurance money can the gift be kept.

Third, the insured is entitled to any surplus that may result from the insurer exercising subrogation rights. This is because subrogation rights extend only to the amount which the insurer actually paid to the insured. Thus, if the insurer then proceeds to bring an action against a third party and is paid an amount in damages, the insurer will be entitled only to the amount which was paid out originally to the insured. Any surplus over this amount has to be paid to the insured.

The case of *Lister v Romford Ice and Cold Storage Ltd* (1957) illustrates the right of the insurer to proceed in the name of the insured against the third party. Mr Lister and his son both worked for the company. The son negligently injured the father. Thus, the company was vicariously liable to pay damages to the father. This award was satisfied by the company's liability insurers, who then used the company's name to sue the negligent employee so that they could recover. They contended that the employee was in breach of the employee's common law duty to act with reasonable care. The House of Lords (by majority) held that this was an implied term in an employee's contract of employment, which the son had breached.

However, this right of the insured depends upon a number of points:

(a) The insurer first has to indemnify the insured in full in respect of all claims made. Only then does the insurer have the right to proceed against the third party.

(b) The insured must not do anything which would prejudice the insurer's subrogation rights; otherwise, liability arises to repay the amount which the insurers have paid. Thus, an innocent insured unaware of this principle of subrogation could, following a car accident, and because his insurance is comprehensive, agree with the other driver (the wrongdoer) not to make any claim against him or her. Such an agreement could prejudice the insurer's subrogation rights.

(c) If the insured has no right to bring an action, the insurer has no right either.

(d) That the insurer has not waived the right of subrogation. It could be a term of the agreement between the insured and insurer, or it could arise where insurers agree among themselves, as where motor insurers in 'knock for knock' agreements agree to indemnify their own insureds regardless of their rights under the law of tort (delict, in Scotland).

As holiday insurance contracts cover the insured for loss of property, medical expenses and third-party liability they will contain subrogation clauses.

Amount of Cover

Holiday insurance policies provide different amounts of cover for the client and his or her property. The travel agent should ensure that clients have adequate cover for their particular needs. This means that they should not be underinsured, because holiday insurance contracts, like other contracts of insurance (except life policies), are subject to 'averaging': which means if the amount insured is less than the value of the loss the insurer will be liable only for that proportion of the actual loss which the amount insured bears to the value of the property. For example, the client has two suitcases of luggage, one (case A) with contents valued at £600, the other (case B) at £400, total value £1,000. The loss of luggage limit clause in the holiday insurance contract is £500. Case A is lost. The amount which the insurer would be willing to pay, following the averaging principle, would be £300, that is, 50 per cent of the value, because the cover purchased is only half of the total value.

In relation to medical expenses for travel in Europe the amount of cover ought to be at least £1 million or at the very least £500,000. For the United States of America and other parts of the world at least £1 million. For cancellation cover the travel agent should ensure that the limit of the cover is high enough to meet the full cost of the holiday. However, it is even more important to ascertain that the cover is for the widest range of the client's particular circumstances, for example a pregnant woman.

The limits on belongings and money are usually set at about £1,000, with a maximum of £200 payable on any one item, set or pair. Generally a high amount of cover will be fixed for medical care and personal liability, while a low limit will be fixed for loss or theft of personal belongings and money. Most policies also exclude claims for small amounts, which means that the client is generally responsible for paying the first £25 of the claim.

SUMMARY

(a) Most tour operators include holiday insurance policies in the holiday package.

(b) The customer enters into a seperate contract with the insurer. This contract is completed when the premium is paid.

(c) The main legal principles upon which contracts of insurance are based are: *uberrimae fidei* (utmost good faith); insurable interest; indemnity; and subrogation.

(d) The travel agent should ensure that the customer has adequate cover for his or her needs. In particular the travel agent should check that the customer is not underinsured.

SELF-ASSESSMENT QUESTIONS

State whether the following statements are correct or incorrect.

1. The insurance contract is governed by the principles of the law of contract.

2. The customer enters into the contract of insurance with the tour operator if the policy offered as part of the package is taken.

3. Contracts of insurance are contracts *uberrimae fidei*, which means that they have to be in writing.

4. The duty of full disclosure relates to material facts.

5. The insurer has the right to regard the contract as void if the duty to disclose is breached.

6. If the insured is ignorant of the duty to disclose the insurer cannot treat the contract as void.

7. Material facts are those which relate to the life, property, liability or the previous insurance history of the insured.

8. Insurable interest means that the insured has to be able to demonstrate ownership of the property.

9. Insurance contracts provide that the insurer will compensate the insured for loss or damage to his or her property or person or for accidental damage to a third party.

10. The insured will be indemnified for replacement value of goods.

11. Subrogation means that the insured cannot make a profit from the loss.

12. If the insured has been over-compensated the excess has to be repaid to the insurer.

13. The insurer has the right to bring an action in the name of the insured against a third party.

14. Holiday insurance contracts do not contain subrogation clauses.

15. Holiday insurance contracts provide limits on the amount of cover available.

12 Employment Law

GLOSSARY **collective agreement** An agreement made between employers and trade unions covering wages, and/or conditions of employment.

constructive dismissal An employee may have been entitled to resign due to the employer being in breach of a fundamental term of the contract.

direct discrimination To treat a member of one group less favourably than members of another group.

indirect discrimination Whilst apparently treating all persons the same, imposing conditions, qualifications or rules which disadvantage members of a particular group.

summary dismissal Dismissal without notice.

AIM There is a considerable amount of detail on the legal regulation of employment in this chapter, and so our purpose is twofold: first, to provide sufficient detail on relevant employment legislation as it affects the travel industry and, second, to provide an overview of employment law. Do not be put off by the detail – it is there so that members can use it as a reference in the future.

Recruitment

Generally, employers have the right to formulate their own policies of recruitment and selection. There are Acts of Parliament which aim to protect certain categories of job applicant. These provisions are to be found in the Sex Discrimination Act 1975 (SDA) and the Race Relations Act 1976 (RRA), which prohibit employers from discriminating on grounds of race, sex or marriage. There are also provisions prohibiting employers from discriminating against rehabilitated offenders; others lay down guidelines for the employment of disabled persons.

Two statutory provisions which must be taken into consideration when recruiting staff are the following.

 ### The Disabled Persons (Employment) Acts 1944 and 1958

Organisations with more than 20 employees must ensure that at least 3 per cent are registered disabled persons. Also, physically handicapped persons have to be preferred for jobs such as car park and lift attendants. Where it would be dangerous to employ a handicapped person the employer is exempt and special permission can be obtained if the employer has no work suitable for a disabled person to do or because no suitable disabled person has applied. Breach of these

Acts is a criminal offence. The Employment Services' Code of Practice on the Employment of Disabled People 1984 also lays down guidelines for employers.

Rehabilitation of Offenders Act 1974

The aim of this Act is to encourage previous offenders to obtain proper employment and to play their full role in society, i.e. to be 'rehabilitated'. It makes it unlawful for an employer to refuse to employ a person on the grounds that he or she has a 'spent' conviction. A conviction is spent after a specified period. The period varies according to the length of the sentence and the age of the offender at the time the offence was committed. The Act contains a table with these details. A conviction will not be spent if it was for a period exceeding 30 months' imprisonment; convictions for life are never spent. A rehabilitated person does not have to disclose a spent conviction to an employer. Certain occupations and professions are not subject to these rules.

In *Hendry and Hendry v Scottish Liberal Club* (1977) Mr and Mrs Hendry were employed as managers of the club. When it was discovered that Mr Hendry had been convicted of possessing cannabis, he and his wife were instantly dismissed. The court held that they were entitled to £576 compensation for unfair dismissal because the sacking contravened the Act – Mr Hendry's conviction had been spent.

Discrimination

In Great Britain the Acts of Parliament which prohibit discrimination are the Sex Discrimination Act 1975 (on the grounds of sex and marital status) and the Race Relations Act 1976 (on grounds of race, colour, national or ethnic origin, or nationality). Discrimination on the grounds of language is not directly prohibited but may amount to 'indirect discrimination', which we shall discuss later. Northern Ireland has its own equivalent of the sex discrimination legislation and, in addition, the Fair Employment Acts 1976 and 1989 prohibit discrimination of grounds of religion. Religious discrimination is not unlawful in Great Britain but may be indirectly racially discriminatory. In 1986 the Sex Discrimination Act was amended to take into account rulings in the European Court of Justice which equalised retirement ages for men and women.

The Sex Discrimination Acts and Race Relations Act are complemented by codes of practice: the Sex Discrimination Acts by the Equal Opportunity Commission's Code of Practice for Elimination of Discrimination on Grounds of Sex and Marriage and the Promotion of Equality of Opportunity in Employment 1985; the Race Relations Act by the Code of Practice for the Elimination of Racial Discrimination and the Promotion of Equality of Opportunity in Employment, prepared by the Commission for Racial Equality.

Employers who fail to observe the statutory provisions are not liable to criminal prosecution except in the case of fair employment legislation in

Northern Ireland. It is not advisable, however, for an employer to ignore the recommendations laid down in the codes of practice as this may be used as evidence in a complaint to an industrial tribunal.

Discrimination is illegal in employment if it is based on a person's sex. It is illegal also to discriminate against a married person of either sex on the grounds of marital status. (It is not illegal, however, to discriminate against a person of either sex because he or she is single.) Many travel agents are reluctant to employ married couples at the same branch. There are two important cases dealing with this matter.

⚖️ (a) *McLean v Paris Travel Service Ltd* (1976). Jeanette Johnson worked as a reservation clerk in a Hertfordshire travel agent. She was sacked the day before she married John McLean, the assistant manager. She was told it was 'company policy' not to have two married people working together. The tribunal held that this was contrary to section 6(2) of the Sex Discrimination Act 1975. Jeanette Johnson was entitled to £117 for unfair dismissal and £200 for injury to her feelings.

⚖️ (b) *Skyrail Oceanic Ltd v Coleman* (1981). The applicant was a booking clerk in a travel agency. She became engaged to a man who worked for a rival firm. Their respective employers discussed this matter, as it appeared there might be a possibility of leakage of confidential information. It was agreed that the applicant's employer would dismiss her. This was based on the assumption that her husband-to-be would be the breadwinner of the marriage. Thereupon, she was dismissed after the marriage took place.

The Court of Appeal held, reaffirming the decision of the tribunal, that the assumption that the man would be the breadwinner was an assumption based on sex, which amounts to sex discrimination.

We have already pointed out that religious discrimination is not unlawful in Great Britain, though it is prohibited in Northern Ireland.

Sikhs and Jews have been recognised as ethnic groups as well as followers of a particular religion and thus are protected under the Race Relations Act 1976. It amounts to direct discrimination if, on grounds of race, sex or marriage, a person is treated less favourably than persons of the other sex or another race. It does not matter that the act was done with the best of intentions, as the three following cases illustrate.

⚖️ (a) *Batisha v Say* (1977). A woman was turned down for a job as a cave guide on the grounds that 'it is a man's job'. The tribunal held that the employer was guilty of direct discrimination.

⚖️ (b) *Grieg v Community Industry* (1979). The applicant and another woman were appointed to a job. The other woman did not turn up for work so the applicant was not allowed to start work because in the past there had been problems with one woman working in an all-male team. It was held that this amounted to direct discrimination. The motive was irrelevant.

(c) *Zarczynska v Levy* (1979). A barmaid alleged that she was dismissed for refusing to obey an order not to serve coloured persons in a pub. It was held that even though she had not been personally discriminated against on grounds of her race, she had been treated less favourably on racial grounds, and was thus entitled to pursue her claim.

Indirect discrimination

Indirect discrimination occurs where a condition is imposed which applies to all persons but which disproportionately affects one particular racial group or sex or married persons. 'Successful candidates must be willing to strip to the waist when doing this job' clearly discriminates against women because, although some might be prepared to do this, the majority would not.

Where the organisation's employees or a section of the workforce are recruited on the recommendation of the existing employees, indirect discrimination can occur against the non-represented minority – black, white, male or female – for example in those situations where employees are recruited by word of mouth recommendation.

 It must be noted that age restrictions may amount to indirect discrimination as the case of *Price v Civil Service Commission* (1977) shows. Belinda Price, aged 36, applied for a job advertised by the Commission and was told that candidates had to be between 17.5 and 28 years old. She claimed this was indirect discrimination because far fewer women than men could comply with this condition *in practice* as many women in this age group start a family. It was held that the applicant was unable to comply with this condition, which was to her detriment. The Commission was instructed to abolish or raise the age limit because it had failed to show that the age requirement for the job was justified.

Victimisation can also occur when an employee has been treated less favourably than the discriminator treats, or would treat, others, on the grounds that the employee:

(a) brought proceedings under the Sex Discrimination Act 1975 or Race Relations Act 1976;

(b) gave evidence or information in these proceedings;

(c) helped the Equal Opportunities Commission or the Race Relations Board;

(d) made allegations of discrimination under the Sex Discrimination Act or Race Relations Act.

SUMMARY (a) Legislative provisions contained in the Sex Discrimination Acts 1975 and 1986 and Race Relations Act 1976 protect employees against discrimination on grounds of sex, race or marriage.

(b) The Race Relations Act covers not only race but also colour, national or ethnic origin and nationality.

(c) It is illegal to discriminate against a married person of either sex on the grounds that he or she is married.

(d) It is direct discrimination to treat a person on grounds of race, sex or marriage less favourably than persons of the other sex or another race, or a single person.

(e) It does not matter that the direct discrimination was done with the best of possible motives.

(f) It is indirect discrimination where a condition is imposed which disproportionately affects one racial group or sex.

(g) Age restrictions may amount to indirect discrimination. Unlike direct discrimination, indirect discrimination may be justifiable.

(h) The Sex Discrimination Act and Race Relations Act also contain provisions against employers victimising employees who have brought or assisted in complaints under the Acts.

(i) The Disabled Persons (Employment) Acts 1944 and 1958 contain provisions to encourage employment of people with disabilities.

(j) Important guidelines for employers are contained in the code of practice in the employment of disabled people.

(k) It is unlawful to discriminate against an employee on the grounds of a spent conviction.

(l) In Northern Ireland the Fair Employment Acts 1976 and 1989 prohibit discrimination on grounds of religion.

Sex discrimination in employment

 The Sex Discrimination Act prohibits unlawful discriminatory acts in relation to employment.

(a) All arrangements for recruiting, including advertisements, must ensure that the job opportunities are available to all irrespective of sex. Even if the advertisement is fair, unlawful acts may have followed. Questions asked of female interviewees, for example, which might be questions to elicit information about marital status or having children, may indicate an intention to discriminate. The arrangements are discriminatory even if no one gets the job advertised.

(b) If an employer offers a job to a woman on less favourable terms than those offered to a man this in itself is discriminatory. The Sex Discrimination

Act does not apply to offers relating to contractual payments of money unless, if the contract were accepted, it would fall foul of the Equal Pay Act 1970 (as amended).

(c) It is unlawful for an employer to refuse to employ a person because of his or her sex merely because other employees will not work with a person of the opposite sex.

(d) There must be equal opportunities to all employees to transfer to more favourable shifts or sites. No employee should be denied promotion by restricting training opportunities. A single-sex training programme is permissible in order to alter the imbalance of the sexes in a job, these imbalances having become apparent during the previous 12 months.

 The Race Relations Act also prohibits discriminatory acts in relation to applicants and employees.

(a) It is unlawful to discriminate in the arrangements made for recruiting. Questions during the course of recruitment indicating an intention to discriminate, and the employer making prejudicial assumptions based on race, could lead to allegations of discrimination.

(b) It is unlawful to discriminate against a person in the terms on which employment is offered.

(c) It is unlawful to segregate people in the same racial group.

(d) There must be equal opportunity in access to promotion, transfer and training.

(e) Assistance with training for particular work may be offered to a racial group under-represented in that work in the preceding 12 months.

Sex Discrimination Act 1975 – genuine occupational qualification

Discrimination on the grounds of sex is lawful if the sex of the person is a genuine occupational qualification (GOQ):

(a) The essential nature of the job calls for authentic male/female characteristics (excluding physical strength or stamina), for example an advertisement for a man to play Hamlet, or a woman to play Ophelia.

(b) The job needs a man/woman to preserve decency or privacy or because it is likely to involve physical contact in circumstances where that person may reasonably object to a person of the opposite sex.

 In *Timex Corporation v Hodgson* (1981) a male supervisor was dismissed by reason of redundancy but a female supervisor, who had less service, was retained. The employers sought to justify this on the grounds that all the other female supervisors were leaving and they needed to keep one female supervisor to deal with the problems of female shopfloor workers, i.e. to take women to the first-aid room, to ensure an adequate supply of tampons and pills for period pains in the ladies' lavatory, among other things. It was held that this was GOQ.

(c) The employee is required to live in premises provided by the employer and the premises are not equipped with separate sleeping quarters and toilets and it is not reasonable to expect the employer to re-equip: for example, single-sex employment on a construction site or a lighthouse.

(d) The job is to be done in a hospital or prison, etc., where people need supervision and the inmates are of one sex.

(e) The employer provides individuals with personal services that promote welfare or education and these can be most effectively provided by one sex, for example a male youth club leader for a boys' club.

(f) The job involves performances of duties outside the United Kingdom in a country whose laws or customs are such that they could not be done by a person of the opposite sex, for example sending a woman to negotiate with a Middle Eastern sheikh.

However, in the case of *O'Connor v Kontiki Travel* a woman was refused a job as a coach driver because it was argued she would have to drive through Muslim countries where women drivers are unacceptable. It was held that this would have been a GOQ had it been the case; however, the only Muslim country the tour was going to was Turkey and no evidence was led that women drivers would be objected to there.

(g) The job is one of two held by a married couple.

Finally, it is unlawful to advertise in a way that indicates the intention to discriminate, for example 'waiter', 'salesgirl', 'postman' – unless the advertisement contains an indication that both males and females may apply.

The Race Relations Act 1976 – genuine occupational qualification

The Act lays down a list of circumstances where it is lawful to discriminate on racial grounds because belonging to a particular racial group is a genuine occupational qualification (GOQ):

(a) The job involves participation in a dramatic performance or other entertainment where a person of that racial group is required for authenticity.

(b) The job involves participation as an artist's or photographic model where a person of that racial group is required for authenticity.

(c) The job involves working in a place where food or drink is provided to the public in a particular setting, e.g. a Chinese waiter in a Chinese restaurant.

(d) The holder of the job provides persons of that racial group with personal services promoting their welfare.

Note:

(a) Employers must ensure that job advertisements are fair and that recruiting arrangements make the jobs available to all.

(b) If the job is the same, then the terms offered to men and women and/or different racial groups must be the same.

(c) Persons cannot be refused the job or be dismissed on grounds of sex or race.

(d) Discrimination is permissible if the sex or race of the person is a GOQ.

Finally, it is unlawful to advertise in a way that indicates the intention to discriminate even if that discrimination would not be unlawful, unless being of a particular racial group is a GOQ.

Contract of employment

The contract of employment, like all other contracts, is formed when there is an offer and an acceptance, i.e. when the employee accepts the offer of a job. It may be oral or in writing, though many employers in the travel industry provide their employees with written contracts.

A contract of employment is subject to the principles of the law of contract which, in theory at least, means that the parties are free to negotiate their own terms and conditions so long as they are within the constraints of the law. However, some employees do not negotiate their own terms; instead they accept those terms and conditions which are contained in collective agreements.

Both parties, employer and employee, should understand all the relevant terms and conditions at the time employment commences.

The sources of these contractual terms are varied.

Express terms and statutory statement of terms

Express terms are those which are expressly agreed as forming part of the contract. The employment contract does not have to be in writing but if a written contract is not given, employees must be provided with a statement of the most important terms of the employment within 13 weeks of commencing work. This is a statutory right under section 1 of the Employment Protection (Consolidation) Act (EPCA) 1978. The terms are:

(a) the identity of the employer;

(b) the identity of the employee;

(c) the date on which the employee's period of continuous employment began, which must take into account any employment with a previous employer which counts towards that period;

(d) the title;

(e) the scale or rate of pay, or method of calculating it, and intervals at which payments are made;

(f) hours of work and normal working hours – here the employer should state whether or not overtime is compulsory;

(g) holidays and holiday pay;

(h) terms and conditions relating to incapacity for work owing to sickness or injury;

(i) pension rights;

(j) length of notice which the employee is obliged to give and entitled to receive;

(k) disciplinary procedure;

(l) grievance procedure;

(m) whether a contracting-out certificate for an occupational pension scheme is in force.

The employer may provide some of these details in a document which is easily available for the employee to read at work. It is not acceptable to require the employee to have to ask the manager each time he or she wants to read it.

Changes cannot be made to the contract of employment without the consent of the employee. If agreement is reached to alter the terms, the written statement must be amended to take account of the change within *one* month. If the employer does not provide the statement the employee may apply to an industrial tribunal to decide what the terms and conditions are.

In order to qualify for the right to a written statement an employee must work a minimum of 16 hours per week; however, he or she is also eligible if he or she has worked between eight and 16 hours for five years. Employment agency workers are also entitled to receive certain particulars of employment from the agency.

Collective agreements

Contractual terms may be derived from collective agreements. These deal with the relationship between trade unions and employees or employers' organisations and, therefore, may regulate an individual's contract of employment. For the terms of these agreements to become legally enforceable they have to be incorporated into the employee's contract. Thus, workers may be employed on the basis of 'the national agreements for the time being in force'.

Works rules

Works rules are devised by the employer and may be incorporated into individual contracts of employment in the same way as collective agreements. Works rules may be the subject of negotiation.

Custom and practice

Custom and practice may be used on occasions to 'fill in gaps' in the employment relationship. The custom and practice must be known, reasonable and generally applied in the trade or profession, however.

Terms implied by the common law

Terms will be implied which will give reasonable effect to the intention of the parties. Terms may also be implied by the custom of a particular industry.

Changes in the terms of employment

Although the terms of employment have been fixed from the outset parties may agree to change them by mutual consent. If the employer changes the terms without the employee's consent and these changes are substantial and detrimental the employee may accept them, or may resign and seek compensation.

Most contracts of employment contain a clause similar to the following:

> *The employee will perform such duties as may from time to time be assigned to him by the manager.*

In so far as these duties are fair and reasonable the employee is bound to do them.

In certain circumstances an employee is dismissed, e.g. because the employer has reorganised the job. If the employee cannot or will not accept the changes, dismissal may be justified if it is for 'some other substantial reason' (EPCA 1978, s. 57(1)(b)).

New technology

The travel industry is one which relies on new technology for its efficient working. Employees will be expected to adapt to new techniques within their contractual terms. It was held in *Cresswell v Board of Inland Revenue* (1984) that the respondents were entitled to withhold pay from staff who refused to co-operate in the introduction of new computers. The tribunal found that the nature of the job had not changed.

Termination

The contract of employment may be terminated by either party on giving the correct period of notice. This is subject to employment protection legislation providing remedies for employees who have been unfairly dismissed.

The *minimum* periods of notice are provided by the EPCA 1978. The minimum period of notice which the employer must give to employees depends upon the employees' length of service:

1 month but less than 2 years' service	– one week's notice
2 years' to 12 years' service	– one week's notice per year of service
12 years' or more service	– twelve weeks' notice

The employee must give a minimum of one week's notice.

These periods of notice may be extended by agreement. Most travel managers and many travel assistants are required to give longer periods of notice than the statutory minimum. Employers may choose to give payment in lieu of notice instead of requiring an employee to work out his or her notice.

SUMMARY
(a) The employment contract is just another type of contract.

(b) Express terms are those expressly agreed by the parties. If there is no written contract then the employer must give the employee a written statement of the most important terms.

(c) Collective agreements, work rules and the custom and practice of the trade or profession may also be regarded as part of the terms and conditions of employment.

(d) Terms will also be implied in the employment contract by Acts of Parliament and by the common law.

(e) The parties may agree to vary the terms of the employment contract.

(f) The employment contract may be terminated by either party giving the correct notice.

Duties of the Employer

These duties are implied by law in all employment contracts, some being based on common law principles, others on legislation.

The duty to pay wages

Prospective employees will be delighted to learn that if there is no express provision in the employment contract about remuneration, the law will imply a term into contracts that the employer must pay for employees' services. Where there is no provision for calculating the rate of pay for the job, employees must receive remuneration which is customary – they must be paid on the basis of *quantum meruit* (as much as they deserve). However, this is measured by the court, not what employees think they deserve.

The most important statutory provisions governing pay are:

(a) Itemised pay statement: every employee who works 16 or more hours a week (eight hours or more where employed for five years) is entitled to receive a written pay statement at or before every payment of wages or salary. It must show:

    (i) gross amount of wages or salary;

    (ii) net amount;

    (iii) if the net amount is divided and paid separately the amount and method of each part payment;

    (iv) any variable or fixed deductions from the gross wages or salary and the purpose for which they are made.

(b) The Wages Act 1986 prohibits employers from making unauthorised deductions from employees' wages or salaries, unless required to do so by Act of Parliament or a court order. An employee may give written consent in advance authorising a deduction. If an employer contravenes these provisions the employee may complain to an industrial tribunal.

(c) Sick pay: the statutory position is governed by the Social Security and Housing Benefits Act 1982 and Statutory Sick Pay (SSP) Regulations (1986) making the employer effectively the DSS's agent in administering his or her employees' sickness pay rights.

In essence, the employer must pay sick pay for the first 28 weeks of illness in a period of incapacity for work. The employer recovers from the state the amount of SSP paid by deducting an equivalent sum from the national insurance contributions he or she would otherwise make. An employee may not claim for the first three days of illness. The main categories of employee excluded from SSP are:

    (i) those who do not pay national insurance contributions;

    (ii) employees over state pensionable age;

    (iii) employees on a fixed term contract of three months or less and persons not employed because of a stoppage at work due to a trade union dispute. In the latter case, however, an employee is not excluded if he or she had no direct interest in the outcome.

(d) If the employer overpays an employee due to a mistake the employer may be entitled to recover the payment from the employee. Employees may be guilty of theft if they refuse to repay an accidental overpayment.

(e) Deduction for industrial action – employers may make deductions where the worker has taken part in a strike or other industrial action.

Briefly the rules governing payment of wages and salaries may be summarised as follows:

(a) The employee is entitled to an itemised pay statement and, in certain circumstances, SSP.

(b) Employers may not make unauthorised deductions from employees' wages or salaries.

The duty to provide work

There is no legal 'right to work'. The employer is under no duty to provide an employee with work.

In *Collier v Sunday Referee Publishing Company Ltd* (1940) Asquith J said:

> *It is true that a contract of employment does not necessarily or perhaps normally oblige the master to provide the servant with work. Provided I pay my cook her wages regularly she cannot complain if I choose to take any or all of my meals out.*

However, some employees are legally entitled to complain if they are not provided with work. Those who are paid by results or commission or on variable shift premiums, or who are given the option to work overtime need the physical opportunity to work. These employees receive a basic wage plus the chance to earn extra. An implied term of a skilled worker's contract of employment is that he or she be provided with a reasonable amount of work to maintain or enhance his or her skills.

The duty to co-operate with the employee

Employers have a duty to treat employees with respect. They should not act in such a way as to make it difficult for employees to carry out their duties. Employees forced to resign because of the employer's unreasonable behaviour may be entitled to claim for constructive dismissal.

The duty to take reasonable care of employees

At common law employers are under a personal duty to take reasonable care for the safety of their individual employees.

What does this mean?

(a) *Personal duty* – an employer will be liable to an injured employee even where the employer has delegated this duty to a manager, foreman, safety officer, etc. and even if the injury results from the negligent act of the person to whom the employer delegated the duty. The employer cannot argue that he or she exercised reasonable care in selecting the manager, foreman, etc.

(b) *Reasonable care* – the employer does not guarantee that his or her employees will not suffer injury; however, he or she must exercise such care as is reasonable in the circumstances to expect from any prudent employer. The greater the degree of likelihood of danger to the employee, the greater the care required to be taken by the employer.

(c) *Individual employees* – the duty of care is owed to each employee individually and not to the employees collectively. Thus, special measures of care will be required for those employees who may be especially vulnerable.

In *Paris v Stepney Borough Council* (1951) the plaintiff, who had one good eye, was employed as a garage hand. He lost his good eye when a metal chip flew off the vehicle on which he was working. His employers had not provided goggles, and the plaintiff sued for damages. It was held that although it was not customary to provide employees with goggles for this work, nevertheless the Council should have provided goggles to this particular employee.

The duty of care may be divided into three constituent parts: the duty to select competent staff (fellow employee); the duty to provide and maintain suitable materials; the duty to institute and operate a safe system of work.

(a) *Competent staff* – If an employee is injured as a result of the act or omission of a fellow employee arising from the colleague's inexperience, incompetence or lack of training, he or she can sue the employer on these grounds.

An employer who is aware of the danger posed to fellow employees by a particular employee may be liable on the basis that he or she failed to discipline or dismiss him or her (e.g. for constant practical jokes).

(b) *Suitable materials* – Where employees must use dangerous machinery, it is for the employer to take reasonable steps to minimise the danger. He or she must weigh up the likelihood of accidents or injury against the cost of safety precautions. Inspections of equipment should be carried out at reasonable intervals and defects remedied without delay.

The Employers' Liability (Defective Equipment) Act 1969 states that an employer cannot escape liability by arguing that the defect is due wholly or partly to the fault of a third party, e.g. a supplier.

(c) *Safe system* – this includes safety of the premises, ventilation, lighting, temperature; lay-out for performance of the work; adequate notices, warnings and instructions.

This rule may apply to single 'one-off' operations as well as to routine repetitive work. The more complicated or unusual the operation, the more detailed the system is required to be.

Obey the law

The employer must obey the law and has a personal obligation to employees to observe certain legislation, for example:

(a) the Factories Act 1961;

(b) the Offices, Shops and Railway Premises Act 1963;

 (c) the Race Relations Act 1976;

(d) the Equal Pay Act 1970;

(e) the Sex Discrimination Act 1975;

(f) the Health and Safety at Work etc. Act 1974.

To allow time off

Certain rights are provided by Acts of Parliament, e.g. the right of certain elected trade union officials to time off for trade union duties; the right of employees to time off for public duties, e.g. to act as a magistrate; the right of pregnant women to time off for ante-natal care; the right of a redundant employee to reasonable time off to look for other work (which right, in contrast to the preceding ones, does require a qualifying period of two years' continuous employment). There is no common law right to time off, only such time as may be agreed between the parties.

To allow holidays

Surprising as it may seem, there is no common law right to holidays. There is also no such statutory right, with or without pay, even to bank holidays except for employees covered by the Banking and Financial Dealings Act 1971.

SUMMARY   The duties of the employer are:

(a) to pay wages;

(b) to provide work for a certain category of workers;

(c) to co-operate with employees;

(d) to take reasonable care for the safety of employees by ensuring there is a safe working environment and competent fellow workers;

(e) to put into practice all the statutory provisions designed to protect employees;

(f) to allow time off for ante-natal care, trade union duties and activities, public duties, etc.

Duties of the employee

The duty to co-operate

The primary obligation of employees is to attend work and to do what they have agreed to do.

Employees are in breach of their duty if they refuse to travel to a site where the employer is able to provide them with work when in the circumstances it would be reasonable for them to do so. Thus, a travel assistant cannot unreasonably refuse to move to another branch.

Employees are not obliged to do more than the contract requires. They are not compelled to work overtime unless that is expressly agreed in the contract (this may simply be the custom of trade, it should be pointed out!). Due to seasonal fluctuations in bookings, travel agency and tour operations staff may be required to work overtime at certain times of the year.

 Under the Health and Safety at Work etc. Act 1974, employees are under a duty to co-operate with the employer as far as it is necessary on all matters pertaining to health and safety in the workplace.

To obey orders

Employees must obey lawful and reasonable orders given by the employer. Employees would, however, be entitled to refuse to obey unlawful instructions, to work on unsafe plant or machinery or to work beyond the contractual requirement except in an emergency. They may refuse to obey an order which exposes them to risk of physical injury or serious infection, unless the contract permits it.

 In *Morrish v Henlys* (1973) Leonard Morrish, a stores driver, was told by his manager to record in his book that he had been supplied with more petrol than he had actually taken. He was told that this was the normal way of making up deficiencies in the records and he was told to falsify his entry. He was dismissed for failing to obey orders. It was held that Morrish had been unfairly treated. He was awarded £100 compensation.

Fidelity

Employees must not put themselves in a position where their personal interests conflict with their duty to the employer. This means that they must not accept any reward for their work other than from their employer (e.g. a secret commission). There are three specific aspects to this duty.

Not to compete with the employer

If the employee engages in part-time employment or 'moonlighting' this must not harm the employer's business, otherwise it amounts to a breach of fidelity and may be restrained by an injunction or an interdict. For example (in Scotland), this could involve doing 'homers' or secretly earning income from a particular trade from customers of the employer. Alternatively, in some cases the contract will specifically exclude part-time employment.

Not to disclose confidential information

While an individual remains in employment the obligation is included in the implied terms which impose a duty of fidelity on the employee. Thus, if an employee copied a list of the employer's customers for use when the employment ended or deliberately memorised this list he or she would be in breach. After the employee has left his or her employment he or she cannot use or disclose information about commercial secrets. In order to decide whether an ex-employee is in breach of this duty the courts take into account such matters as the nature of the employment (is confidential information habitually handled in the course of the job?); the nature of the information (can the material be classed as a trade secret or is it highly confidential as to require protection?); whether the employer informed the employee the material was highly confidential. In practice employers will usually insert restraint clauses in the employment contract.

Invention and copyright

Whilst the contract of employment will normally outline the legal ownership of employee inventions, the Patents Act 1977 amended by the Copyright Designs and Patents Act 1988 states that an invention shall belong to the employer only if:

(a) it was made in the normal course of the employee's duties and that it might reasonably be expected to result from these duties; and

(b) the employee has a special obligation to further the interests of the employer's business because of a particular responsibility arising from his or her duties; or

(c) although the invention was not made in the normal course of the employee's duties, it was made in the course of a specifically allocated duty and an invention might reasonably be expected to result from that duty.

Even where the employer patents the invention, an employee may be entitled to a 'fair share' of the benefits, taking into account criteria such as the effort and skill expended by the employee and the likely benefits to the employer.

Under section 4 of the Copyright Designs and Patents Act 1988, if the employee produces written work in the course of his or her employment (if he or she was employed to produce that work) the employer is the first owner of the copyright.

Restraint of trade

The object of a restraint of trade clause in an employment contract is to protect the employer's business against disclosures by an ex-employee or attraction of the employer's customers to a competitive business set up by the ex-employee.

In determining the validity of these clauses the court must weigh up the need for reasonable protection of the employer's business interests against the right of ex-employees to future employment. The aim of a clause, to be valid, must be to prevent the employee from soliciting former customers, rather than stopping the employee from working at all. A typical example of such a clause might be a travel agent's practice including a contractual clause that the manager will not work for another travel agency within five miles during the first two years of leaving.

The area of restraint must be reasonable; a worldwide restraint may be valid only where the employer's business is of a similar extent. The size of the area and its relationship to the employer's connections are factors to be considered.

An employer who breached the employee's contract (e.g. by failing to give the required notice) is unlikely to be able to enforce a restraint clause.

Normally, restrictive clauses will be enforced by injunction or interdict.

 In *Strathclyde Regional Council v Neil* (1984) Neil raised a series of objections to a clause in her contract of employment to the effect that she had to return to the employer for at least two years after a paid training leave. If she did not do so, she would have to refund an amount proportionate to the unexpired portion of the contracted minimum period of service.

The court found against her on the following grounds:

(a) this was not an unlawful restraint of trade because the employee was not prevented from using her skills when she left the Council;

(b) there was no restraint on her liberty beyond that normally involved in a contract of service;

(c) there was no evidence of force or other unfair means as would invalidate her consent to the contractual term;

(d) the terms of repayment did not amount to a penalty clause.

Obviously this case has important implications for traineeships and day release agreements.

To take reasonable care

It is an implied term of the contract of employment that employees will use reasonable care in performing their duties. A breach of this duty may entitle an employer to dismiss summarily an employee. If damage or injury is caused the employer may recover this from the employee.

 In *Dennis v Campbell* (1976) a betting shop manager broke his obligation to take care when he gave credit to a punter, contrary to instructions and trade practice. He was ordered to make his employer's loss good when the punter defaulted. However, it is usually the practice to avoid such litigation – the employer's insurance company actually pays the damages.

SUMMARY The duties of employees are:

(a) to co-operate with the employer by doing what they are contracted to do;

(b) to obey lawful orders;

(c) to be loyal to the employer by not competing or disclosing confidential information;

(d) to take reasonable care so as not to harm other employees.

Health and Safety at Work etc. Act 1974

The common law duties of employer and employee have been examined above. The aim here is to look at their rights and duties under this Act. The main purpose of the Act is to strengthen the protection of people at work.

Older legislation such as the Factories Act 1961 and the Offices, Shops and Railway Premises Act 1963 remain in force; however, the provisions of this Act will gradually replace them as new regulations and approved codes of practice come into force.

Two bodies, the Health and Safety Commission (HSC) and the Health and Safety Executive (HSE), are established under the Act. The HSC consists of a full-time chairman and representatives from both sides of industry and local authorities. Its duty is to promote the objectives of the Act and formulate health and safety policies. The HSC has three full-time members appointed by itself and their duties are to carry out the day-to-day work of the HSC and to enforce the legal requirements under the Act.

To whom does the Act apply?

The Act covers 'all persons at work', regardless whether they are employees, employers or self-employed. It also protects persons who are affected by work activities, for example neighbours, passers-by and customers. It therefore applies to people rather than to premises.

Duties of employers

There is a general duty on every employer 'to ensure, so far as is reasonably practicable, the health, safety and welfare at work of all his employees'. The matters which this general duty on employers includes are:

(a) to provide and maintain plant (equipment and appliances) and systems of work which are, as far as is reasonably practicable, safe and without risk to health;

(b) to arrange, so far as is reasonably practicable, the safe handling, use, storage and transport of articles and substances;

(c) to provide the necessary information, instruction, training and supervision to ensure, so far as is reasonably practicable, the health and safety of employees;

(d) to maintain those premises under their control in a safe condition without risks to health;

(e) to provide safe access to and egress from working premises;

(f) to provide and maintain a working environment that is, so far as is reasonably practicable, safe and without risks to health and is adequate as regards facilities and arrangements for the welfare of employees at work;

(g) to prepare and, as often as may be appropriate, revise a written statement of the general policy with respect to the health and safety at work of the employees and bring this statement and any revision of it to the notice of all employees. This does not apply where there are less than five employees employed at any one time;

(h) to conduct their undertakings in such a way as to ensure, so far as is reasonably practicable, that persons not in their employment (clients, etc.) who may be affected by any work are not exposed to risks to their health and safety.

Duties of employees

These are:

(a) to take reasonable care for the health and safety of themselves and persons who may be affected by their acts or omissions at work;

(b) to co-operate with their employers as regards any duty imposed on them relating to health and safety;

(c) not to interfere intentionally or recklessly with, or misuse anything provided for health, safety or welfare (for example, fire extinguishers).

Enforcement of the provisions of the Act

Inspectors appointed by the HSE have the power to enter any premises, at any reasonable time, if they have reason to believe there is any dangerous situation. They may bring on to the premises any equipment they need (see Chapter 4: Business Premises).

In relation to people their powers enable them to require any person to give them information that is relevant to their examination or investigation. These persons will have to answer the questions and be required to sign a declaration as to the truth of their answers.

What happens if the Act has been contravened?

In this event the inspectors may:

(a) issue a prohibition notice – this prohibits the activity giving rise to the risk until remedial action specified in the notice is taken; such a notice is issued if there is a risk of serious personal injury;

(b) issue an improvement notice – this requires the fault to be remedied within a time specified in the notice;

(c) prosecute – a court action, in the criminal courts, which may be in addition to (as well as instead of) issuing a notice (in Scotland the decision whether or not to prosecute is taken by the Procurator Fiscal);

(d) seize, render harmless or destroy any substance or article that they consider to be the cause of imminent danger or serious personal injury.

Readers will probably consider that a travel agent's shop is an extremely safe place to work. However, it is only necessary to think of minor faults such as trailing wires, worn or loose carpets and tiles or piles of brochures left carelessly on the floor to imagine the accidents that may follow and for which the employer will be liable.

SUMMARY

(a) The aim of the Health and Safety at Work etc. Act is to promote health and safety at work through statutory provisions.

(b) Employers, employees, the self-employed, customers, passers-by and neighbours are protected by the Act.

(c) The Act imposes a duty on employers to provide safe machinery and working conditions.

(d) Employees have a duty to care for the health and safety of themselves and others who might be affected by their acts and omissions.

(e) The provisons of the Act are enforced by inspectors, who may enter premises to make any investigation. If the Act has been contravened, they may issue a prohibition notice or an improvement notice, or prosecute.

Maternity rights

A working woman who becomes pregnant has the right under the EPCA 1978 to:

(a) time off for ante-natal care;

(b) be paid for her absence at the clinic at the appropriate hourly rate.

This right is acquired merely by being an employee.

There is no right under the EPCA to maternity leave, though the pregnant woman has the right under the Act to return to work. She also has an entitlement to maternity pay, provided under the Social Security Act 1986.

The right to return to work

A pregnant woman has the right to return to work, after the end of her confinement, in the same job in which she was employed, on the same terms and conditions. This is provided in sections 45–48 of the EPCA 1978. The working woman must have:

(a) worked for her employer for two years, if she works more than 16 hours a week; or

(b) worked for five years if she works more than eight hours but less than 16 hours a week, and in either case must

(c) continue to work up to 11 weeks before the expected date of confinement, although she is allowed up to 29 weeks' leave after the birth of her child.

In addition, she has to give her employer three weeks' notice in writing before she leaves and before returning to work. Also under the Act, a woman has the right, subject to a two-year qualifying period, to bring a complaint of unfair dismissal on the ground of pregnancy. To rebut this allegation, the employer would have to show that the woman was, as a result of her pregnancy, incapable of doing the work she was employed to do, or that she could not continue in her job without breaking the law.

The right to maternity pay

This right is governed by the Social Security Act 1986. To qualify for maternity pay a woman must:

(a) continue to work until at least 15 weeks before the expected date of confinement;

(b) cease work a full six weeks before the expected date of confinement in order to qualify for the full 18 weeks of paid maternity. If she does not, there will be a reduction of one week from the 18-week period for every week worked after the sixth week before confinement;

(c) have worked for the same employer for a period of two years prior to her pregnancy. If this is so she will be entitled to maternity pay at the higher rate of 90 per cent of net pay for six weeks, and at a reduced rate for a further 12 weeks, a total of 18 weeks in all. If she has worked for the same employer for more than six months but less than two years, she is entitled to a flat rate of £39.25 a week for the full 18 weeks.

If the woman has worked for less than 26 weeks she does not qualify for maternity pay. She can, however, claim state maternity benefit, if she has the correct number of national insurance contributions. If she had opted for the reduced rate of contributions she is excluded from claiming state maternity benefit.

SUMMARY

(a) The working woman who becomes pregnant has rights under the EPCA 1978 to time off for ante-natal care and to return to work after her baby is born.

(b) Under the Social Security Act 1986 she has the right to maternity pay.

(c) To return to the same job, she must have worked for two years (or five years, depending on the hours worked a week) with the employer.

(d) To qualify for full maternity pay she must have worked for the same employer for two years.

(e) If she has worked for the same employer for more than six months but less than two years, she gets the flat rate of maternity pay.

(f) If she has worked for less than six months she may be entitled to state maternity benefit.

Dismissal

This section deals with the way the contract of employment may be terminated. There have been several legislative changes in recent times, nevertheless the old common law grounds also remain.

Terminate at common law

The ways in which the contract of employment may be terminated include:

(a) by a supervening event;

(b) by notice given by either party;

(c) by breach of contract;

(d) by summary dismissal.

Each of these will now be looked at in turn.

Termination by supervening event

The employment contract will be automatically terminated by an event such as the compulsory winding up of a company or permanent closure of the employee's place of employment. The contract of employment is also terminated if a receiver is appointed by the court.

Termination by notice

Either party can terminate the contract by giving the proper notice to the other. At common law this implies a reasonable length of notice depending on the circumstances. This will usually be taken as the period of payment (e.g. weekly or monthly). However, the period will be expressly stated in the written particulars of employment and subject to minimum periods of notice laid down in the Employment Protection (Consolidation) Act.

Termination by breach

If one of the parties breaches an essential term of the employment contract, that contract is terminated if the other party 'accepts' this repudiation.

Termination by dismissal without notice

At common law a dismissal with proper notice is lawful. There are also some occasions when summary dismissal or dismissal without notice is lawful. In deciding whether summary dismissal is justified, the principle applied is whether the employee's conduct shows that he or she has disregarded the essential terms of his or her employment contract. That is, if the employee's conduct amounts to gross misconduct.

An employee summarily dismissed may bring an action for wrongful dismissal in the court. The only remedy available is damages, the measure of which will be such wages, bonuses, etc. as the employee would have earned if due notice had been given.

Termination under statute

Section 54 of the EPCA 1978 provides that, subject to exceptions (e.g. those over retirement age, those employed for less than two years continuously), 'every employee shall have the right not to be unfairly dismissed'. To claim a remedy for unfair dismissal an employee shall be treated as dismissed by the employer under the following circumstances.

(a) *Direct dismissal.* When the contract is terminated by the employer with or without notice. The words used to dismiss must be clear and unambiguous and should set a date for the end of the employment. Such words are to be distinguished from those used in the heat of the moment. Problems arise where the words used are ambiguous and the employee has interpreted them as a dismissal. It is the tribunal's job to try to ascertain the employer's intention behind the words used.

In *Kendrick v Aerduct Productions* (1974) the employer told an employee to 'fuck off!'. The question was whether this was to be construed as 'you're fired!' or merely a term of abuse. It was held that the words used constituted dismissal. The tribunal decided that the words were to be interpreted as a reasonable man would interpret them.

However, in another case, *Futty v Brekkes Ltd* (1974), the same expression was interpreted as meaning 'clock off!' and did not, therefore, amount to dismissal. It is not the words used that matter but the intention behind them.

(b) *Fixed term contracts.* The expiry of a fixed term contract without its being renewed is deemed to be dismissal.

(c) *Constructive dismissal.* The Act provides that an employee may be entitled to resign and claim that he or she has been dismissed (constructively) if the circumstance shows that the employer's conduct makes it unreasonable for the employee to continue working there. The most common situation is where the wage or salary has been cut or status reduced. It may also arise from a material change in shift patterns or an order to move to new premises some considerable distance away (only if not agreed to in the contract). Sexual harassment may lead to constructive dismissal.

The employee must inform the employer in writing of his or her intention to treat the matter as constructive dismissal if the employer continues the action of which he or she is complaining. The burden of proving that he or she has been constructively dismissed lies with the employee.

Examples of the type of conduct by employers which have justified employees claiming constructive dismissal include:

(i) unilaterally changing employees' terms to their detriment;
(ii) not treating staff with dignity, using foul language and verbally abusing them.

Reasons for dismissal

In unfair dismissal claims the employer must state the reason for dismissal; if he or she cannot put forward a reason approved by the EPCA 1978, the dismissal will be automatically unfair. These statutory reasons for dismissal are divided into three groups.

(a) Potentially fair reasons, which are related to the conduct, capability or qualifications of the employee; to redundancy; or where the employer would be contravening a duty or restriction imposed by law if he or she allowed the employee to stay in the job; some other substantial reason.

(b) Automatically fair reasons, which include dismissal for taking part in industrial action, provided all the participants are equally dismissed.

(c) Automatically unfair reasons, which are: dismissal of a woman because she is pregnant unless she is incapable of doing the job; dismissal for trade union membership or refusal to join a trade union or for trade union activities; where the dismissal was because of the transfer of the business except in limited circumstances.

Fairness of dismissal

The Act (as amended by the Employment Act 1980, s.6) provides that in all cases where dismissal is not automatically unfair, the tribunal must consider:

whether the dismissal was fair or unfair, having regard to the reasons shown by the employer, which shall depend on whether in the circumstances (including the size and administrative resources of the employer's undertaking), the employer acted reasonably or unreasonably in treating it as sufficient reason for dismissing the employee. That question shall be determined in accordance with equity and the substantial merits of the case.

It is therefore, the task of the employee to prove he or she was dismissed and it is for the employer to show that the reason for the dismissal falls within the category of 'potentially fair reasons' laid down in the Act.

These reasons will now be considered.

Incapability

Capability refers to 'skill, aptitude, health or any other physical or mental quality'. Qualifications means 'any degree, diploma or other academic, technical or professional qualification relevant to the position which the employee held'.

Therefore, this reason can be divided into incompetence or health.

(a) *Incompetence*: In *Lowndes v Specialist Heavy Engineering Ltd* (1977) the applicant was dismissed after five serious and costly errors. No written warnings were given and he was not allowed the opportunity to state his case. Nevertheless the tribunal held that the dismissal was fair. (*Note*: if this case were heard now it would be unfair on procedural grounds due to more recent case law.)

In *Lewis Shops Ltd v Wiggins* (1973) Wiggins ran a boutique in Southend. She was warned several times about her standards and when she did not respond to these warnings she was dismissed. The evidence showed that the atmosphere of the shop was 'seedy and lethargic'. The tribunal held that dismissal was fair because she had had many opportunities to improve her standards.

⚖️

In *Taylor v Alidair* (1978) an airline pilot made a single, but serious error of judgement when landing his passenger plane, which resulted in considerable damage to the aircraft. His employer, who was on board, suspended him. At the board of inquiry which followed he was dismissed. The tribunal held that dismissal was fair because his mistake was serious.

Lack of qualifications is a ground for fair dismissal only where holding the relevant qualifications is a requirement of the job, for example for a driver to hold a licence of the required class.

(b) *Health*: There are two main types of case in which ill health may lead to dismissal of an employee. The first is where the employee has been absent for a specific medical reason and dismissal is contemplated because of the needs of the business and the fact that the employee is unlikely to resume duties under the contract for the foreseeable future. The second arises where dismissal is thought necessary because the employee is persistently absent for short periods for related or unrelated health reasons. Before dismissal an employer will need to consult with the employee concerned, obtain up-to-date medical reports (with the employee's consent), caution the employee that his or her employment future is under review, and have regard to business needs. Any alternative work should also be considered.

Where medical evidence shows that an employee will never be able to carry out his or her duties again, the contract may technically come to an end by 'frustration'. This is not held to be a dismissal in law.

⚖️

In *Tan v Berry Brothers* (1974) the applicant was a cellarman at a wine merchant. He had a good attendance record in his first year of work. In the second year he was absent from work due to sickness on 16 days. In the third he was dismissed after being off sick for 50 days out of a possible 70. The tribunal held that because the business required someone reliable the dismissal was fair.

⚖️

In *International Sports Ltd v Thomson* (1980) the employee had been absent from work for about 25 per cent of the time. She complained of a variety of problems including dizzy spells, anxiety, bronchitis, viral infection, cystitis, dyspepsia and flatulence. All of these were covered by medical certificates. She had been warned several times by her employer and then was given a final warning. Before deciding to dismiss her the company consulted a doctor who saw no reason to examine her as none of her previous illnesses could be verified, there being no common link and no chronic illness.

It was held that dismissal was fair as the employer had been reasonable in that the employee had been warned and been given the opportunity to present her case.

The tribunal will consider such factors as the size of the business and the amount of disruption caused by the employee's absence, medical evidence and consultation carried out with the employee.

Misconduct

It is helpful if the employer gives examples of what he or she considers to be misconduct. This may mean giving specific rules relating to smoking in certain areas or clocking in someone else's card, for instance. Foul or abusive language may also be held to be misconduct. (Whilst such language may be acceptable on a building site, it is hardly appropriate in a travel agent's.) It is also necessary to distinguish between misconduct which is so serious that an employee may be summarily dismissed and that which merits prior warnings.

Absenteeism and lateness are types of misconduct that depend for their gravity on the extent and reason for them. Misconduct has also been held to have been committed in these situations:

(a) refusal to wear appropriate clothing for the job (e.g. the company uniform);

(b) an employee has carried on sexual relations during working hours;

(c) refusal to go on a training course;

(d) wearing provocative badges contrary to warnings.

Certain matters so clearly amount to misconduct that listing them is unnecessary. Where an employer wishes to dismiss an employee on grounds of misconduct he or she must show that the matter was given prompt and thorough investigation and that the employee was warned about this conduct – unless it was so serious that summary dismissal was appropriate. It must not have been a matter which he or she has condoned in the past unless staff have been forewarned that it is no longer acceptable. The employee must be provided with an opportunity to state his or her case.

Where notice has been given that certain conduct is considered a dismissable offence and the employee has ignored it, it is likely to justify dismissal, as the following case illustrates.

 In *Dalton v Gold Medal Biscuits* (1974) Mr Dalton had worked with the company for 22 years with unblemished service. He was instantly dismissed when it was discovered that he had clocked in a friend's card. The friend was ready to work at that time. There was a prominent notice above the clock stating that the clocking in of a fellow employee's card would justify instant dismissal. This was repeated in the employees' handbook. It was held that dismissal was fair.

Criminal acts committed in the course of employment, e.g. theft, fraud, violence and industrial espionage, may all justify dismissal. Criminal acts outside the course of employment may justify dismissal if they affect the employee's work,

Legal restrictions

An employer may fairly dismiss an employee if required by an Act of Parliament or a regulation to do so (e.g. a person employed as a driver may be dismissed if he or she has been banned from driving).

Redundancy

An employee may be fairly dismissed for redundancy. A redundancy situation occurs when the dismissal is due to the closure of the workplace or when the requirement for employees to do work of a particular kind has diminished or will diminish at the place where the employee is employed. If the employee does not have a mobility clause in the contract, then if one office closes he or she will be redundant even if the business is relocated elsewhere.

Requiring employees to perform their work in a different manner (transferring to computerised instead of manual systems, for instance) will not normally constitute a redundancy situation.

Although redundancy is a potentially fair reason for dismissal, the dismissal must still be carried out fairly, with proper consultation. The redundant person must also have been fairly selected in cases where there are a number of employees who could be made redundant and the employer has to select individuals.

Redundant employees with two years' continuous service are entitled to a redundancy payment based on age and length of service.

Some other substantial reason

If the dismissal is not for any of the reasons discussed above, it can be for some other substantial reason and still be fair, but the employer must act reasonably both in the reason for the dismissal and how the dismissal is carried out. This is not a catch-all clause enabling employers to dismiss for no good reason.

Examples of a potentially fair reason include:

(a) reorganisation for business reasons resulting in a change to terms and conditions which the employee has refused to accept;

(b) pressure from major clients to dismiss an employee where not doing so could damage the employer;

(c) bad publicity connected with the employee reflecting on the employer.

Remedies for unfair dismissal

Reinstatement

The reinstated employee will be treated as though he or she had never been dismissed. Thus, continuity of employment is observed and added to actual service, any wage increase and interim benefits accrued during the absence must be paid.

In reaching its decision the tribunal will consider such matters as whether the employee wants the job back; whether the employer will be able to comply with a reinstatement order and whether the employee caused or contributed towards the dismissal. Therefore, harmony in the working environment and the personal attitudes of the employer and employee will be taken into account.

Re-engagement

The employer is ordered to employ the person not in the same job but in one which is comparable with the previous position. The tribunal decides the terms of the re-engagement.

Compensation

Compensation comprises the basic award, the compensatory award and, in certain circumstances, an additional award or a special award.

The basic award is calculated by reference to the following table:

Age	Amount per year of service	
Under 22	half a week's pay	maximum period of 20 years
Service between ages 22–40	one week's pay	maximum pay of £205 per week
Service between ages 41–64	one and a half weeks' pay	maximum of £16,150

The compensatory award is calculated on the basis of loss sustained, for example net wages and pension rights. The maximum payment is £10,000. The employee must mitigate the loss, which means that he or she must find, or strive to find, suitable alternative employment. If the employer fails to reinstate or re-engage an employee, an additional award may be made by the tribunal. This additional award may also be made if the dismissal was on the grounds of race or sex discrimination.

A special award may be made where the dismissal was on the grounds of trade union membership or non-union membership.

(*Note:* these amounts are reviewed from time to time.)

SUMMARY (a) Some of the common law grounds for dismissal are a supervening event, by notice, by breach or by summary dismissal.

(b) The only remedy for dismissal at common law is damages.

(c) The Employment Protection (Consolidation) Act 1978 sets out the grounds of fair dismissal.

(d) Employers must show that the reason for dismissal was on one of these grounds.

(e) Employees must show that they were in fact dismissed.

(f) Employees may establish that they were constructively dismissed if they can show that the employer acted in an unreasonable manner.

(g) The main grounds of fair dismissal are:
   (i)   incapability, including ill health;
   (ii) misconduct;
   (iii) legal restrictions;
   (iv) redundancy;
   (v)   'some other substantial reason'.

(h) The remedies for unfair dismissal are reinstatement, re-engagement or compensation.

(i) Reinstatement is distinguished from re-engagement in that in the former employees are treated in all respects as if they had not been dismissed.

SELF-ASSESSMENT QUESTIONS

State whether the following statements are correct or incorrect

1. Employers must employ disabled persons.

2. Employers do not have to employ anyone who has a spent conviction.

3. Anti-discrimination provisions are found only in the Sex Discrimination Act 1975 and Race Relations Act 1976.

4. It is illegal to dismiss a person because he or she is married.

5. It is illegal to dismiss a person because he or she belongs to a particular religious group.

6. Indirect discrimination occurs when a person is treated less favourably than others of the same sex or marital status.

7. Employers are acting in a discriminatory way if female applicants for a job are asked whether or not they intend to have children.

8. Discrimination on the grounds of sex is lawful if the sex of the person is a GOQ.

9. The written notice containing the most important terms of employment is the contract of employment.

10. Other sources of express contractual terms are collective agreements and works rules.

11. Provisions in other Acts may be implied into the employment contract.

12. An employment contract containing a variation clause allows the employer to alter the terms of the contract.

13. The common law duties of the employer are to pay wages and take reasonable care of employees.

14. Employees would be in breach of their duty if they refused to obey an order which put them in physical danger.

15. Employees are in breach of their duty if they do work secretly and earn income from that work which should be earned by their employer.

16. Health and safety inspectors pay regular visits to premises in order to check that the building is sound.

17. Contravention of the Health and Safety at Work etc. Act leads to a civil action in the courts.

18. The employment contract can only be terminated by either party giving notice.

19. Wrongful dismissal entitles the employee to bring a claim before an industrial tribunal.

20. Unfair dismissal relates to dismissal under statute.

Appendix
Answers to self-assessment questions

1. Introduction to law (p.1)

2, 4, 5, 6, 7, 9 and 10 are correct.

1. Ignorance of the law excuses no one.

3. Fines and imprisonment are criminal law sanctions. There are no punishments in civil law. The sanctions of civil law include rendering agreements invalid or unenforceable, compensation, damages, etc.

8. By-laws have the full force of law.

If you got all the answers right you should continue on to the next chapter. If you got more than one wrong you should re-read this chapter before moving on.

2. The legal systems of the United Kingdom (p.11)

England and Wales

1, 3, 7, 8, 9, 10, 11 and 12 are correct.

2. England and Wales have the same legal system.

4. Most criminal cases are heard by the magistrates' courts.

5. A majority verdict of 10–2 is sufficient.

6. Appeals from the magistrates' court are heard by the Queen's Bench Division of the High Court.

Northern Ireland

1, 2, 4, 5, 7, 9 and 11 are correct.

3. Appeals from the Crown Court are heard by the Court of Criminal Appeal.

6. Magistrates' courts hear minor civil cases.

8. There are no juries in the county courts.

10. The House of Lords is the highest court of appeal in Northern Irish civil cases.

12. The Law Society of Northern Ireland is the governing body for solicitors. Barristers must be members of the Inn of Court of Northern Ireland.

Scotland

2, 3, 5, 6, 8 and 9 are correct.

1. The Scottish legal system evolved independently from that of England and Wales and has been considerably influenced by Roman law.

4. Minor criminal offences are dealt with by district courts.

7. The High Court of Justiciary (Court of Appeal) is the highest court of criminal appeal in Scottish cases.

10. The Outer House of the Court of Session is a court of first instance. Appeals are heard by the Inner House.

11. The Court of Session sits in Edinburgh. It does not go on circuit.

3. Business organisations (p.23)

2, 3, 4, 6, 7, 10, 12, 13, 14, 15, 18 and 19 are correct.

1. The Business Names Act 1985 applies to sole traders and partnerships when not trading under their own names or when the firm's name is not the same as those of the partners.

5. If the ownership of the family property has only recently been transferred, the trustee in bankruptcy may be able to prove it was transferred to defeat the creditors.

8. A partnership in Scotland has a separate legal personality (section 4(2) of the Partnership Act 1890).

9. As a partner Betty is liable for the civil wrongs of other partners only if the wrongful act or omission arose in the ordinary course of the firm's business.

11. A retiring partner or deceased partner's estate will remain liable for that business of the firm as yet unsettled at the date of retirement or death, unless he or she has made an arrangement with the firm's creditors.

16. As the company has no certificate of incorporation it has no corporate personality, and therefore cannot act as a principal.

17. Directors have actual authority but also apparent authority to do all those acts usually done by a director. Any limit on their authority has to be notified to third parties.

20. It was decided in *Tesco Supermarkets Ltd v Nattress* (1972) that a company can commit offences because the acts of the directors who control the company become the acts of the company.

If you have given more than two wrong answers, then you should reread the chapter.

4.   Business premises (p.43)

1, 2, 7, 8, 9(d), 10, 11, 13 and 14 are correct.

3. Cafés, restaurants, hotels, etc. are in a separate 'use class' from that to which travel agencies belong, i.e. 'shops'.

4. A betting shop is not considered to be a shop for the purposes of the Use Classes Order.

5. This may undermine the structure of the whole building and thus requires planning permission.

6. Painting of the exterior of premises does not require planning permission *unless* it is for advertising purposes.

9. **(a)** The 1957 and 1960 Acts govern the liability of occupiers of premises, whether or not they are the owners. The Acts apply to all, not just commercial, premises.

   (b) The duty is to ensure that visitors are safe rather than to ensure that the premises are safe. This could be achieved by excluding visitors from dangerous premises.

   (c) The degree of care owed to trespassers is less than that owed to visitors but, increasingly, the standard of care is becoming the same.

12. A first-aid box must be provided in all premises in which persons are employed.

15. Health and safety inspectors have power under the Act to enter upon premises at any reasonable time; they do not have to be accompanied by a policeman.

5.   The tour operator and travel agent relationship (p.54)

3, 4, 5, 7, 9, 12, 13, 15, 16 and 18 are correct.

1. Legal status means finding out what legal principles apply.

2. Travel agents may act as tour operators.

6. There is no legal requirement for a formal deed; an oral contract is sufficient.

8. The conduct of the parties could also imply that the principal has appointed the agent to act for him or her.

10. The travel agent also has implied actual authority.

11. Any withdrawal of, or limitation on, the agent's authority must be communicated to third parties, otherwise the contract is valid.

14. Travel agents may delegate performance.

17. Principals have a duty to pay their agents if they have done what they have undertaken to do as well as to reimburse them for expenses and to compensate him or her for any liabilities.

If you got more than five answers wrong you should reread the chapter carefully; if you got less than five wrong, check back on the subjects you are unsure about.

6. Consumer protection legislation and the travel industry (p.63)

1, 3, 4, 8, 10, 13, 15, 18, 19 and 20 are correct.

2. It is his or her job to encourage competition.

5. It reports on references made to it by the Director.

6. The MMC investigates whether a monopoly situation exists and if it considers that it does and that consumers' economic interests are being harmed it will report accordingly.

9. Any restrictive agreement has to be registered and if it is against the public interest it will be declared void by the Restrictive Practices Court.

11. The TOSG Travel Fund Ltd is an insurance fund which compensates holidaymakers if a member company fails.

12. The Act prohibits the fixing of minimum prices.

14. The Act would consider such inducements as positive competition.

16. Section 14 imposes criminal liability on 'any person' acting in the course of a business.

17. There is no offence committed under the Act if the statement is not false at the time it was made.

21. The defences of due diligence, act or default of another, or reliance on information supplied are available, plus if the defendant can show the price was not in an advertisement or that it did not relate to the availability of goods, services, etc. from him or her.

If you got five or more answers wrong you should read the chapter again.

7. The law of contract (p.85)

1, 2, 6, 7, 9, 11, 15, 16, 18, 20, 23 and 24 are correct.

3. A contract is legally binding as soon as the offer has been accepted. In the case of a holiday contract it is legally binding when the booking has been confirmed.

4. It is an essential requirement of the English law of contract that there must be consideration, but it is not a legal requirement that it should be reasonable or sufficient.

5. It is preferable that the package holiday contract should be in writing but it is not a legal requirement.

8. Religious discrimination is not unlawful.

10. This would amount to sex discrimination under the Sex Discrimination Act 1975 and race discrimination under the Race Relations Act 1976.

12. It is not illegal but the contract may not be enforced against the person under 18 years of age.

13. The contract is legally binding unless the intoxicated person was so drunk as to be

incapable of understanding the contract and sought to cancel it immediately on becoming sober.

14. Express terms may be set out orally, in writing or partly orally and partly in writing.

17. The travel agent may choose to do so but is not legally bound to do so.

19. These conditions would be enforced if they passed the reasonableness test.

21. The client made an error of judgement and that does not entitle him or her to cancel the holiday unless the error was induced by the tour operator or travel agent.

22. The statement that the pool was being built was a true statement. An indication of the completion date would be a statement about the future, not a statement of existing or past verifiable fact.

If you got all the answers right then you are doing very well; there was a great deal to learn in this chapter. Twenty correct answers is still very good.

8.   The Package Travel, Package Holidays and Package Tours Regulations 1992 (p.103)

1, 2, 6, 7, 9, 10, 12, 13, 15, 19, 20, 21, 22 and 25 are correct.

3. They only replace existing provisions where these conflict with those contained in the Regulations.

4. They also apply to domestic packages and are applicable to some business travel arrangements.

5. Transport is not an essential element of a package. A package must contain two out of three elements specified, i.e. transport, accommodation, other tourist services.

8. These are specifically included, provided that the arrangements are put together as a package.

11. The information must be provided 'before the contract is concluded'.

14. He must have been *prevented* from going ahead with the packages.

16. The time limit is 30 days.

17. Provided that the maximum number required was specified in advance and the consumer was notified in accordance with the Regulations, no compensation is payable.

23. The regulations are enforced and prosecutions made by the local weights and measures authorities (usually labelled 'trading standards departments').

9.   Settlement of disputes (p.121)

1, 2, 5, 6, 10, 11, 12, 15, 16, 17, 18 and 20 are correct.

3. The tour operator may cancel the holiday if it is necessary to do so as a result of hostilities, political unrest or other circumstances amounting to *force majeure* or if the client defaults in payment of the balance. (NB: 4.5 of the Code of Conduct.)

4. A contract is only 'frustrated' if, *without the fault of either party*, some event occurs which renders further performance an impossibility, renders it illegal or so radically alters the circumstances that the contract becomes quite different from that originally intended.

7. The *conciliation* service is provided by ABTA officers.

8. The holidaymaker has a choice – he or she may use the arbitration service *or* raise an action in court.

9. Once the holidaymaker has agreed to go to arbitration he or she is bound by the arbitrator's decision.

13. The county court arbitration is conducted by the district judge of the court.

14. Claims for less than £1,000 are usually dealt with under the 'summary cause' procedure.

19. Special damages may be awarded where the client has brought his or her special circumstances or special needs to the tour operator's attention at the time that the contract was entered into.

21. The plaintiff may be entitled to claim damages in a foreign currency if his or her losses were incurred in that currency.

10. Carriage of passengers and their luggage (p.133)

1, 4, 5, 7, 8, 9, 12, 13, 15, 17, 19 and 22 are correct.

2. Although a non-fare-paying passenger may have no claim based on the law of contract, he or she may have a claim under the law of tort (delict, in Scotland).

3. He or she does not guarantee the safety of the passengers but does owe a duty of reasonable care, and the relevant standard is very high.

6. It is not negligence, but the carrier may be held liable if he or she fails to protect passengers from annoyance or injury caused by the drunken passenger.

10. British Rail expressly excludes such liability in its conditions of carriage.

11. The carrier is an independent contractor and, therefore, the doctrine of vicarious liability does not apply.

14. Travel agents usually act on behalf of the airline company and therefore do not enter into contracts of carriage as principals. If they issue tickets in their own names, that is, as principals, they will be bound by the Warsaw Convention.

16. The Montreal Protocol No. 4 states that the carrier is liable for delay to passengers and their luggage.

18. As liability is 'strict' rather than 'absolute', carriers have available to them the defences of having taken all the necessary steps and the contributory negligence of the passenger.

20. This Convention was brought into force by section 14 of the Merchant Shipping Act 1979.

21. They are covered by the Convention for the International Carriage of Passengers and Luggage by Rail 1961.

11.   Insurance (p.154)

1, 4, 5, 7, 9, 10, 13 and 15 are correct.

2. He enters into the contract with the insurance company.

3. *Uberrimae fidei* means utmost good faith and refers to the fact that there is a duty on both parties to the contract to disclose all material facts.

6. Innocent non-disclosure is no defence. The insurer may treat the contract as void.

8. The insured has to be able to show that financial suffering will be caused by the loss.

11. Subrogation means that the insurer, after fully indemnifying the insured, may have the right to sue a third party for damages or for breach of contract.

12. The insured will have to account to the insurer if more than full compensation for loss has been received. Any gift which has been received for the purpose of mitigating the loss must be accounted for to the insurer.

14. Holiday insurance contracts will contain subrogation clauses.

12.   Employment law (p.161)

4, 7, 8, 10, 11, 12, 13, 15 and 20 are correct.

1. Organisations with more than 20 employees have to employ disabled persons although this legislation is not enforced.

2. It is unlawful for an employer to refuse to employ certain rehabilitated offenders because of 'spent' convictions. (There are exceptions.)

3. There are other Acts such as the Fair Employment Act 1989 of Northern Ireland and codes of practice published by the Equal Opportunities Commission and Commission for Racial Equality.

5. This is not illegal in Great Britain, but it is in Northern Ireland. Religious discrimination may, however, be indirectly racially discriminatory.

6. This is direct discrimination.

9. This is not the contract of employment.

14. Employees would not be in breach if they refused such an order.

16. Their duties are to enforce the provisions of the Health and Safety at Work etc. Act.

17. It is an offence to contravene the Act and proceedings are brought in the criminal courts.

18. The employment contract may be terminated at common law and under statute.

19. This is dismissal at common law and the dismissed employee brings a civil action in the courts where, if he or she is successful, the only remedy is damages.

Index